Lewis C. Reimann

1951

Return to Bob Barnett

Dudes of the Nineties

Between the Iron and the Pine

A BIOGRAPHY
of
A PIONEER FAMILY
and
A PIONEER TOWN

BY

LEWIS C. REIMANN

Lithoprinted in U.S.A.
EDWARDS BROTHERS, INC.
ANN ARBOR, MICHIGAN
1951

DEDICATION

This factual account of my boyhood days in Iron River, Michigan, is dedicated to my loving Mother who bore me, nursed me, cared for me, guided me through my youth and believed in me. To her I owe all that I am and all that I aspire to be. It was she who bore the burden of a large family, suffered when we were hurt, comforted us in our disappointments, deprived herself so we might have more, and saw her hopes and dreams come true when her children fulfilled her fondest hopes. My sainted Mother, my guide and inspiration.

FOREWORD

When a Chicago financier was invited in the early Eighties to invest his money in the infant iron mining and lumber industries of Iron County of the Upper Peninsula of Michigan, he sniffed:-

"Iron County? Hell, it's too far away from anywhere to ever amount to anything!"

Little did this man of money expect that the giant white pine of that virgin land would go into the building of most of the homes of his native Chicago and other thriving young cities of the middle west. Nor that the iron ore dug from its fabulously rich mines result in the defeat of the Kaiser and Hitler. He had no way of knowing Iron River was to be the home of Carrie Jacobs Bond whose songs were to be sung the world over. Nor that I, one of the Reimann Baker's Dozen, would write this saga of the North seventy years after he made his brash statement.

How did all this come about? How did this backwoods community, hidden in the dark pine-covered hills in that far-away land, become a great factor in the building of this nation?

Well, here is the tale, written in a distant city by the author as he sits before his fireplace recalling his boyhood days at the turn of the Century.

If the language is rough in spots and the scenes are rugged at times, it is my design to present the life of the day as it really was. If some of the characters and events resemble some of the real events and characters of the past, living or dead, it is purely intentional.

The Author

ACKNOWLEDGEMENTS

While this book was written out of my own recollections of the early days in the Iron River District, many others have contributed to its success by refreshing my memory on some of the history and anecdotes and by assisting me in finding some of the "Oldtimers" who were free in telling me about those early days of struggle "Between The Iron and The Pine."

Among those who contributed this valuable material were Jim Murphy of Elmwood, Mrs. A. W. Quirt, her daughter Mrs. Lila Quirt Purcell, Mrs. Hjalmer Magnet, Bob Solberg, my brother William Reimann and his daughter, Ruth, Leslie Fisher, Mrs. Herbert Fisher, John J. Corbett, Joe Brown, John Ennis, John Westerberg, Mannie Krans, George Breen, Dominic Dascola, Io Oshins, Gus Ruus, Mary Lorenz, Otis Meehan, Mrs. Kathryn Richardson Chandler, Charles E. Good and many others.

Others were Walter F. Gries of Ishpeming, who contributed some Cousin Jack tales, N. J. Nolden of Escanaba for Indian stories, Martin LaVoilette of Stambaugh, mining stories, Mary Mertins for her story on the Stealing the Court House, Alton P. W. Hewett for Choose Your Partners, William Duchane, editor of the Escanaba Daily Press for the Dan Seavey story, Charlie Larson of Escanaba for some Finnish stories, and for editorial advice were George Reeves, the author of "The Man From South Dakota", Clarence H. Dykeman, author, and Professor Carlton F. Wells of the University of Michigan.

These good people have my gratitude for helping to make this saga a success.

CONTENTS

Chapter I

BETWEEN THE IRON AND THE PINE

A Boy's Eye View
Cheaper By The Baker's Dozen
Over The Hill

Chapter I

BETWEEN THE IRON AND THE PINE

A Boy's Eye View

The little log house, in which most of the Reimann tribe saw their
first light of day unattended by a doctor, stood on the peak of mile-high
Stambaugh Hill overlooking the Iron River valley and the stream below.
It was a crude two-story cabin with a sleeping attic and an attached log
barn, just a speck in the surrounding wilderness of pine, hemlock and
maple. The young village of Iron River lay below in a triangular piece
of ground, hemmed in tightly on two sides by dark towering, timbered
hills and by a little stream, called the Iron, on the third.

On all sides as far as our eyes could reach was the vast forest ex-
tending over the rugged hills. The giant white pines topped the hardwood undergrowth like a velvet cloth laid over the landscape, waving
and undulating when the north winds blew across them, a soft vista of
green and black. Roads radiated out in several directions from the scattered town, - highways over which rugged men and great teams struggled
to bring down the millions of logs to the rollways on the river bank and
to the steaming sawmill at the edge of wilderness.

To the northwest and the southwest rose the dark upper structures of
mining shafts and great stockpiles of red iron ore dug from the bowels
below the ground which once was covered by a virgin forest.

Between the Iron and the Pine men struggled to wrest a living. Lumberjacks came from the woods of Maine and the forests of northern
Europe and miners from the mines of England's Cornwall and south-
Europe; and others, like my father, came without previous skill at
either industry, to make places for themselves wherever they could in
the crisp and rugged environment which lived essentially on lumber
and iron ore.

To the men who worked the mines and the woods for pay, life in the
Northern Peninsula was harsh and demanding, and the goal was one of
wealth distant; but to a boy who saw only people, people with familiar
names and familiar faces, life was vivid and colorful. The Main Street
of Iron River appropriately enough was paved with red iron ore rock
and its raised walks were of plank from the green pine forests, but the
color I saw then and remember now was the color of the people.

If on an early morning I were to follow the red iron rock topped road
down Stambaugh Hill as the fog lifted off the Iron River stream, cross
the little plank bridge to the village and walk up the hill to Main Street,
I would come first to Frank Camin's ice house and root-cellar beer
vault, where Frank's big steel-grey Percheron stood patiently hitched
to the beer wagon preparatory to supplying the local saloons with the
cooling "brew that made Milwaukee famous", kegs piled high and topped
with chunks of lake ice mixed with marsh hay to keep the contents cool.

3

The big grey's legs and belly were red from the ore dust of the streets.

"Billy the Drunk" stumbled along the plank sidewalk from his fitful sleep in the town lockup to make his rounds of the back doors of the saloons for his "eye-openers". Unwashed, long-haired and fragrant, he earned his shots of whiskey by cleaning the big brass spittoons in the taverns.

The town ice wagon was making its rounds distributing lake ice to the saloons, butcher shops and private homes. A tribe of Chippewa Indians waited at the front of Pat Kelly's general store--squaws with their papoose strapped to their backs, bucks sitting on the high wooden sidewalk, beaded moccasined feet dangling over the edge--impatient to have their shopping and trading over before the saloons opened.

Miners in their red, ore-soiled clothes hurried along the walks on their way to work, carrying their dinner buckets. Lumberjacks in their "stagged" woollen pants, mackinaws, battered hats and caulked boots, strolled the early morning street, their red, bleary eyes showing the effects of "the night before." Clerks were sweeping the walks in front of their stores and setting out their street displays of bargains in mackinaws, butter churns, axes, peavies and farm implements.

Teams of powerful Belgian and Percheron horses stopped for a drink of cool water at the town watering trough, on their way to some construction job or hauling loads of stove wood. Stray dogs, reviewing the dog-history of the night before, smelled around the street and fireplugs, picking fights with weaker mongrels. Cows moved down a side street on their way to their milking, their udders distended, followed by sleepy-eyed, barefooted boys.

Dr. Frank Bond, the husband of the not-yet famous Carrie Jacobs Bond, hurried along home with his little black bag after an all-night vigil at a child birth. The delivery boy was loading up his wagon before Hay Davison's bakery, to supply the families in the outlying mining "locations."

Smoke curled up from three hundred homes as housewives prepared breakfast for their men and hungry school children. The whistle at the cooperage mill blew a doleful blast to warn its employees that work would start promptly at seven. The Catholic Church bell rang out its invitation to early mass. The Chicago & Northwestern Railroad engine was shunting and bumping its loaded cars of logs and lumber onto a siding to make way for the local freight train due in a few minutes.

Roosters crowed their welcome to the new day and scratched dung hills for their harems. Late rabbits scooted between houses to their safe hiding places for the day. Half-wild cats wound in and out under the high wooden sidewalks looking for mice. A blanketed buggy horse stood tied to a half-gnawed post at the wooden sidewalk before a saloon, restless, pawing deeper into the already deep hole under his feet, awaiting his drunken master sleeping it off from the night before in the back room of the drinking place.

This was the street scene which greeted the eyes of a boy as he walked through the village of Iron River on a misty morning in the early 'Nineties. Here were gathered from distant states and far

The Reimann's Baker's Dozen
Author back row left

countries the men and women who sought a living in a new, raw and un-
sentimental region of fabulous resources yet to be exploited. Once
there they were faced with the problem of eking out a living for themselves and their children from the virgin material that grew in the hills
or the metal that lay deep under the ground, or from the services which
lay between. It was a struggle that is world-old, - the struggle to wrest
from nature food, clothing and shelter, to secure a fair wage from in-
dustrialists who financed the lumber companies and the mining syndi-
cates or to find employment between the Iron and the Pine. Failing in
this struggle the alternatives were to move to a less rugged scene
where life was more stereotyped and secure, or "go over the hill" to
the County Farm.

Cheaper By The Baker's Dozen

Our family was of sturdy stock. Two of my sisters were born in
Germany where my father had his fill of regimentation and military
service. His brother had found new opportunity in the middle west, at
Racine, Wisconsin, and sent back such glowing accounts of high wages
and easy freedom that soon the family was on its way across the stormy
Atlantic. But here they found that seasonal employment as a stevedore
was not enough to meet the needs of the growing family. Sailors on the
Great Lakes brought down tales of a fabulously rich land and work opportunities in the Upper Peninsula of Michigan. Packing their few sticks
of furniture in a box car and loading the family on the train, they set out
for Stambaugh, Michigan, in the iron and pine country, without promise
of work or a place to live.

With his only assets a mortgaged team of mules and a buckskin suit
bought from an Indian squaw, father set himself up in the draying business. Babies came along regularly every year or two until there were
a total of fourteen — six boys and eight girls. A dysentery took the
second boy, leaving a baker's dozen to feed and clothe. None of us was
born in a hospital or with the assistance of a doctor. Midwifery flourished and we survived.

To find names for each of the thirteen must have been a great task.
The ceremony of christening each child was a serious and elaborate
affair in our church and home. Each of us was swathed in a long embroidered christening dress and carried on a pillow to the little German
Lutheran Church on the hill overlooking the green valley of the Iron River below. Each child had several god-parents from among our family
friends and each was given several names. Mine were Ludvig Frederick Johannes Karl, - after my father and three godfathers. Later, for
convenience and to save embarrassment, I changed mine to Lewis
Charles. Both parents and god-parents "stood up" with the child in
solemn ceremony as the minister baptised the baby and secured the
promise of each god-parent to provide for the child in the event of the
death or disability of the parents.

After the church ceremony and adjournment to the home, the

christening party was supplied with a big dinner and liberal quantities
of beer. As the party reached its climax, my parents placed on the
table a Bible, a handful of earth, a stick, and a piece of money. The
child was then held over these articles and encouraged to reach for
them. If the baby touched the Bible, it was predicted that he would become a minister; if the stick was picked up, he would become a teacher;
if the coin, he would become rich, and if the earth, he was destined to
an early death. This superstition was borne out only in one case. Our
parents failed to record our choices, but apparently only one reached
for death and one for teaching. One died at six weeks of age. None of
us became rich; none are ministers; one became a teacher. All eight
girls became wives and home makers. The five brothers entered into
business and professions. The thirteen are still living at this date with
a total age of 783 years.

As the family grew the struggle to provide for them became grim. A
pair of skinny mules and a buckskin suit could not keep up with the demand for food, shelter and clothing. Competition in the draying business became serious. The small town of Stambaugh offered little prospect of increasing the family income. My father faced the alternative
which faced every other big family. If he couldn't discover an iron
mine, or become a logging contractor he had to resort to social welfare, which meant the Poor House over the hill. He had to do something else.

With the same courage that they used when they left the Old Country,
my parents bought, without a down payment, a big house on Main Street
in the now thriving village of Iron River, down in the valley below Stambaugh. Here they set up a boarding and rooming house for miners and
lumberjacks. Father continued his draying business with a new team of
chestnuts, while mother and my sisters participated in the arduous work
of running the new establishment. The girls learned early how to cook
under mother's skilled instruction and example. Making several dozen
beds, cleaning the big house, cooking and waiting on table for the stream
of hungry men was part of the daily routine. The women did all the
washing and ironing for the family and the sheets and pillowcases for
the roomers. They arose at four o'clock on Monday mornings to do the
washing over hot, steaming washtubs and corrugated washboards, and
hung it out on long lines in the back yard, before preparing breakfast
for the boarders and the hungry brood of children. The night before
the clothes were placed to soak in tubs and boilers were filled with rain
water on the kitchen stove for heating in the morning. This work done,
the girls grabbed a quick breakfast and were off to school, returning
when school was out to do the ironing and prepare the evening supper.
Filling lunch pails for the two dozen or more workmen was a daily
chore and required careful buying of food and split-second planning.

After several years of running the big rooming and boarding house
and gradually paying off the contract on the house, my parents began to
talk of building a home and retiring from the business. Some of the
girls were married and the problem of engaging adequate hired help
made the continuation of the establishment a difficult one. Lumber was

plentiful. Plots of land around the edge of the village were available.
But the cost of a home large enough for our still big family meant a
considerable outlay of money. The large boarding and rooming houses
in the mill town of Atkinson, twelve miles distant, were being torn down
and sold, since the timber in that area had given out.

It was agreed that they would erect a home on some lots they had
previously bought in the Barrass addition on Carnegie Avenue. But
where was the necessary money coming from? Surely to pay for the
big boarding house on Main Street and to raise a family of thirteen
drained all our cash resources. One day as they were discussing the
prospect, mother went down into the cellar under the kitchen and
brought up two fruit jars filled with gold pieces which she had carefully and secretly saved over the years since moving to Iron River.
Her brown eyes sparkled as she dumped the gold onto the kitchen
table. Our eyes bulged in wonder at her foresight and thrift. Gold
and silver were the principal medium of exchange at the time. Little
paper money was in circulation. We had what it took, thanks to mother!

Proudly the next day my father and I drove the team to Atkinson to
haul the first load of lumber for our new home. Within two months,
with the whole family working under the advice of a Swede carpenter,
the house of fourteen rooms was up and we were moved in, leaving the
days of boarding house drudgery behind for good. Our new home was
typical of the day. It had a grand parlor and a sittingroom, with kitchen, pantry and bedrooms radiating off from them. The parlor was
usually kept closed until special guests arrived. It had a moldy odor
from having been kept closed from fresh air. The shades were always
down to prevent the sun from fading the curtains and the woven rag
carpets. Like most parlors, it was furnished with black horse-hair
covered chairs and sofas. Unless one had his feet firmly on the floor
he was in danger of slipping off the smooth surface. Short ends of
horse-hair stuck up in the seat and added to the discomfort of the
occupant. The chairs were stiff and uncomfortable and heavily carved.
A foot-pumped organ stood in the corner and gave out wheezy tones.
Most families had a prospective musical "genius" who had to be coaxed
to show off bashfully his or her talents to the assembled "company."

A great kerosene lamp with a highly colored and painted globe hung
from the ceiling, giving off a doubtful light "for all in the room". These
lamps could be pulled down by a chain and pulley for filling with kerosene, trimming of the wick, cleaning the glass "chimbley" and lighting
and were the prize pieces in the home. The carpet was usually made
by local women out of rags saved by the family from worn-out suits
and skirts, dyed to the taste of the owner. These carpets were spread
over the floor and tacked down around the baseboards and swept with
a broom after "company" left. Once a year they were taken up and
hung on the clothesline outdoors to receive a beating at the hands of
one of us boys. This was a job we hated and mother had to keep a wary
eye on us until all the dust was beaten out. The windows of the parlor
were never opened except on the hottest days, thus giving the room a
flavor all its own. When company left, the door was tightly closed

again and we were forbidden to enter the sacred place until the next
guests arrived.

Saturday night was the time for the weekly scrub-up and baths for
the whole family, "whether we needed it or not."

There was no running water. We had no bathtubs or waste disposal.
While supper dishes were being washed, we boys carried buckets of
water from the rainbarrels under the eaves and filled the boilers and
kettles set on the kitchen stove. A washtub of tin or wood was placed
in the middle of the kitchen floor and and the hot water poured in. The
youngest lined up first and took turns at getting into the tub. Amid
screams and laughter and cries of "Soap gets in my eyes!" we were
soaped from top to bottom with homemade softsoap, scrubbed to a red
glow, then dried with a rough towel while we stood before the hot kitchen stove. Several children bathed in the same supply of water. Then
the tub was carried out into the yard, to be emptied and filled again for
the next "batch" of children.

Our soiled clothes of the week were piled in a heap for Monday's
wash, while we got into our night shirts (pajamas unknown) and sent
off to bed, to be ready for Sunday School the next day with clean clothes
and "bright and shiny faces."

Girls used no lipstick, rouge or nail polish. They did powder their
faces, when they "went out", with cornstarch to take off the shine and
give them that alluring, soft look. Long hair was "a woman's pride and
crowning glory." It was carefully shampooed, at home, combed and
brushed endlessly, then coiled around the head in braids and tied with
broad, bright-brocaded ribbon. Pompadours became fashionable in the
late 'Nineties and "rats" were used to puff up the hair over the front of
the head. Hourglass figures were affected by the younger women and
they "made even the minutes count." The smaller a girl's waist the
more attractive and delicate she was thought to be. Bustles made of
wire, basket-like affairs covered with cloth, were tied behind to accen-
tuate the slimness of the waist. Older girls and women wore whalebone
corsets, high in front and low around the sides and back, to complete
the hour-glass effect. They were worn so tightly that we wondered how
they could swallow enough food to keep alive.

Since most of the men wore mustaches or beards, and even the dudes
left long "sideburns" and shaved the rest of the face, we tried to force
the issue by shaving early. At the first appearance of "down", we made
experiments with our fathers' straight-edge razors. I found an old razor left by one of the roomers—a big, heavy instrument shaped like a
knife instead of hollow ground and diligently honed and stropped it for
weeks before trying my first shave, which almost led to disaster and
my mother's concern lest I cut my own throat. It was months before
I had enough "down" to shave off and before I could wield the stiff
blade without sad results.

To prove our arrival at manhood we raised mustaches which we
thought more attractive and more masculine. But after a few weeks
the ridicule of our parents and friends ended in shaving the upper lip
until we could show more for our effort. The "battle of the brush"

persisted until the advent of the safety razor and until the town barber shops hung out the "No More Shaving" signs.

The two village barber shops advertised "Baths 25 Cents", but during my summer vacation when I worked as a lather boy in one of the shops I remember only one person ever taking a bath there. He was a traveling salesman courting a saloonkeeper's daughter. Here it was my duty to become acquainted with all the shaving customers who had their own private shaving mugs arranged on a shelf on the side wall. These mugs were inscribed with the owner's name in gold. John Airey's mug bore the head of a bull; Ed Lott, the horse dealer, had the head of a stallion on his mug; and Josh May, the shift boss at the time, had as his seal a pick and shovel. As each customer came in, I found his mug, ran hot water into it and with the shaving brush worked up a stiff soap lather, then handed it to the barber.

Christmas vied with the Fourth of July as one of the most thrilling events of the year. With a large family of children and a limited family income, our Christmas celebrations were necessarily simple but perhaps for that reason were very important to us all. Mother and my older sisters knitted most of their spare time during the year to make practical gifts: mittens, scarves, mufflers, wristlets, stockings and socks. Each child saved up some money to buy presents for the others and the stores were carefully groomed to find gifts that came within our financial range, which was not an easy undertaking. We spent hours looking over the possibilities in the shops.

We had no fireplaces on which to hang our long hand-knitted wool stockings, so they were spread over the chairs and sofa and the window sills of the sitting room the night before Christmas. Mother was careful to explain that the front door must be left unlocked to let Santa Claus in, as the small chimney of our heating stove was too small and much too hot for such a fat man and his big pack. Fir trees were plentiful just for the chopping. Ours was decorated with strings of cranberries and popcorn prepared by the girls the week before. A few tinsels saved over the years and a bright "angel" at the very peak completed the trimmings.

No one slept after four in the morning and our parents found it difficult to keep us in bed until the proper time. We were all up at daybreak. When mother called to us that Santa had been there we rushed down to find what he had left in our long woolen stockings. Every stocking contained an orange—the only time in the year we tasted oranges—some barberpole stick candy, a pair of knitted stockings, mittens or a muffler, a pocket knife, a small mouth organ, a popcorn ball made of home-popped corn and molasses, a hair ribbon or a small doll. Nothing elaborate or costly, but our hearts were full of appreciation for the small gifts made by hand or purchased out of meager savings.

Church Christmas parties were held on Christmas Eve or on Christmas night. Programs of "pieces" spoken in droning voices by members of our Sunday School and a talk by the minister or Sunday School superintendent made up the entertainment. We had little interest in this part of the evening, for our minds were on the climax which was sure to follow. Excitement reached its peak when Santa Claus appeared at the church door to the tune of sleighbells borrowed for the occasion from Bill Moss' livery stable and passed out small paper sacks of candy, peanuts and popcorn balls to every child present, whether he was a member of the Sunday School or not. The result was that Sunday School attendance increased to an all-time high a few weeks before Christmas, then dropped to a new low immediately thereafter.

The Christmas season was a time of sleigh rides with teams and big bobsleds, home parties in almost every home where there were children, and the exchange of gifts between families and friends. Great home meals were prepared for days ahead. Turkeys or chickens were often the gift from the butcher shop to its best customers at Christmas time, and because of our big family and our boarding house trade we rated high with the butcher at that time. Two or three brown roasted fowl filled to bursting with sage dressing and sewed up with white "store" string, mashed potatoes with a chunk of melting yellow butter on top, turnips, rutabagas, sour cabbage, pickles of many varieties, wild blueberry and raspberry preserves and jellies, stewed prunes and tomatoes, homemade sausages and headcheese from our fall butchering were heaped on the overburdened family table. Three or four kinds of pies with their rich brown crusts and juicy fillings bubbling up through the cuts, several frosted chocolate and coconut cakes and homemade ice cream topped off the great meal. One Christmas my father killed the fatted piglet and mother roasted it whole and placed it on the table with a bright red apple in its mouth and surrounded it with spiced red crabapples and browned potatoes—an old German custom. As we gathered around the loaded table, our eyes could not close for the blessing, so eager we were to pile in to that Christmas banquet.

After the big dinner we kids spent a strenuous afternoon skiing and coasting down the steep hills around town or ski-joring behind our galloping horses, to return a few hours later, ready to consume a great supper of the left-overs.

And so, though we were far from wealthy, our family always found plenty in that zone where plenty was to be had—effort and foresight always wrung enough from the garden spot, the little farm and the surrounding woods to keep a roof over our heads and a very good table indeed.

Over The Hill

But to the aged, the sick and the crippled the Upper Peninsula was not always so kind. The County Poor House was a name that hung over us like a vague threat long before we knew what it was. We had heard our parents and others speak of people going "over the hill to the poor house", but to us kids it was like the threat of the policeman or ghosts. It did not touch us and never could, we thought. People spoke in whispers of old folks disappearing from the local scene and going off

somewhere to the other side of the county. There was a stigma attached
to it which we did not comprehend. "Isn't it too bad about old Mrs.
Swanson? You'd think her children would . . . . After all, her late husband supported seven. Now seven can't support one."

One day my father and I drove our team and wagon to the County Poor
House on the other side of the county for a load of potatoes to feed our
many boarders. On the way we passed standing timber yet untouched by
an ax and little farms cut out of the forest by sturdy pioneers. The land
was rich both above the surface and in the soil, but its wealth was for
the young and strong, not for the old and sick. As we drove the team
into the grounds we saw an assortment of old men and women wandering
about or sitting listlessly on benches in the shadeless yard of the main
building. This was a box-like affair, two stories high, with an outside
unenclosed stairway leading to the second floor.

We entered the main door to seek the manager. In a big sitting room
were other old people sitting around singly on chairs and rough benches,
with dull, lifeless faces, staring into space. None of them looked up as
we entered. The room was bare of curtains or easy chairs, the floor
was of rough boards and there was an absence of books, magazines and
newspapers.

When the manager, a coarse-looking individual with a week's growth
of black and grey beard and a scowling face, appeared and saw us, his
expression seemed to say: "Who are you to invade my domain?" As
he entered the room the occupants seemed to shrink from him and look
in the other direction. We told him our business and asked to be shown
through the place, which he was reluctant to do. He took us through the
hallways where we could look into the bedrooms, which were as bare as
the sitting room—with single low cots covered by straw mattresses,
thin blankets and no pillows. There was a straight chair in each bedroom and a rickety dresser, no curtains or pictures except those which
had been pasted on the walls by the occupants. Three of the rooms
were barred across the doors and windows with iron rods, for the more
violent cases, the manager explained. Those confined in these rooms
were mental cases who were seldom allowed out of the room or building. A small space under the door provided room for trays of food to
be shoved under. Beneath each cot was a pot or "thundermug", most of
them well filled. The odor of the rooms was almost stifling. Every
bedroom in the building had an occupant, and some had two or three.

"This place is always overcrowded," put in the manager.

The manager's wife was paid by the County Poor Committee for
meals at a fixed rate. It was evident from the appearance of the patients
that their fare was far from ample. A farm was operated in connection
with the institution, and those residents who were able to work at all
were required to do so. During the heavy planting and harvesting seasons a few additional workers were hired. A large barn held cows and
horses and the chicken house was filled with poultry, which supplied
the eggs. Most of the meat and vegetables used were raised on the
place. An attempt was made to make the farm and institution self-
supporting, but each year, the manager told us, there was a deficit

which was made up out of the County Poor Fund. To reduce the deficit some of the eggs, milk and other produce was sold, leaving less than enough for an adequate diet for the inmates. The load of potatoes we hauled away helped reduce the deficit but also reduced their food supply. The County Poor Committee was the supreme law on admittance and supervision. No provision was made to entertain the unfortunates or to give them reading matter or recreational facilities. "They wouldn't appreciate it if we did," commented the manager. Despite the fact that these poor or incapacitated were subject to almost unbearable conditions and treatment, there was seldom a complaint on their part or on the part of the citizens of the county. The inmates seemed completely cowed and without interest in life once they were committed to the place. They were failures, weren't they? Why didn't they provide for their old age? Why did some of them spend their hard-earned money on drink and women? Why didn't their children take care of them when they reached the age of senility? But how much could a man save out of his $25 per month's pay in the woods or his $1.75 a day in the mines? How could he raise a family and save against the day when he could no longer swing an ax or drill iron rock in the mine?

At the end of the farm was a small shack-like building which my father said was the Pest House. Here were housed all serious contagious cases of indigents brought in from all parts of the county. These sick people had little care, for contagious diseases were looked upon with fear. Only people who had had smallpox, scarlet fever or measles were allowed to render them any service other than to shove in a tray of food under the door. They were permitted to walk within a restricted area at night, then were driven back into their pest hole to be locked up for another twenty-four hours. We did not go near the place, for it was believed that just a breeze blown from it in our direction would spread the disease. If a person survived the Pest House, he was fortunate.

Old age pensions were unknown. Should anyone have suggested old-age support, he would have been set sown as a crackpot. Let them save their money like we did! Aged, infirm, mental derelicts and those who were in their last stages of alcoholism from the rot-gut sold in the cheap saloons had only one place to end up, and that was the place "over the hill", unless relatives or kind friends took them into their own homes.

Contagious diseases were quarantined in the homes of the victims. The doors were placarded with a big sign in red ink: "SMALLPOX. DO NOT ENTER UNDER PENALTY OF THE LAW." Whole families were confined to their homes until the days of incubation were passed. Where there were several children in the family who had not had the disease, it sometimes took months for all of them to be exposed and cured. The father, whose income was needed to keep food and other necessities coming in, was often required to live away from home for several weeks or sleep in the woodshed, where he prepared his own meals. Hospitals rarely had isolation rooms. If a diseased person had the means the hospital board might at times be persuaded to let

him occupy a special room. Nurses were scarce and relatives had to
provide nursing care in most cases of illness or accident.

There were no widows' pensions. When the breadwinner was taken
by disability, accident or death in the woods or in the mines, the mother
or the older children had to fill in the gap by seeking work as maids or
housekeepers or at the local cooperage mill. In our community, where
death struck often and unexpectedly, finding domestic help was no problem but the wages were pitifully small for the amount of work required.

Everyone worked long hours, including laborers, businessmen and
housewives. Electricity had not yet come in. There were few telephones, no power but that furnished by steam and horse.

In my later 'teens I got a job delivering groceries and meat in town
and the surrounding mining "locations." I took the place of the regular
deliveryman for a month while he was on summer vacation, an almost
unheard of privilege. I had to be up at six o'clock to get my breakfast,
feed, water, groom and harness the team and be at the store at seven.
After returning from an all-day trip, I ate my supper and returned to
the store to wrap up orders for the next day's delivery, sometimes
working until ten at night and for small wages.

These long hours led to my attempting to organize a union of clerks
and deliverymen in all the local stores. I called a meeting of those involved, explained the necessity for organizing and proceeded with the
election of officers. We drew up a set of reasonable demands for
shorter hours and more in the pay envelopes. Everything went well until the return of the man whose place I had taken at the store. He attended the first meeting after his return and was elected to an office
in the union.

When his employer, Finley Morrison, got wind of the movement, he
put pressure on his man, with the result that he withdrew from the or-
ganization and persuaded many of the others to do the same thing, under
threat of reprisal from the merchants. Barney Krom, the owner of a
big drygoods and general store, who had started his career as a drygoods peddler, remarked that I was a dangerous person and should be
ridden out of town on a rail. By and large it behooved a young man in
those days to remember that to him who hath, more shall be given, to
learn the ropes of one industry or the other, and to satisfy himself with
climbing hand over hand. Hard money came hard, via the machines,
out of the lumber or the ore. But of the two sources, the woods and its
lumberjacks remain clearest in my mind.

Chapter II

THE PINE

Getting Loused Up In The Lumbercamp
Men O' The Woods
Lumber Camp Personnel
Cutting The Big Stuff
The Spring Drive
Stealing Timber

Bide Waters and George Fisher, "River Hogs"

Chapter II

THE PINE

Getting Loused Up In The Lumbercamp

A dozen roads led out of the village to the lumber camps deep in the woods, like spokes of a great wheel of which Iron River was the hub of trading and source of supply. Up these winding roads went hundreds of lumberjacks, long strings of horse teams and equipment early in the fall, to return only after the spring "breakup" and the start of the drive. The town was quiet again and we saw little of the timber crews except when the camp foreman came to town with his spanking team of trotters hitched to a buckboard looking for men who had walked to town when their small caches of whiskey gave out, or to check on incoming supplies and equipment. The supply teams made the trip to town twice a week and stopped at the warehouse next door to our boarding house for a load of food or woods tools.

One of my heroes among these men was Frank Kline, the supply teamster. He hauled for the Menominee River Lumber Company operating on the Brule River near the Wisconsin line. I knew when he was due in town and I was always there to greet him when he opened up the warehouse. He kept me supplied with raisins, prunes and brown sugar, filling my pockets until they bulged. At one time he fed me so much brown sugar that I had a run on our Chic Sale building for days.

One winter Frank invited me to spend my two weeks' Christmas vacation at the camp which he supplied. My mother willing, I took the twenty-mile trip with Frank and a sleigh load piled high with frozen quarters of beef, whole hogs, barrels of flour and sugar, cases of tobacco, dried beans and peas and other supplies which could withstand the below-zero weather.

Frank was the most skilled "team skinner" I ever saw. While he loved every hair in his horses' thick hides, he never hesitated to use his snaky, sixteen-foot lash on a balky or uncooperative horse. Holding the six long reins in his right hand and his whip in his left, he guided the six horses as skillfully as a "river hog" handled his pikepole or peavy on the drive.

On the way to the camp Frank told me of the most serious experience of his long life as a supply teamster. Late one afternoon in the fall, he said, he was on his way to camp with a wagon load of supplies when he heard the howl of a wolf off to his right. Another wolf answered in the rear. Then another, on ahead. His horses picked up their ears and started to walk briskly. A big grey wolf crossed the road a hundred feet ahead of his lead team and a whiff of the wild animal odor struck the horses' nostrils. The lead team plunged ahead, jerking the other horses into a run. Down the rough road they went at a gallop. Soon they were out of control and the high wagon lurched from side to side

over the deeply rutted road. The wolf howls continued and the horses
became panicky. Sitting on a high pole seat above the load, Frank was
swung from side to side in a twelve-foot arc. Seeing that he could no
longer control the runaways, he watched for his chance and grabbed an
overhanging limb of a big maple tree. Climbing up into the tree, he saw
his six-horse team and wagon disappear down the road. Frank sat in
the tree all night with the wolves holding their circle around him until
another supply team came the next morning and rescued him.

Frank found his horses down the side of a cliff, one with a broken
leg and the load of supplies scattered over forty acres along the road.

"Weren't you afraid the wolves would get you, Frank?" I asked.

"No, I'd rather have them after me than hurt one of those damn jug-
heads I'm driving. I love every bone in their heads."

Frank said that when he reached town after his scare he related his
experience to a lawyer friend.

The attorney advised him to make out a will before he returned to
his hazardous work.

"You know," the lawyer said, jokingly, "when you go into the next
world, you can't take it with you."

"Hell," said Frank, "if I can't take it with me, I won't go!"

These and other tales whiled our time away through the long morning and we stopped at a "halfway" camp for dinner and to feed the
horses. Blanketing the animals and putting on their nose bags filled
with oats, we entered the cook shed. Old August greeted us like long
lost lumberjacks and piled the food high on the rough table. Frank
wore black knitted woolen mittens inside his horse-hide woodchopper's
mitts, an ideal combination for sub-zero weather. He took the woolen
mittens out and hung them on the warming oven over the cook stove to
dry. After getting thawed out we had a typical lumber camp dinner of
beef stew, boiled potatoes, canned tomatoes, bread and butter, huge
wedges of dried apple pie and steaming cups of coffee flavored with
condensed milk and sweetened with brown sugar. Frank remarked to
me that the coffee was strong as hell and black as his boots, but since
there was no accounting for camp cooks, we passed it off. When we
were ready to leave for the last leg to the camp, Frank could not find
one of his woolen mittens. We all searched but no black woolen mitten.
Frank had a hunch and reaching into the coffee pot under the warming
oven with a long cooking fork he fished out his knitted mitten, shrunken
to one-third of its original size.

When we reached the lumber camp after dark and had stabled, fed
and unharnessed the horses and unloaded the supplies, we headed for
the cook shack. Frank introduced me to Jacques, the dark French-
Canadian cook, and explained that I was to be the camp guest for two
weeks. Jacques was delighted and shook my hand until my arm ached.
I wondered why he would welcome another mouth to feed. I did not have
to wait for the answer. The "cookie", or chore boy, who is the cook's
"Man Friday", he explained in thick accents, had walked out on him the
day before and he needed another one badly.

"By gar, you work for me, you get regular wages, fifteen dollar da mont', chuck, a place to sleep, easy job. All right, yes?"

That sounded good to me, who was expecting just free board and a bunk for two weeks. But I didn't know what I was letting myself in for. For an apron he handed me a flour sack, which advertised "Minnesota's Best", and set me to peeling two bushels of potatoes as a starter. Late that night I stumbled into an upper bunk in the crew's bunkhouse after the lumberjacks had gone to sleep, too tired to think of what was in store for me the next day.

It seemed I had hardly struck my bunk before the cook called me at four o'clock to start the day. With eyes half open, I staggered into the cook shack to the tune of his swearing—half English and half French invective, only part of which I could understand. I soon realized why the previous boy had walked out. The cook was a tyrant and a slave-driver. His word in the cook shack was law, to me and to any of the men who entered. He threw my flour sack apron in my face and ordered me to set the long red oilcloth covered tables with tin plates and cups for ninety men, lug on big pots and bowls of food and pour two-gallon pitchers of piping-hot coffee.

This done, I was sent out to strike the large iron triangle with a hand sledge hammer, summoning the men to breakfast. I stood aside as I counted eighty-two men rush past me. Within a few minutes the heaping table was bare again and the men were on their way to the cut-tings four miles down the river.

Jacques showed me how to wash and scald the tinware in the big double sink. The scraped dishes were put into a wire basket, then dunked and sloshed around in the near-boiling, soapy water, then the basket was lifted to the second sink compartment which contained clear boiling water just off the stove. Thus sterilized for two minutes, the tin dishes were stacked on edge on the drainboard and left to dry by themselves. The heavy table knives, forks and spoons were placed in a big pan of boiling water on the stove and left to simmer a few minutes, dumped into a heavy sugar sack which was shaken back and forth by the cook and me to drain off the water, then the contents were spread onto one of the eating tables to dry of their own steam—sanitary and quick. Next came the work of packing the noon lunch. Outside the shanty door stood a two-runner sled on which a big wooden box had been built to carry the mid-day meal. Into this we lifted great pots of steaming stew, stacks of sliced camp-made bread, a wooden pail of jam, a crock of farm butter, gallons of black coffee, condensed milk and sugar along with bowls and utensils. Hitching old Jerry, a retired spring-halted strawberry roan, to the sled, we set off down the skidding road to find the cutting and skidding crew. Old Jerry needed no guiding. Lifting his left hind foot high into the air at each step, he struck down a well-trampled road, his ears peaked and his nostrils flared for sounds and sights.

Though muffled to the ears, I soon could hear the chuck of axes as they bit into the frozen trees and the singing of crosscut saws from a distance of half a mile. As we drew near the scene of operations big teams passed us, emitting clouds of steam from the sweating hides

and straining at the great logs they drew on travois. Mackinawed teamsters, taut reins in one hand and a long whip in the other, waved a mit-
tened paw at the new "cookie" and clucked to their horses.

As I drove my whanigan near a fire in the middle of the woods, I
heard my first cry of "Timber! Look out! Here she come!" which
was preceded by quick strokes of the saw and the scurrying of sawyers
to places of safety. A two hundred-foot pine cracked at the butt, swayed
uncertainly for a moment and plummeted down, crackling through the
underbrush, to land with a booming thud. I stirred up the fire and set
my stew pots around to keep them hot and laid out the other food where
the men could reach it handily. Then taking a big battered pan, I beat a
tattoo with a cooking spoon. The heavy noises in the woods stopped immediately, horses whinnied, chains clanked musically, a pair of bluejays flashed over the closing circle and landed in a spruce nearby. I
stirred the stew with the big spoon.

Suddenly, as if in a play, the actors in this woods drama stepped into
the snow-covered stage, dressed in their colorful costumes of red, blue
or green mackinaws, their rubber-soled boots and bright sock-tops,
"stagged" woolen pants tucked in at the bottom, and tasseled caps,
carrying the "properties" fitted to their part in the act—their axes,
saws, canthooks or teamster's whip. The teams of horses now blanketed were ringed around the outside of the circle, hungrily munching the
oats and hay laid out on the snow for them and watched, without ceremony, the men as they lined up at the stew pots with tin bowls and
spoons in hand to ladle out the hot, fragrant food, place two or three
slices of thick bread and a hunk of butter on top, pick up a mug of coffee
as it was poured out by the straw boss, then find a seat on a nearby log
or upon a heap of fresh-cut pine boughs on the snow.

The first serving was rapidly "inhaled." The men came for "seconds"
and "thirds", each time taking away another mug of coffee which they
poured in liberal quantities of brown sugar and condensed milk. Next
came the dessert out of the whanigan box, - pies, doughnuts, raisin
cookies and dried raisins. There was no skimping on food in this or
any other lumber camp. Once out of town and away from liquor and
women the lumberjack lived to eat and ate to live.

Their stomachs full, the men pulled pipes out of their pockets, filled
them with strong he-man Peerless tobacco or cut-plug, tamped it down
with calloused forefingers, juggled live coals from the fire on their calloused hands and lighted their pipes. As they smoked, good-natured
banter began the rounds. The new "cookie" came in for some ribbing
for his greenness and awkwardness. When the foreman stood up, the
crew put on their mittens, shouldered their tools and returned through
the deep snow to work until dark. The two bluejays made bright spots
on the snow as they picked up the crumbs. Trace chains jingled again
as the horses stretched themselves into their collars, and the axes
cracked again in the pines.

My afternoon back in the cook shanty was a busy one. There were
bushels of potatoes to peel, onions to cry over and slice, pans and
cooking utensils to wash and a stack of bread to cut. Old Jacques

taught me the trick of slicing fresh-baked bread by heating the knife on the cookstove every few slices, and how to open number ten tin cans of tomatoes with two strokes of the cleaver. When I messed up a can on my first try, the old fellow yelled:

"Such ha half-baked cookee I never see. You mus' 'ave been put in with da bread and taken out wit' da cookies, you damn fool!"

Shortly after dark the men returned from the cutting. The teamsters stabled, unharnessed and fed their horses, while the others washed up at the end of the log bunkhouse, using hot water from the boiler on the big heater in the middle of the room. The cook directed me to strike the big iron triangle to summon the hungry men to supper. Silently they filed in and went at it. What stacks of food they put away! My young legs were weary from running back and forth to keep the table supplied. I wished I had had roller skates, like Paul Bunyan's cookees had.

After supper the men were busy, sharpening their axes, putting a razor-edge on their crosscut saws with steel files, or mending torn and worn clothes. A few started a game of blackjack with dimes as the stake. By eight o'clock everyone was in the bunkhouse, sitting on the edge of his bunk. A young jack brought a fiddle and played "The Irish Washwoman", "Turkey in the Straw", and a few jigs to the accompaniment of the stomping of heavy boots.

Pipes were pulled out and the rancid smoke curled up to the low ceiling. Peerless, a mixture strong enough to remove the enamel from a beginner's teeth, was the favorite smoke. A few men cut fine chips from their plug tobacco and smoked that. The Swedes, Norwegians, Danes and Finns seldom smoked, but chewed Copenhagen snuff from a flat, round box which fitted snugly in their hip pockets. This "Snuss", black, powdery and powerful, was placed under the lower lips and kept there until the "dynamite" was dissolved. No camp with a Scandinavian crew could operate without a huge supply of "snuss" in the store. Cigarettes were never smoked in a lumber camp. They were called "coffin nails" and "pimp sticks" by the shanty boys. Anyone coming into camp smoking a cigarette was suspected of moral turpitude or of being low enough to rob his own grandmother. Cigars were expensive and rarely smoked except at Christmas time or when the foremen treated the boys for a big production of logs on the landing.

The "deacon's seat", a wide log bench at the end of the bunkhouse, was filled by old Barney, the champion camp story-teller, and a few of the old case-hardened men recognized for their leadership and skill in the woods. This seat was jealously guarded by the oldsters and was a place of honor won only by years in the camps. Any greenhorn attempting to occupy it was promptly ousted by catcalls or a heavy hand on the scruff of his shirt. Barney led off, between puffs from his Peerless loaded pipe, telling of his latest exploit with a woman in a Pentoga brothel. When the handclapping subsided, Jerry Mahoney spit a quid onto the hot heater and told of his last fight in Kate Piper's saloon. Each occupant of the "deacon's seat" added his own account of town exploits. The camp fiddler then raised his instrument to his shoulder and played a sad lament before the men turned into their bunks, clothed in their woolen underwear.

The air in the bunkhouse was cloudy with tobacco smoke and the rancid odor of drying socks and the sweat of men. One of the young men reached up to pull the rope to open the skylight in the roof to let in fresh air. Barney sprang at him like a tiger and pulled him away, cursing:

"You God damn greenhorn! Where were you raised? You city dude, don't you know that that damn night air is poison?"

In an instant the men were out of their bunks in a heated argument over the comparative merits of bunkhouse air and fresh night air.

The skylight remained closed, but not before one of the younger punks piped up from his top bunk:

"No wonder there is so much fresh air in the woods. These damn old cristers keep all the stinking air locked up in the bunkhouse."

By nine o'clock I was dead on my feet and climbed to my top bunk. I had hardly dropped off to sleep before I had visitors, which I had been too tired to notice the night before. My neck and feet were full of needles. As I opened my eyes in the dim lantern light, they seemed to drop from the roof onto my face and stung me in a dozen places at one time. I hid under the rough woolen blankets, but they crawled down in and attacked my tender skin in all its exposed places. I slept fitfully all night despite my fatigue. When the cook roused me at four o'clock to begin my arduous rounds of the long day, I was happy to get out of my infested nest. I learned from Jacques that the nightly raids of innumerable bedbugs hidden in the cracks of the logs and wooden bunks were the bane of lumbercamp life, to be endured like snow, ice and long hours of work.

Most lumberjacks were immune to these pests but I found dozens of welts on my body. The more I scratched the worse they itched. I was born fifty years too soon. There was no effective bedbug disinfectant. One just bore them, for fifteen dollars a month. I was thoroughly loused up with bedbugs and "greybacks", huge body lice, that stuck to every seam in my clothes. At the end of my two weeks' "vacation" I was literally crawling with vermin, to the horror of my mother when I reached home. She put me through the only delousing process then known—all my clothes were boiled and my head liberally doused with kerosene.

My two weeks in the lumber camp filled me with a new respect for those hardy men who spent most of their lives in the pines for pitifully small wages, wet to their hips in freezing weather and little to look forward to except a few days or weeks in drunken carousals and cheap women, but left me with no desire to seek wealth by their route.

Men O' The Woods

Along every road that radiated from Iron River lived men who had taken up claims or squatted on small pieces of land, to live a life of quiet or to escape from the hampering confines of town.

Fred Miller was one such homesteader. He had previously owned a section in Stambaugh township where iron ore was discovered.

Uninterested in becoming wealthy, he had sold his mineral rights to the
Oliver Mining Company, which developed the Riverton Mine and paid
Fred a surface rent on which he lived happily in his woods retreat on
Little Hagerman Lake, twelve miles from town on the Brule River road.

Fred had a few acres of clearing, raised ten or twleve bushels of
potatoes and an assortment of vegetables. All his meat, except saltpork
and an occasional slab of rusty bacon, came from the woods, lakes and
streams round about. He was a fat, jolly man, almost as round as he
was tall. He always reminded me of Santa Claus. His belly shook like
a bowlful of jelly at a good story. He had no beard, but a grey, flowing
mustache stained yellow under his nose from his pipe.

With him lived Frank and Joe Dittmeyer, nephews whom Fred took
under his hospitable wing. These young men were skilled woodsmen
who could blaze a trail without a compass, track a wounded deer for
miles through the wilderness, trap like Indians and fish as successfully
as an Icelander. There was no woods skill at which they were not expert. Frank, the elder brother, became a close friend of Stewart Edward White and was one of the principal characters in the author's
"The Blazed Trail." Joe was the first white child born in Iron River,
his parents having come from "down below", as southern Michigan was
called. He was born in the log house which was a part of the big boarding house which my parents bought when they moved from Stambaugh to
Iron River.

Fred Miller and the Dittmeyer boys came to town monthly for their
supplies and a few rounds of drinks with their friends, usually making
the trip in with Frank Kline, the supply teamster for the Menominee
Lumber Company camp on the Brule. The trip home was made by a
hired team and wagon or buckboard. My father and I took them home
on one such occasion. On the way out the bottle went the rounds every
time the horses rested on top of a hill. By the time we arrived at Little
Hagerman Lake, Fred and the Dittmeyers were ready to "sleep it off"
in their cabin. Their sleeping shack was separate from the cook shack.
The bunks were screened with cheesecloth against the hordes of mos-
quitoes which came up from the marsh nearby. We dumped them into
these bunks, drew together the screen and soon heard their heavy
snores.

My father directed me to get some lunch for the two of us before we
started the trip home. While he was watering and feeding the horses
in the lean-to barn, I searched for something edible to cook. It was my
first experience at preparing a meal. I found some salt pork incrusted
with a layer of salt. This I fried in a frying pan over the wood stove
and gave it an extra salting. Then I fried some eggs in the salty grease
and served it to my father with bread and coffee thick as syrup. Neither
of us could eat the salty mess and right there my father, no cook himself, gave me a lecture on "freshening" rather than salting salt pork.

On our way home we picked up Mickey Ryan, a lumberjack who,
carrying his "turkey", was on his way to town after being fired at the
lumber camp for picking a fight with the straw boss. Mickey was a
rough and tumble artist with a wide reputation. He stopped off at Kate

Piper's saloon for "a few drinks" and asked my father to take him back to another camp the next day. Mickey entered the saloon and yelled at the crew gathered at the bar:

"I'm the man who beat your father," and looked around for a challenger. There were no takers. He spotted his friend, little Danny Kane, a shacker on the Brule, down for the day. Grabbing Danny around the waist, he swung him onto a table and ordered him to sing. Danny, afraid of no man or beast, sang the hated song: "I Could See the Marks of Poverty on his Dirty Irish Face." Mickey knocked Danny off the table and drove him out of the saloon with a stove poker for his reflections on the Irish.

The district was full of woods characters who spent a few months in the camps and lived a precarious existence in town in the off season. "Deadwater" Joe, a river driver, was more cunning than most. He was always broke in town, begged his meals and mooched his drinks, but always kept a wad of money hidden in his socks, for "hard times", he said. He fought lumberjacks when they came down with their stake at the spring breakup and he usually lost in the fight, but managed, while rolling on the floor during the struggle, to get his hands into his opponent's pockets and come away with a fat roll of bills.

Many of the woodsmen were expert rifle shots and supplied their own meat from the deer herds which abounded in the tall timber and lake shores. Andy Chamberlain lived at James Lake and staged a party for his friends one Fourth of July. Well lubricated with rotgut from "Pigface" Conley's saloon at Elmwood, the men began to boast of their skill with a deer rifle. Mike McGraw went into his bedroom and came out with a 30-30 rifle and told Andy to hold an onion up in his fingers and he'd show them some real shootin'. Andy held the onion in his finger tips and Mike promptly shot it to pieces.

Chris Conway lurched up unsteadily and said: "Hell, that's no shooting at all, at all. Here, Andy, hold up this matchstick and I'll show you some expert shooting."

His gun wavered and exploded. Andy lowered his hand and found he had three fingers missing.

Clarence McDermott, lumberman, teamster and farmer, lived alone a few miles from town on the Ice Lake road. He and Tom Murray were drinking partners and had many bouts with old man John Barleycorn. Both were crack shots with a revolver and when in their cups would boast of their prowess with a Colt 45. Once when they were liquored up they sat in their chairs in Clarence's house and took turns at trying to part each other's hair with bullets. There were several misses and the walls were pocked with bullet holes. Steadying his arm on a table, McDermott took another shot and put a permanent crease in Murray's scalp where he usually parted his hair with a comb.

McDermott immediately swore off and didn't drink for years. Then one day he met Murray and the boys at a bar and went on a terrible "tear." He and Murray stood with their feet on the brass rail and drank until they had to be carried into the back room. Clarence died only a month later. Just before he died, he confided to his friend: "Be

Jaysus, I used to be able to take it by the quart. It must be that damned
rotgut they sold us at Billy Hill's."

Dick Nevers worked in the lumber camps as a teamster and as a
foreman on the drive. He was one of the highest paid men, for he was
sober, steady and a leader among the men. Nothing was too hard for
him to tackle. Log jams were a challenge to him. White water held no
fear for this man of the woods. He worked hard all winter, saved his
money, then came to town when the drive was over and spent it all in a
protracted spree. Every year for many years he planned to go to the
Minnesota State Fair at Minneapolis, but each year his money was gone
before he could make the trip. Finally one year he managed to get as
far as St. Paul. Jingling the money in his pocket, he stepped into a
saloon "just for one little drink." Three days later he found himself
lying behind an abandoned barn on the outskirts of the city, pockets
empty and his head feeling like an empty barrel. When he sobered up,
he walked to Minneapolis and the fairgrounds, only to find the place
empty and the exhibits gone until the next fall.

Milwaukee breweries did a great business in our town. Schlitz and
Blatz were always on tap. It was used as a "chaser" by the whiskey
drinkers and as a beverage by most others. "Rushing the growler" was
a favorite pastime. This meant buying beer by the pail at fifteen cents
a fill and consuming it away from the taverns—in homes or behind the
barn or on the job. Heavy kegs of "halves" or "quarters" were bought
for larger home parties, picnics or family reunions, to be topped by a
cake of ice to keep it cool and "tapped" by knocking out the bung and
inserting a beer faucet.

Fred Bisonette and Joe Kapusta ordered a "quarter" to celebrate
Fred's birthday. They invited Frank Krauser and Charlie Mottes to
share their treat. Fred set the keg upon his kitchen table, knocked out
the bung and drove in a wooden faucet. As the beer foamed out into the
bucket, they sat around drinking the brown brew.

Joe smacked his lips a few times, then looking at Fred, said: "This
beer don't taste right, Fred. Where did you get it?"

"Why, this is some of Frank Camin's Schlitz. Why, what's the matter with it?"

"Well, you taste it again. See what you t'ink."

Tasting the beer a second time, Fred stopped, looked at the glass in
his hand and said, "No, b'crise. It don't taste right, does it?"

When they got the same opinion from Frank and Charlie, Frank said,
"There is something wrong with this damn horse piss. Mebbe it is poi-
soned. We better have it tested."

So they took a bucketful down to Emil Ammerman's drugstore and
asked Emil to test it. Emil took the bucket to the drug counter in the
back of his store and poured some liquid into it. The beer turned
green. Coming to the front, he said to Fred and Joe, "It looks to me
like your horse got diabetes."

Danny Kane lived up the road on the Brule River beyond Fred Miller's place and frequently came by Fred's on his stout spotted Indian
saddle pony on his way to town for supplies. On his way from town one

day Danny came trotting his pony into Fred's yard with a hundred pound sack of Minnesota's Best Flour tied behind the saddle. Fred and the Dittmeyer boys came out to greet Danny and remarked: "That's too big a load for that little pony, Danny. Why don't you get a team and buckboard to haul your stuff in?"

"Why," said Danny. "That pony can carry Fred and his two hundred and fifty-five pounds like a damn and run with him."

"Well, let's try it," replied Frank.

So they led the pony to a high stump and boosted Fred into the saddle. The pony trotted off down the road without effort.

"Now, let me put that hundred pound sack of flour behind Fred," suggested Danny.

When this was done, the pony set off again, carrying his heavy load with ease.

"Hot damn," yelled Danny, throwing up his battered hat. "That should be worth a quart of good whiskey!"

The Dittmeyer boys were expert fishermen and hunters. We had many trips together. They had a dugout canoe made from a big pine log which they used to fish pickerel and bass on Little and Big Hagerman Lakes. A small stream ran through their clearing where we netted minnows for bait. We caught great fifteen to twenty pound pike and large mouth bass up to twelve pounds. In the early days "headlighting" deer was permitted, or at least overlooked. Frank and Joe fastened a carbide light to their caps to "shine" the deer's eyes as they paddled noiselessly around the shallow shores of the lakes, one carefully "feathering" the canoe paddle in the stern while the other sat in the bow with his rifle in readiness. When they saw a pair of eyes reflecting their light, the bowman raised his rifle, shined his light along the sights and pressed the trigger. This was the easiest method of furnishing the camp with fresh venison.

Another method was to make a "saltlick" by pouring salt on the ground around the roots of a big tree. The hunter waited on a scaffold built in the limbs of a nearby tree for a deer to come for the salt. These beautiful creatures could smell the presence of a saltlick from a great distance. Deer made deep trails to the lick by their frequent visits. A hunter needed only to look for fresh deer tracks to learn if deer were using the lick and what the chances were of getting a deer there.

Some of the homesteaders and shackers living in the deep woods used a still easier means of getting their meat. On finding a well-used deer trail through the woods, they set a rifle or shotgun loaded with buckshot between crotches of two small trees, pointing across the trail at the height of a deer's neck where it entered the body. Attaching a string to the rifle trigger and stretching it across the trail, they tied it to another tree. There they left it. When the rifle report was heard, day or night, they merely went out and brought in the dead deer.

This method, however, sometimes proved of doubtful worth. Tom Bangs and his son Bill lived in one of those lonely spots in the woods and secured their meat in this fashion. One day his son came home from town with a pack of supplies on his back and decided he would take a shortcut which came out upon a deer trail near the cabin. Dusk overtook him as he was nearing home when his leg bumped into the string stretched across the trail. His father found his son bleeding like a wounded deer and carried him to the shack where he applied a tourniquet above the bullet hole in his upper thigh. The next day he packed the boy on his own back to a neighbor three miles through the bush and had him hauled to town to a hospital where his leg was amputated at the hip.

Paul Minckler, a sawmill operator and lumberman, went "headlighting" for deer near his own lumber camp one night. He made a circle through the woods without success. As he came near the camp again he saw two pairs of eyes in his headlight's glare. He shot twice and brought both animals down in their tracks. They were a valuable team of young horses he had just bought.

Old Louie Hunter was a woods recluse living on Oberg's farm near the Brule River, where we fished for speckled trout. He had a running cancer on his nose which he kept covered with "court plaster." His nose dripped continually. We went fishing one day and passed the farm to see Louie splitting wood in the yard. He invited us in to have a lunch. He wanted us to try some of his sour dough pancakes and maple syrup. We entered the shack and sat down in the kitchen-bedroom-parlor. Louie began to stir up the batter. His sore nose began to run in the heat and dripped into the sour dough. We lost our appetite for pancakes and suddenly remembered that we had left our fishing tackle down at the river.

"Cannibal" Jack was a big, round-shouldered, easy-going town character who loved the woods, hunting and fishing and spent every minute he could steal away from his wife and children off in the woods. We met him fishing on Cook's Run one summer when the big ones were not biting too well.

"How's fishing, Jack?" I asked him.

"Hell, it's just no damn good. All I got was little ones."

"Let's see them, Jack."

Just then he pulled an under-sized speckled out of the water.

"He's too small to keep, ain't he, Jack?"

"Yes, he's too small to take home but this is what I do with the little ones."

Taking the little fish off the hook he bit it in two and proceeded to eat it raw.

We visited Mike McGraw's place on the Deerskin River over in Wisconsin where he and his wife, Jen, lived the year around. Mike was glad to have company, for Jen was a tartar and a hellcat when she had too much liquor under her apron.

"Come in, boys, have a lunch," welcomed Mike. "Jen and I are livin' high. I shot a big black bear last week and the blueberries are ripe. Jen likes bear grease in her blueberry pies."

At that he called into the shack: "Jen, we got two hungry kids to feed. Make them some blueberry pie."

Jen stuck her snagtooth face out of the low door and yelled back: "I ain't got no wood. How in hell do you expect me to bake pies without no wood?"

Mike turned to us in disgust: "Ain't that just like a woman? I just bought her a nice new ax and the woods is full of wood. Now she says she ain't got no wood!"

John the Bull, another escapee from civilization, was a dam tender at the Brule for the Menominee River Lumber Company. Part of his meat came from the stream he watched over. Speckled trout gathered in large schools below the dam during spawning season in an attempt to go upstream to the small creeks to lay their eggs. Locked there below the dam they were an easy prey for John, who would sit at the top of the dam and shoot them with his rifle.

John could neither read nor write, although it was rumored that he was of royal birth. He ordered his supplies from memory. During the long winters when he was alone, the only way he knew what was in the cans was to see the picture on the label. When the supplies were brought in on a wagon over the rough roads in the fall the labels were often torn off. He ate whatever he opened and sometimes lived on sauerkraut or canned tomatoes for days.

John got his nickname from the fact that he broke in a pair of enormous bulls to yoke and did all his farm and woods work with them. They weighed over a ton apiece and were his love and joy. They would often stick their big heads into the low doorway of his windowless shack and darken the interior until he ordered them away. When they became unruly he yoked them together and turned them loose that way for a week at a time for punishment. They seemed to know the reason for this treatment and a cross word from John would calm them down.

The bulls had a reputation for being dangerous to strangers and acted in the capacity of watchdogs on the place. Everyone gave them a wide berth. One day a gang of river drivers crossed the dam on their way to a log jam down-river, their peavies and canthooks slung over their shoulders. The bulls saw them approaching and, with rumbling bellows, charged them. The men stood their ground with their implements thrust before them to meet the charge. John came out of his hovel to see what the disturbance was all about. He gave the bulls a sharp command and they turned back to the barn shamefacedly.

John's shack was built of logs and banked with sod. The only door was so low that he had to crawl into it on hands and knees. One day a neighbor, who had missed seeing John for several days, stopped in to investigate. The bulls were standing before the shack, bellowing and pawing the ground with their huge front feet. He went for another homesteader and together they drove the bulls off into the barn and locked them in. The men crawled in through the door and found John dead in the bunk, smelling none too sweet.

Using John's old dugout canoe, they buried him in a shallow grave on the river bank. When they returned the next day with the sheriff to dispose of John's belongings, they found that the bulls had dug up the grave and had butted the body out on the ground. They reburied the remains and piled up a great heap of stones over the grave. Within a week one of the bulls died of grief. The mate was sold to a homesteader who used him to pack in his supplies from Iron River to the village of Alvin, across the Wisconsin line.

Queer individuals who had found it hard to adjust themselves in other parts drifted into the new country to find peace and a new start. Pat Belleville was one such. He was born without hair and never did grow any hair, fingernails or toe nails. He wore a red wig which he never took off in the presence of other men. He worked in the lumber camps but was never friendly with the crew. He did his work well, was sober and thrifty. His misfortune made him resentful and defiant to everyone but the foremen. He hated everyone and no one liked or associated with him. He was a lone wolf. As he grew older he became more and more eccentric. He would disappear into the woods and stay for two or three days at a time. One spring two of the lumberjacks followed him on one of his jaunts. He stopped in a clearing, drew a circle in the snow and shaking his fist to the heavens defied God to come down and fight him. Yet when a thunderstorm was in progress, Pat hid in his bunk and would not come out for his meals or go to work. He ended his days in a locked room in the County Poor House.

In his sober moments, the typical lumberjack and woodsman was a gentle creature, liberal with what he had, hospitable to visitors and shy in the presence of women. To beg a meal was beneath him, but when on an extended bender, his craving for strong drink was overpowering and he would at times go to extremes to get it. Sober he was proud, generous to a fault, asking no favors, and as "independent as a hog on ice."

Dave Craig, a young lumberjack and river driver, was one such modest individual. Money burned holes in his pockets and he gave with a lavish hand to his friends while it lasted. No chronic drinker himself, he was generous to his thirsty friends. A few weeks after a long log drive down the Menominee River, he found himself in Green Bay, Wisconsin, without money or friends. A proud man, he refused to jump a freight, the usual transportation of busted men. He started to walk to Iron River, a distance of 143 miles. He "counted ties" on the railroad bed. On the second day hunger gnawed at his innards but he would not beg. When he reached Menominee he dug his hands deep into his pockets and came up with a lone dime. Going to a store he bought a package of Peerless tobacco and "lived off" that until he reached home, his shoes worn through, his socks in shreds and his feet bleeding from the sharp cinders on the railroad track. He came "home" to our boarding house where we staked him until he found work again. Upright and industrious, he courted three of my sisters in succession but was unsuccessful with each.

By the people who came from "down below", it was believed that a lumberjack was a species somewhat lower than a human being. Val Gooth, a Hollander, built a sawmill at Indian Lake, then brought his family to live with him. Coming into town on the Chicago & Northwestern train, he and his wife and fifteen year old daughter stopped at the Boynton House for supper and the night. Andy Boynton had a special table for his more refined out-of-town guests and rough tables for his lumberjack trade. When they were seated in the diningroom before a table with white linen, the daughter became fascinated by the rough men eating and cursing at the other end of the room. Leaning over the table, she whispered to her father, "Those men over there. They are eating the same food as we are. I thought lumberjacks ate hay."

"No, dear," replied Val Gooth, "they really are part human."

That lumberjacks earned some of these accusations can be illustrated from the experience some of the ladies from "down below" had in a hotel in Iron Mountain. Some of the mill operators were entertaining some big Chicago lumber buyers and their wives. They engaged a special diningroom and put on a typical lumber camp meal. The ladies had expected something real fancy and didn't relish the coarse grub furnished by their hosts. Some of them were not hesitant in expressing their disappointment.

"Well," whispered Fox, the big mill owner, to one of the committee, "let's give these god damned dames a real party!"

Going down into the bar, he found a jolly bunch of men just down from the spring drive.

"Boys," he said, "we're throwing a big party upstairs. Lots of food, plenty of good whiskey and some women. Come on up, all of you."

"Whoopee," yelled Joe Behnan. "I'm hungry for whiskey and women. To hell with the food. Let's go up, boys."

Up they went, stomping in their caulked boots, and into the private diningroom. What they saw there took the zip out of them. They were not accustomed to such refinement. Those women didn't look like the "ladies" they had known. Shyly they sat down at the tables, staring at the beautifully dressed females and fingering the glasses of liquor poured out to them. The party looked as though it would be a failure despite this local color from the woods. The silk and voile dresses on the women and the rough mackinaws and open plaid shirts of the men made a striking contrast in the room.

But as the mill owners plied the jacks with more and more liquor, the woods boys overcame their shyness and entered into the spirit of the occasion. Throwing off some of their inhibitions in the presence of the fair sex, they were off, telling some of their favorite lumber camp stories. One of the jacks staggered up to one of the ladies and asked her to dance with him. When she refused, he hit her a resounding slap on the buttocks and went on to the next.

One of the mill owners, thinking to relieve the embarrassing situation, said to her, "Don't pay any attention to them. They think they are in a whore-house."

Lumber Camp Personnel

Each camp had its own complete personnel. The lumber camp operator selected his own foreman, called the "head push", whose responsibility it was to push the work and the men along to complete the cutting and hauling before the spring thaws stopped the operations.

Courtesy Hines Lumber Co.

Lumber Camp Crew

Courtesy Hines Lumber Co.

Dinner in the Pines

The foreman picked his own camp crew. Foremen were chosen for
their thorough knowledge of lumbering, their ability to handle rough
men and for their reputation for being able to whip any jack who became
insubordinate. Whenever a lumberjack questioned the authority of the
foreman he was promptly subdued by the latter's heavy fists and heavy
boots.

Men who got into fights were allowed to finish them unless they resorted to knives or guns. If they carried open grudges which impaired
their work, they were given their pay checks and told to take their "turkeys" and get to hell for town. Should a foreman be bested in a fight,
he lost the respect of his men and had to be dismissed. Fighting was
not a matter of merely boxing while on your feet. It was slug, kick,
bite, chew, butt, gouge and "putting the boots to 'em."

The "walking boss" was a super-foreman who supervised several
camps and had a pair of fancy trotters and a cutter or buckboard to
take him from one camp or crew to another. A variety of "straw
bosses" worked under the foreman and the "walking boss", directing
the smaller crews and jobs in different parts of the woods. The camp
clerk was the timekeeper, ordered the supplies of food and equipment.
He also made out the payroll and wrote the checks, ran the little store
where the men bought tobacco, "snuss", mittens, socks, mackinaws,
underwear, caps and other necessities. He checked the incoming supplies and sent out orders with the teamster who supplied the camp.

The "scaler" measured the logs with the Scribner rule as they were
hauled and decked at the rollways on the river bank and marked them
on the end with the company's identification hammer for easy sorting
when they arrived at the sorting booms down the river at the end of the
drive. He was required to record his measurements and send them to
the owners or lumber company operating the camp. Upon his honesty
and accuracy depended the amount of payment made to owner, or homesteader and the amount collected from the mill or lumber buyer. It
was an infrequent occurrence for the scaler to be bribed by one party
or the other to render a more favorable account of the amount of timber cut and hauled.

The supply teamster was the most envied of all the crew. He made
several trips to town each week to bring in food and equipment, so he
enjoyed both town and camp life, while most of the crew went into the
woods in the early fall and did not come out to town until the spring
breakup or after the drive was finished. He slept in the office building
with the bosses and others belonging to the upper staff, and enjoyed a
higher wage than anyone else except the office crew and the bosses.
This "horse-skinner" had unusual skill with the six reins and the long-
lashed whip with which he controlled six-horse teams. I have seen him
"pick off" a balky lead horse twenty feet away with his long whip, yet
his horses were his pride and joy. No one was allowed to handle or
feed them but he. They were always ready to "pull their hearts out"
for him when a loaded wagon became stuck in the deep, muddy ruts in
the poorly kept supply roads.

The blacksmith in his log smithy was an important and indispensable craftsman in every camp. He was one of the most skilled employees and worked long hours when the need arose. He shod all the big horses, which was a backbreaking job, mended broken sleigh runners, shaped bunks for the log sleds, eveners, whiffle-trees and neckyokes, put new links in broken chains, sharpened peavies and canthooks and did an endless number of repairs. More often than not he worked late into the night to equip the men and the teams for their work the next day.

The filer was the aristocrat of the crew. A skilled and experienced artisan, he carried on his work in a little room which few were allowed to enter. Wearing glasses for his fine work, he was an artist with a metal file. He retooled the crosscut saws which had been worn down by the sawyers cutting the timber. He was paid well and enjoyed a freedom no other man in camp had. Like the blacksmith, he worked at an exclusive trade and was jealous of passing on his technique to others. Usually he was a family man, sober, and thrifty, consequently saved his money and had contempt for those who spent their stake within a few days of reaching town.

"Road monkeys" made up the road repair crew, building and maintaining the tote and supply roads as well as the iced highways over which the great loads of logs were hauled. A "road monkey" was not required to have a special skill, as the work to be done was obvious and there was always a "straw boss" to supervise the job. "Road monkeys" began their work early in the fall in order to have the roads ready when the heavy work of hauling supplies, skidding logs and hauling the timber to the rollways got under way. They filled holes on the road bed, built rods of corduroy or log bridges over swampy terrain, cut out and filled in "turn-outs" to allow teams to pass each other and kept the roads clear of falling trees and brush. It was a lowly job and the pay was low. Every "road monkey" looked forward to the day when the foremen would promote him to a more lucrative position.

The "straw boss" was an under boss who took charge of a small crew in a section of the operations and was expected to direct his crew and also work along with the men. His ambition too was to acquit himself in such a manner as to merit a better and better paying job.

The rest of the crew was made up of sawyers, swampers, teamsters and sprinkler men, mentioned in another chapter.

The scale of pay depended upon the skill and experience of the individuals. The ability to handle men, use an ax, pull a saw, drive a team, etc., and the labor supply, determined the rate of pay.

Experienced foremen received from $75.00 to $100.00 a month; the "walking boss" who supervised several camps, from $80.00 to $120.00; the scaler from $50.00 to $65.00; sawyers, $26.00 to $30.00; blacksmith, $35.00 to $45.00; filer, $30.00 to $40.00; swamper, $20.00 to $26.00; teamster in camp, $26.00 to $30.00; supply teamster, $45.00 to $60.00; road monkey, $20.00 to $26.00; clerk, $26.00 to $30.00; "riverhog", $2.00 to $3.00 per day; cook, from $60.00 to $100.00, according to his ability to save; cookie, or chore boy, $15.00 to $25.00. Meals and a bunk were included.

Most of the lumbering was carried on by large companies financed

by outside capital. The companies bought several sections of timberland from the government or from homesteaders at a few dollars an
acre. Frequently the foreman was directed to encroach on adjoining
timber not included in the original deal. "Round forties" were those
lands which surrounded the purchased tract and were stolen when not
watched over by the owner. Occasionally small operators entered the
field and many of them amassed considerable wealth in their private
ventures. Whenever these smaller, independent loggers began operations in adjacent territory, the competition between them and the big
companies became keen. The big fellows tried with various means to
crowd the little fellows out of business. Crews were raided by the
promise of higher wages and better chuck. Dams were blown up after
the company's logs had been driven down the river, to prevent the private operator's logs from being floated down to the mills. When the
logs owned by both reached the sorting booms above the mills, crews
were paid extra for stealing the timber by shunting it into company
booms. The large companies frequently sold their logs under cost to
bankrupt the private men in the competition of the open market.

The crews of the small operators were usually intensely loyal to the
boss and many fights took place between rival crews whenever they met
in the woods, on the drive or in saloons. Many of the private companies
lost their "last red shirts" bucking this competition. Some had mortgaged their teams, equipment and their logs to set up in business. The
big companies were never loved and always feared by their competi-
tors and even by their own crews.

The smaller operators were disdainfully dubbed "haywire outfits",
because they usually had equipment which was bought as cast-offs from
the big companies. Their credit was limited and their equipment had
to be repaired frequently with wire used in baling hay. Haywire was
the logger's and the farmer's friend. Most teamsters carried several
strands of haywire to make necessary emergency repairs on the road
and woods. There was nothing as handy and as effective as haywire
for woods and farm use.

Camp cooks were temperamental, irascible, independent and tyran-
nical. They were the hardest worked and the most imposed upon of
any members of the camp crew. Early and late meals, unexpected
guests who were never turned away hungry, critical men and undepend-
able "cookees" made their lives hard. It was the privilege of lumberjacks to criticize the food whether it was good or bad, for this was
their opportunity of "blowing off steam", even though their griping was
not justified. Many of the cooks were heavy drinkers and had a bottle
of booze hidden for occasional nips, a practice which added to the
troubles of the foreman. Frequently the camp would awaken for a
day's work to learn that the cook had taken his "turkey" for a "walk"
the night before, leaving the foreman to rustle up a substitute cook
from among the crew until someone went into town to find another.

The tables in the cook shack were always piled high with a large
variety of food—cookies, pies, cake, pickled meats, cheese, bread
and butter. The coffee pot was always boiling on the big wood-burning

range. No one was ever charged for a meal or two. Drifters from other camps were given a meal and a night's lodging to help them on their way.

The "cookee" was usually a boy in his teens who had quit school to live a life of independence, or a broken down lumberjack who could no longer withstand the rigors of woods work. He was the butt of the cook's temper and the crew's teasing. He was loved by the shanty boys but none of them would admit their affection for him. His pay was low and he dressed mostly in the cast-off clothes of the lumberjacks. He was called "chore boy", "crumb chaser", "gut-hammer" or the "cook's devil". Up at the cook's call by three or four o'clock, he ran his legs off setting the tables, carrying tons of food, splitting wood for the cook-stove, keeping up a supply of hot water, "swilling" the pigs, packing lunch for the noon meal and taking it to the scene of the cuttings. It was his responsibility to awaken the crew in the bunkhouse by striking a hammer on the big circular saw or iron triangle, "gut-hammer", hung before the cook shack and calling:

"Get up. It's daylight in the swamp. The grub's on the table and the S. O. B.'s in the bunk."

There were frequent changes in "cookees", for they received no open sympathy for their work. They stood it until they could no longer "take it", then drew their pay at the office and hooked a ride back home with the supply sleigh.

Once a lumberjack entered the cook shanty, he was required to eat his meal in silence. No talking was permitted beyond the request to "pass the beans" or to pass the "wagon grease" (butter), etc. These were busy men and they had no time to waste talking at meals. Should a stranger, unaccustomed to the tradition, open up a conversation at the table, he was met with open frowns or a kick under the table. If that did not suffice, the cook told him off. The cook was master of all he surveyed in the cook shanty, although his authority was limited to its four walls.

But once in the bunkhouse, the men indulged in lively and spicy conversation. Talk centered around the accomplishments of the day, the big loads of logs hauled, the accidents to the men, what they planned to do with their poke after the spring breakup, the women in their lives, ribald stories, or teasing the weaker ones.

Invariably one of the men in the crew was the self-appointed leader, as was Barney who worked at a camp where I spent two weeks as a boy. He was the recognized, unofficial boss. His stories were the most salacious, his voice the loudest, his frame the biggest and wherever he sat was the head of the room.

Barney was a big, bull-necked Norwegian, square-headed, with fists like hams and a cold blue eye that could stare down even the toughest foreman. The men did not stir out of the bunkhouse after breakfast until Barney stood up and gave the signal. They quit work at night when Barney laid down his ax and shouted in his big voice that shook the tree-tops:

"All right, you bullies! Time for beans and saltpork!"

Whenever there was a complaint over working conditions or the food, Barney was the arbitrator with the foreman. Whatever deal he made with the boss was accepted by the men. He was the first man in the woods in the fall and the last one to leave in the spring. He had a loyal following and could be relied upon to round up a crew for the camp. Whoever had him in his employ could be certain of having a satisfied gang. The men stuck with him wherever he worked. In town he herded the men, watched over their pokes when they were drunk and in the fall rounded them up again for the camp. He was feared and respected by the saloon keepers and bartenders while looking after his friends in their cups. He could swing a mean fist and a devastating caulked boot. He was the perfect exemplification of the hard-working, hard-living and hard-drinking lumberjack of the day. He was a true "bull of the woods."

When the lumber camps closed at the spring breakup and the thawing snow and ice prevented further cutting and hauling of timber, hundreds of professional lumberjacks appeared in town, wild for whiskey and women, two things always associated in their minds. Hungry for the strong stuff, they cashed their checks, which sometimes ran into a hundred and fifty or two hundred dollars, at a local saloon, and with a roll of green money in their stagged pants, they went on an orgy of drinking until they were full as ticks, treating and "loving" until their money ran out, or until it was taken away from them by the saloon keepers or bartenders or hangers-on. What the saloons did not get, the "bawdy-house ladies" got. Then, bleary-eyed, broke and at loose ends, the big he-men of the woods went from saloon to saloon looking for easy treats from their former companions or ran accounts until the next pay-off.

To keep the men in the saloons as long as their money lasted, each saloon had snack lunches at the end of the bar or on a table where the men could help themselves, thus eliminating the necessity of getting a meal at a boarding house. Cheese, pretzels, crackers, salt and smoked herring, rye bread and sardines were there for the taking. But if a busted lumberjack came to the lunch table too often, he was driven away with a curse:

"Go 'way, you drunken bum. That's for our good customers!"

Then again after the spring drive, another but smaller and tougher crew of men descended upon the town for their celebrations—drinking, fighting and "loving" at so much a "throw." It was all a part of the life of the era of the big pine and hemlock. Rough men, living in primitive fashion, away from the civilizing influences of town and city life, working long hours in the snow and wet, most of them single and free from family responsibilities, sought release in the only way they knew.

But it should not be thought that all of the lumber and drive crew lived that way at the close of the logging season. A few were married men with families, with a piece of land to farm and ambition to get ahead. Some even aspired to become lumber camp operators some day. These men hoarded their hard-earned money for a better day. At the breakup they headed for home and family to turn the check over to the little woman for safe-keeping. Some of these, after a few winters in the camps, turned to farming or business as a safer and more profitable vocation.

A few wiser lumberjacks, remembering what happened last year, cashed their checks at local grocery stores and deposited some of their money with the storekeeper as a reserve stake to draw on after their first spree was over. Deposit receipts were not required of the storekeeper—just a handwritten notation on his books that Jack Lumberman had a credit of seventy-five dollars to be drawn upon when he sobered up.

Most lumberjacks had no restraint over their money when they entered a saloon. The place was filled with their friends and it was "your right hand to your partner, left to the bar, and your money was gone." Often men who owned teams of horses and worked in the woods near town found themselves deep in debt and their horses and rigging mortgaged to the saloon keepers whom they patronized at night.

Reverend Westphal of the First Presbyterian Church spent much of his time trying to stem the tide of carousing and to reform some of the more intelligent lumberjacks when they came to town. He was stopped by one of the men of his acquaintance and was asked for the loan of a dollar "to sober up on."

"What will you do with it? Spend it on whiskey?" asked the Reverend.

"No, sir," replied the 'jack. "I want it to buy some medicine I heard of. I get stiff in the joints."

"Well," shot back the minister, "if you kept out of those joints, you wouldn't get stiff."

Cutting the Big Stuff

Saturday nights and Sundays were times of leisure in the camps. The men stayed up later Saturday nights and played cards for small change or for plugs of chewing tobacco or packages of Peerless, the universal smoke. Few were lucky enough to get a pass to go to town, even if transportation were available. The foreman was very reluctant to let the men off, for it invariably meant losing hands to an extended spree in the saloons.

The camp boss attempted to offer some diversion in the shape of a gramophone, books and magazines, but these were soon discarded for devices of the men's own planning. The most popular reading material was the Police Gazette with its pictures of prize fighters, horse races and hippy women whose costumes left little to the lumberjack's imagination. On Saturday nights before Christmas the foremen staged a lumberjack dance in the cook shanty. The tables were stacked against the walls. Sand was thrown on the floor. A camp orchestra consisting of a fiddler and an accordion player supported by a mouth-organist played square dances, waltzes and the schottische to the stomp of heavy-booted feet. Since there were no women in the camp, half of the men were "women" with red handkerchiefs tied around their heads or flour-sack aprons around their waists. There was considerable jealousy over who would be "women." To keep the peace it was necessary to require the "women" to become men and men to become "women" at the intermission, which was enlivened by Irish jigs or clog dances.

Sunday morning breakfast was an hour later than on week days and the tempo of the day was relaxed. The axemen ground and sharpened their favorite axes until the blades could shave the hair off their arms. These axes were carefully hidden in their bunks and woe to anyone touching them. Some axemen would rather have another touch their women than handle their axes. There was a special Sunday dinner with suet pudding and other light touches. Sunday was also "boiling out" day, when the men changed their clothes and boiled out the lice and nits clinging to them in big iron kettles out of doors. Red underwear was hung on every bush and tree about the camp site. Occasionally when the men found big "greybacks" (lice to you) they pitted them in fights against each other with plug tobacco or boxes of "snuss" as stakes.

If the weather was unfavorable the men spent the afternoon in the bunkhouse telling stories and bragging of their prowess with logs, liquor and women, on whom their minds constantly dwelt. One tough jack who boasted about the fact that the authorities in his home town in Maine had requested him to leave for good, insisted that he could always recognize any woman he "had been with", for he said:

"When I kiss 'em, I brands 'em at the same time."

Some of the men were proud to display their "lumberjack smallpox" —scars on their faces and bodies gotten from caulk kicks in drunken brawls in town or on the river drives. Some had parts of an ear missing, nostrils slit or a finger crippled from these fights. Each was a mark of distinction.

Liquor was forbidden in camp, but it was a hard edict to enforce. Some had bottles hidden in their "turkeys" or ditty bags. No one was so low as to steal whiskey from another man's "turkey" unless he was in the last stages of delirium tremens and began to see pink snakes or flying elephants, which was not infrequent after a trip to town. In case of such dire need any lumberjack was ready to share his liquor with his suffering brother.

In the absence of hard liquor some of the men bought "Hoffman Drops", a highly alcoholic mixture which they diluted with water for drinking, sending some of them berserk. "Pain-killers" in various forms were brought into camp for "rheumatism" or bad tooth aches. "Hinckley's Bone Medicine" was ninety per cent alcohol and could be bought at some of the camp stores, but it had to be rationed out sparingly by the camp clerk if he wanted a full work crew the next day. It was called "liquid dynamite" and was highly explosive to the "innards."

Lumberjacks were great whittlers. In their leisure time evenings and Sundays some whittled on soft pine, fashioning chains inside of blocks of wood, wooden fans with notched edges for souvenirs for girl friends, toys and figures of big-hipped and heavy-breasted women.

Before daylight on Monday mornings the cry of the cookee: "It's daylight in the swamp" found the men ready to roll out for another day of grueling work in the deep pine woods. The breakfast call on the gong in front of the cook shanty brought them out to a breakfast of beans baked with blackstrap molasses, stewed prunes, fried salt pork, fresh baked bread or pancakes piled high with corn syrup and butter and steaming coffee sweetened with brown sugar and evaporated canned milk. The men were silent around the red, oilcloth covered table groaning with the heavy, nourishing camp grub. They stowed it away with both forks and knives into bulging cheeks. For those who liked it, black tea, strong enough to "float an ax" was gulped down by the quart. The zero weather, the deep snow and the heavy-muscle work demanded hot, nourishing and sustaining food. Some of the men filled their shirt pockets with big, round raisin cookies and doughnuts, for their mid-morning snack, before leaving the table.

When the cutting crew was sent into the big pine at the beginning of the winter's operation, saw and ax men were divided into pairs and were spread out by the foremen into the timber at safe intervals. Armed with a ten foot crosscut saw, two double-bitted axes honed to a razor's edge, a bottle of kerosene and a pair of steel wedges and a sledge hammer, they were ready to attack the big trees.

The head cutter located a tree, looked up to see which way it leaned and how it would fall naturally, then pointed out the direction of the probable fall. Then each man cleared out the underbrush around the tree to give wide clearance for their swinging axes. A piece of brush or low-hanging limb catching the ax as it arced down became a danger-ous boomerang and could seriously injure the axman.

Taking off their woolen mackinaws, the men proceeded to tramp down the snow around the tree to gain a solid footing. Then standing on the side of the direction of the fall, they began cutting a notch about three feet from the ground and ten inches deep, one cutter swinging his ax from a right hand position and the other from the left. It was advan-tageous for a woodsman to be ambidextrous in the use of an ax or saw, for they could change positions as their arms tired.

Laying their axes aside, the cutters began to cut the tree trunk with the crosscut saw, on the side opposite the notch, and from four to six inches higher. The resinous sawdust flew at each pull of the saw and made a fragrant pile on the white snow. As these yellow mounds grew they scented the air with a sharp odor so strong that one could taste it in the atmosphere—perfume to the hardy lumberjack. The men seldom rested in their steady back and forth pull on the saw until the tree be-gan to sway and crack unless the tree "pinched" the saw. When this happened, one of them drove a steel wedge into the cut, widening it un-til the "pinch" was relieved. Then sawing vigorously, they awaited the first cracking sound of the uncut part of the trunk and watched the top of the tree as it began its slow arc through the air. Then quickly seiz-ing the saw from the cut, they yelled:

"Timber! Here she comes!", so all nearby could hear, then stepped back to a place of safety behind another tree. As a shiver ran through the top branches, the giant of the woods began its descent, slowly at first, then with accelerated speed. As it struck the ground, snow flew up in a white cloud. The branches acted like springs and threw the tree back off the earth several feet, then it settled down into the deep snow like a dying animal.

The men had to be constantly on the alert when a tree started falling, for at times it would lodge against another, rest there momentarily, then shake loose and fall clear. At other times the lodging would spring the tree butt back and pin any "greenhorn" to the ground under its tons of weight. If a tree did not dislodge itself, the men had an even more dangerous task, for they had to cut the tree against which the first one lodged, a tremendously risky undertaking requiring the skill and caution of seasoned timber cutters, for they faced the double danger of working under the lodged tree and of being pinned down by both.

Once the pine was on the ground, the men sprang upon its trunk with their double-bitted axes in hand and proceeded to trim off the branches with deft swings of the sharp blades that made a clean cut down to the inner bark. No protruding limbs were permitted, for they acted as a brake when the big horse teams dragged the log to the skidway. When the trunk was trimmed, it was marked off by ax cuts into log lengths of from twelve to sixteen feet. Taking their crosscut saw again, the men began to cut through the tree. Here again the skill of the sawyers came into play, for as the tree lay on uneven ground, it would pinch the saw, so that it could not be pulled through the cut. Wedges were used to pry open the cut. If that did not suffice, the men would cut a small sapling from the woods to lift the log until the cut opened, then sawed it through.

The resin or pitch in the pine offered another obstacle, for the saw became gummed up and made it difficult to pull. Here a liberal application of kerosene on the full length of the saw solved the problem by dissolving the pitch.

As the log was marked off into proper lengths with an ax, the saw was placed into the ax cut and gently drawn back and forth until the saw cut was an inch or two deep. Then the sawyers swung into action. Planting their feet firmly on the snow, they pulled back and forth in an easy rhythm. The saw was never pushed. Each man gripped the saw handle lightly with his fingers, never pressing down or pulling up, but letting the saw "ride" through to the bottom of the log. Once the correct rhythm was set, the arms and body in motion, sawing was not too difficult. Occasional rests allowed the muscles to relax. "Riding the saw" meant pushing down on the forward or back stroke. "Stop dragging your feet" meant that the partner was a "greenhorn" or an amateur sawyer.

The logs were left where they lay until the skidding team hooked on and hauled them to the skidways, where they were piled up until the big logging sleighs took them to the rollways at the river bank.

Each skidding team had a teamster whose sole responsibility was to feed, water, groom, harness and drive the team. The "swamper" was the skidding teamster's assistant. He handled the chain attached to the eveners behind the horses, cleared a path for the horses with his ax, hooked the chain or skidding tongs onto the end of the logs or rolled the logs onto a v-shaped travois for easier pulling.

"Snaking" out the logs was a work of skill on the part of the

teamster, swamper and horses. Once the horses were hitched to a log
and a semblance of a road was cut through the brush, the teamster
spoke quietly to his big Percherons. Drawing the reins or "lines" taut
he held the animals back until their feet were straightened out and they
were in position to exert their full strength against their collars. At a
quiet chirp from the driver that was hardly audible fifteen feet away,
and the command: "Come, Dan. All right, Tom," the powerful team
eased into its harness and started the log on its way. Snow flew, brush
cracked and the horses steamed. Swinging around a fresh-cut stump at
the command, "Haw, boys," the horses turned left, then "Gee," back to
the skidding road and off to the skidway a few hundred feet away.

Steel chain was one of the most useful and most used means of hauling, decking and holding piles and loads of logs together. Each camp
had tons of chain of various sizes and uses, from a half inch to two
inches in diameter and from twelve to a hundred and fifty feet in length.

On the skidways were small piles of logs to be hauled out on the big
sleighs to the rollways on the river bank, where they would await the
spring drive. The sleighs used to haul the great loads of logs were from
eight to ten feet wide at the double runners and shod with inch-thick
steel. Twelve and fourteen cross beams or bunks were fastened across
the sleigh with a "king bolt" in the middle in order that the bunks could
be swung back lengthwise on the return trip so that sleighs could pass
each other more easily at the "turn-outs." The sleighs were drawn to
the side of the skidways and the logs were rolled onto the bunks, at
first by the loading and decking crew with canthooks, then as the pile
became higher, decking chains were placed around the middle of the
logs and the logs pulled onto the high load with horses. The entire load
was bound by chains at each end and was ready to go. The teamster
climbed to the top and drew up his reins. Again speaking quietly to his
horses, the driver reined his team to the right to "break" the runners.
Then straightening the animals out for a forward pull, he eased them
into their collars. Digging their sharp-shod feet into the ice and snow,
the horses started the load. Once the load, weighing from ten to fifteen
tons at times, gathered momentum, it did not stop until the rollway was
reached.

Each teamster endeavored to haul a record load. There was spirited
competition and lively small betting between the drivers. In the bunkhouse each crew bragged about the loads hauled during the day.

While the foreman sought to have the roads laid out along creek
courses, the roads often had to run over hills and down into valleys.
On the upgrade hauls, extra "tow" teams were stationed to hook onto
the sleigh tongue to help the load over the steep spots. On the down-
grade, sand and straw was scattered over the sleigh tracks to check
the flight of the big loads. Here whips flashed and men shouted picturesque oaths. Runaway loads were feared and were not infrequent,
resulting in death or injury to teamsters and horses. "Sluicing" a team
meant letting a load of logs get away on the downhill haul. Should a
sleigh runner strike an icy spot the sleigh would rush forward and get
out of control, pushing the horses at breakneck speed down the hill,

occasionally sending the animals and the load crashing off the road into
the woods, crushing horses and drivers to death. It was a disgrace for
a teamster to let this happen even though the "road monkeys" had not
taken the necessary precaution of properly sanding or covering the
down hill with straw. If the teamsters survived one of these "sluicings",
he was considered unfit to handle horses thereafter and was "grounded"
to some menial job in the camp or summarily discharged in disgrace.

Some of the logging roads traversed lakes and streams over deeply
frozen ice. This too was dangerous work, for some of the loads weighed several tons. At times as the heavily loaded sleighs passed over
the lake, the ice could be seen waving up and down like a rubber mat.
To avoid danger of sinking through the ice, teamsters took the precaution of unhitching the teams from the sleigh and attaching a long chain
to the end of the tongue from which it could quickly be unhooked should
the ice give way and the team driven to safety. My father's sleigh broke
through the ice one winter, only to be held up by a bottom layer of ice
long enough to allow him to disengage his team. Once a load broke
through it sank to the bottom of the lake, dragging the horses down to
their death.

"Drive-outs" or side turnouts were made along the roads for the
passing of teams on their treks back and forth from the skidways to
the rollways. Horses were the chief power at the time, although I recall in my early boyhood seeing forty teams of long-legged oxen which
were used by the Sawyer-Goodman Lumber Company in their lumber
operation. These were the last oxen used for that purpose. When I saw
them they were stabled in a big barn in town in the late spring, being
fattened up for sale as "beef" to Chicago packing plants.

Horses, or "hayburners" as they were called by the disrespectful,
were shod by the camp blacksmith with heavy iron shoes which had
sharp caulks at the toes and heels to enable them to navigate the iced
roads. A flat or smooth-shod horse was entirely helpless in the woods.
The teamster had to be skillful to prevent the horses from "caulking"
themselves or each other as they maneuvered through the woods or on
the roads. Each winter several horses were laid up or had to be shot
because of deep "caulking." Every teamster was an amateur veterinary
and had a cure for every horse ailment—nitre of saltpeter for colic
when a horse had gotten loose in the stable and had eaten too much
oats; pine tar for a cold; lard for severe chafing from the harness;
gall-cure or water from boiled hemlock bark for galled shoulders and
neck. Sloan's Liniment was the ready standby for cuts, bruises and
stiffness. There were always one or more horses laid up from injuries,
colic or overwork. With good horses selling at $600.00 or $700.00 a
pair, these great, patient and powerful animals received better care
and more consideration than an ailing lumberjack who worked for from
$25.00 to $30.00 a month and "found."

The horses were given the best of care by their teamsters. While
the teamster fed, groomed and watered his own team, a stable "boy",
usually a retired teamster, did a night shift in the big barns, watching
over the horses and reporting any mishaps or sickness which

developed during the night. The best timothy hay, steamed oats, corn and ground-feed were fed in great quantities to keep these fine beasts in prime condition for their strenuous work. The teamster decorated his charges, out of his own pocket, with long red horsehair tassels which hung from the bridles. Some bought tall red and yellow pompoms to fasten over the heads. The horses' collars were covered with wide leather "housings" trimmed with shining brass medallions, to keep snow and rain from wetting the necks and shoulders and chafing them raw. Celluloid rings of red, white and blue studded the harnesses and reins.

At the spring "breakup" those teams which were not used on the river drives were let out to pasture on company farms, to rest up and gain weight for the next fall and winter. Most of the horses had large, hard callouses or galls on their shoulders from their collars and bare spots on their bodies where the harness had worn off the hair in the cold weather. The galls were carefully treated with gall-cure or hardened with hemlock water. A horse never chafed in warm weather. The cold of winter stiffened their body hair and made it brittle. These spots were rubbed with animal oil or lard to start the hair growing again. The horses fared well during their vacation on the farm and were ready for another season in the late fall.

The largest load of logs ever hauled out of the woods consisted of 36,055 feet of virgin Michigan pine. The logs averaged eighteen feet in length. The height of the load was thirty-three feet and three inches. The weight was one hundred and forty-four tons. This load was decked by a chain and a team of horses. It was hauled by a team on iced roads to the Ontonagon River, then rafted in the spring to the nearest railroad where it was loaded onto nine flatcars and shipped to the Chicago World's Fair to be used in buildings there. As many as forty million feet of logs were taken out of the woods by one outfit in one season.

Logs from ten inches up were cut and taken out for lumber, the rest of the tree to lie and rot to make humus for tree growth of the future. It took seven years for the tops and branches to decay. There was no attempt to pile them up, for that was too expensive a procedure when it was believed that "Michigan pine would supply the world's needs forever." Forest fires kindled by the dry, resinous "slashings" completed the destruction which the lumber camps began.

The roads over which the big loads were hauled were iced by means of water sprinklers built at the camp. It was a great plank box mounted on a sleigh which had runners bent up at both ends and two tongues, so it did not need to be turned around, but could be pulled forward or back. On the top of the tank was a large opening into which barrels of water from a creek or lake were drawn up on skids by horsepower. At each end of the tank were openings through which the water poured into the sleigh tracks on the road. These openings were plugged with large wooden bungs which were knocked out when the sprinkling began. Icing the hauling roads was done at night when the temperature was below freezing and the other teams were in the stables. In the morning the road tracks were a glare of ice and made easy pulling for the big sleighs.

Home from the Drive Shaved and Shorn

At John Larson's camp on the Paint River two men operated the
sprinkler. On one night when the temperature was below zero, as the
team was hauling the great tank along the road spilling water in the
track in preparation for the next day's work, a band of timber wolves
which had been starved by the long, cold winter began to howl in the
woods around the sprinkler as it proceeded. The team became frightened by the howls and the odor of the wolves and then became unmanageable. They refused to move ahead and became entangled in the traces
and reins. Realizing that it would be impossible to do the work, the
men finally managed to unhitch the horses and turn them loose singly,
letting them make a run to the stables at the camp three miles distant.

The wolves followed the horses for a short distance, then came back
and circled in the woods around the tank, keeping up their unearthly
howling. The men knocked the plugs out of the water tank and let the
water run over the road. Then they crawled into the empty tank
through the hole on top and stayed there all night. At daybreak the
first team of log haulers came down the road and frightened the wolves
away. The men crawled out of their icy shelter, almost frozen stiff.
The horses had made it to the stables where the stable boy let them in.
The animals had become so badly frightened that they were no longer
fit to be used on the road sprinkler at night, but had to be put at skidding logs in daylight.

Crotched or joined double logs were called "schoolmarms." With
the jack's mind continually on sex when not on liquor, the appearance
of a crotched log in a deck brought out the remark:

"It's my turn at the schoolmarm. You had her last time."

These double logs were particularly dangerous to handle, they
pointed out, for they never rolled where they were wanted and would
at times make a dangerous flip in the wrong direction, pinning an un-
wary jack beneath.

Rotted or "shaky" butts of trees were left in the woods. Years later
the Diamond Match Company bought up these abandoned butts and split
logs and had them lumbered off for matchwood. This in itself was a
profitable business, for the match company could use every inch of
sound wood left on the ground. This was a sort of "gleaning after the
stealing." Harry Sunn and his father, local woods contractors, had the
contract to locate and ship the left-over timber at a neat profit.

Michigan pine which was to "last forever" was cut and sawed up in
one generation. It built millions of homes in the middle west, furnished
masts for ships sailing the Great Lakes and the Seven Seas and piled up
fortunes for those who were in on "cutting the big stuff."

The Spring Drive

The most romantic and dangerous feature of the lumbering business
was the "spring drive", when the logs cut and decked on the rollways
during the long winter months were floated down the rivers to the saw
mills at their mouths. All winter long the crews felled and cut the pine

into board length logs, hauled them to the river banks, stacked them up fifty and sixty feet high, awaiting the spring thaws when the snow and ice melted and flooded the streams.

After the regular crew in the camps could no longer work because of the thaw and were given their winter's pay checks, the younger and more skilled men were hired as "drivers" or "river hogs" to loosen the roll-ways, start the logs down the flooded streams and through the various dams which held back the rushing, icy waters. With "peavies" and long pikepoles they rolled, pried and guided the logs into the water and kept them going down the rivers.

Each dam has a "sluiceway" or narrow apron of water through which the logs were guided and shot through to the boiling water below. These dams were made of logs and earth in the narrow parts of the rivers and had been constructed or repaired the previous summer or fall. As the drive developed these dams were periodically closed to "build up a head of water" to float the logs above, then opened by a ratchet device to let the water down again to shoot the logs through. Each dam had a "tender" who lived in a tent or log cabin near the stream. He was on watch day and night. His was a responsible job, for a too-low head of water or too much pressure on the dam from above could ruin the drive and "wash out" the lumber operator's entire investment by a too long delay in opening the gates.

The "river hogs" wore caulked boots half way up their calves, two or three pairs of woolen socks, "stag" woolen pants cut off at ankle length and loose at the bottom to let out the water; heavy woolen underwear, red or dirt-grey, heavy plaid woolen shirts and a stocking cap. They had to be nimble, rugged and tough. It was work for he-men, only, who could take the cold, wet and grueling work without becoming ill.

These sharp-shod "hogs" were said to be able to "ride a bubble of water to shore." Among their own kind, they were exhibitionists. To prove their skill they often took great risks when others were looking on. They staged log-riding contests, standing on a big log, peavy poised for balance and riding through the dam, like rodeo performers mounting a broncho and staying with him to the finish. Drownings were frequent and expected. The extra pay and the thrill of dangerous moments were worth the risk. When a driver lost his life by drowning or by being crushed in a log jam, his body was often buried on the river bank in a simple ceremony, with a crude plank as a headstone. His caulked boots were taken off his feet and hung on a tree overhead, so he might enter the Kingdom barefooted like a little child. Unless relatives later claim-ed the remains, here his body passed into eternity and the dust.

"Greenhorns" and recent immigrants who worked in the woods were seldom selected by the drive foremen. Their inexperience often was an added risk to the safety of the other members of the crew and to the success of the drive. It was work for practical men who could size up a situation and act quickly to meet it. This was no place for timid, in-decisive men. It required nerve, reckless daring, muscular coordina-tion, nimble feet and a quick brain.

Oscar Peterson had been over "from the old country" less than a

year when he decided to try his hand in a lumber camp. He worked for
Herman Holmes on the Brule and made a fairly satisfactory "road monkey." He was slow of motion and slow of brain but he was willing. When
the spring breakup came, Oscar decided he would like to add to his
wages by going on the drive. Herman hesitated, contemplating the risk
both he and Oscar would be taking by having a slow-witted Swede in the
hurly-burly of a drive.

"I'll take you, Oscar, under one condition," Herman told him. "The
first time you fall off a log, you'll get your pay and go back home."

"By yiminy, das skol be ole right mitt me, Horman," replied Oscar,
offering Herman a chew from his box of Copenhagen "snuss." "You vill
see I make you von damn gude driver."

Everything went well until the drive reached Burnt Dam. Here the
head of water was high and the logs were passing through the dam at
racehorse speed. The main body of the crew walked along the river
bank, not daring to get caught on a log in the rushing water. As they
stood at the dam pikepoling the logs into the apron, they heard a yell
upstream and saw Oscar riding high on a big pine, coming at the rate
of thirty miles an hour. His blond hair was blowing over his eyes, his
mackinaw was gone and his pikepole was waving frantically to keep a
balance on the careening log.

As Oscar and his steed neared the dam, the crew yelled: "Jump,
Oscar, jump! You're going through the dam. You'll get drowned."

Oscar had no choice. The water was sucking his log cross-wise of
the current. As the log struck the dam gate, it stuck there. Oscar was
thrown into the rushing water as it poured over the dam and disappeared.
The crew ran down below the dam and saw Oscar's towhead bobbing up
and down in the water. As he passed a little island where a few logs had
stranded, his feet struck solid ground. Dragging himself up on land, he
lay down dripping and vomiting water. The whanigan boat was maneuvered to the island and brought him back limp and bedraggled.

Herman Holmes ran down to where the men were hauling Oscar out
of the boat, and shouted at him:

"You God damn square-headed Swede. Why didn't you jump when we
told you?"

"Vell, Horman, it vas like dis. How cood I yump ven Aye had no ting
tu stand from?"

The men were fed from a cook's tent or whanigan boat which moved
down the river as the drive proceeded toward its destination. The men
worked from twelve to sixteen hours a day. If a log jam developed, they
worked day and night, stopping only to snatch a lunch and to swill down
buckets of steaming coffee brought by the drive's cookee. Often they
walked several miles back to their sleeping tents and their meals. At
times there were two sets of cooks and cook tents or whanigans, which
were moved downstream either by wagon or flat-bottomed boats.

As the drivers rode the floating logs, they were frequently thrown
into the icy water by a "burling" or spinning log, to clamber back up
again between two other logs, holding on to their peavies, to resume
their operations. No driver ever changed clothing after a ducking. In

fact few had a change of clothing, except socks. To lose one's peavy
when being thrown into the water was considered disgraceful. The men
were fed four and five times a day but always lost weight on the drive.

Most of the logs had their bark knocked off by boulders in the stream
or by bumping and grinding against other logs. Some logs were called
"key" logs because of their buoyancy and their dependability for carrying men without sinking into the water deeply. Others were "deadheads",
for they became waterlogged and heavy and could not carry their human
load. These "deadheads" sank to the bottom of the river bed after being
in the water for several days and had to be abandoned there until a sal-
vage crew could be sent up to pull them up with long pikepoles and raft
them down to the mills chained to floating logs.

The three main driving rivers were the Brule, the Iron and the Paint.
These converged to form the Menominee which finally flowed into Lake
Michigan. All along these streams were erected lumber mills to process the logs into lumber. Several lumber companies operated in the
upper parts of the streams and dumped their logs into the drive at the
same time to take advantage of flood waters. It was necessary to stamp
these logs at the end with initialed hammers for easy identification when
they reached the company mills or sorting ponds. As the drive entered
the mill ponds, drivers were stationed at sorting booms with long pikepoles to sort and guide each company's logs into the proper boom, where
they were later drawn into the mill for sawing.

Once the logs were delivered to the mills the crew was dismissed,
given their pay checks, travel money home and sometimes a bonus for
a quick and successful drive. Shouldering their "turkeys", the men
scattered, the married men to their homes and their families and the
single ones to their home towns and their favorite hangouts to spend
their hard-earned stakes in saloons and bawdy houses. Walking into
town in their caulked boots and rough clothes, they headed first for a
barbershop for a haircut and a "store" shave, then the saloons swallowed them up. The plank sidewalks and the sawdust sprinkled saloons felt
the bite of their long caulks and frequently served as beds for their tired,
intoxicated bodies.

Should the drive pass near a town on its way to the mills, the foremen had to take precautions to hurry the logs through before the men
realized the nearness of saloons. Bob Solberg tells how when the drive
came down the Iron River and reached the Stambaugh bridge where the
"river hogs" caught sight of the town, they threw their peavies and
pikepoles into the water and headed for the nearest saloon for a few
hours of refreshment and relaxation. After the drive had passed and
the water returned to its natural level, Bob and his young buddies fished
the tools out of the water and sold them locally for fifteen cents apiece.

It must be pointed out in justice to those rough men of the woods that
normally they were soft-hearted, gentle and liberal with their money. A
companion with his last dollar, or without one, could always get a loan
"until next spring." Women and children on the streets were safe from
molestation despite the presence of reeling, cursing men. Fights? Yes,
for that was part of their code. No self-respecting lumberjack ever

backed away from a rough and tumble battle, but once the winner was decided, the combatants went arm in arm to the bar to call it square. It was only in his cups or in delirium tremens that a 'jack was dangerous. Then even his best friend became an enemy. But of all the lumberjack fights I ever witnessed, I never saw one pull a knife. Most of the tough fighters were friendly and harmless when sober. But when they were full of whiskey or brandy they often became madmen, whom no one dared cross without incurring a battle.

One of our Upper Peninsula towns had 105 saloons in the heyday of lumbering and mill work. Two of the worst characters were Dick and Alex Gravelle, French-Canadian halfbreeds who had drifted down from Quebec. Dick was six foot four in his stocking feet and Alex was six foot six and was never known to wear socks. Both men were built like bulls, thick of shoulder, deep chested and bull-necked. They worked in the lumber camps and the spring drives until their fighting and drinking made them personna non grata to all foremen.

These brothers gave the saloon keepers a hard time by starting fights, breaking up the furniture and destroying backbars and smashing the liquor supply. Saloonkeeper Eric Jensen got tired of this constant wear and tear on his emporium. Going to Peshtigo, Wisconsin, he hired a gentleman of character known locally as "The Terrible Dane", who was five foot five and wore a nineteen-inch collar, as a bouncer in his saloon. Eric brought him in especially to deal with the Gravelle boys.

The Dane didn't have to wait long. When the roughs heard of the new bartender, they came in to throw him out through the swinging door. Jensen and "The Terrible Dane" were behind the bar when they entered. Dick demanded drinks for both of them and "damn quick." Jensen stalled them off while the Dane slipped around to the front of the bar. Dick made for him and led with a hammer blow that never landed. The bouncer ducked, caught Dick around the waist and threw him to the floor. In their struggle they rolled through a door into a back room, biting, slugging and gouging. Alex reached for Jensen across the bar but the latter stepped back and pulled out a rifle and pointed it at him. Alex tried to knock the gun out of his hands but was shot through the cheek, killing him instantly.

Jensen then went to join his helper. He found Dick on the floor under the Dane who had a strangle hold on his antagonist's throat. Pointing the rifle at Dick he ordered him to give up, which he refused to do and attempted to kick the rifle away. Jensen pulled the trigger and shot him through the temple. Dick died within a few days.

Jensen was exonerated at the trial but a few years later committed suicide from remorse. The sheriff and the coroner examined the house in which the Gravelles lived and found skeletons of four men who had met violent deaths there and had been buried, presumably by the brothers.

Stealing Timber

It was a common practice in the early days for big lumber companies, financed by outside capital, to buy several sections of pine timber for a few dollars an acre, then to steal an equal amount from the surrounding territory. Since their cuttings were not closely watched by government inspectors or owners who lived at a distance, the foremen were directed to disregard boundaries whenever it seemed fairly safe. Huge fortunes were amassed in this way and were passed down to descendants of the lumber barons.

The term "round forties" came from the practice of the logging companies cutting off all their purchased timber and then continuing to cut far beyond the boundaries of the land which they had bought. The "forties" all around the original purchase were cut "by mistake" and dumb foremen blamed for the error.

If a lumberjack asked such a foreman where the line was, the usual reply was:

"When you come to the blazed line, look as far as you can see, then cut up to there."

If a cutter protested that the timber was owned by a neighbor or a homesteader, he was promptly "sacked" and placed on the company's blacklist as a trouble-maker and an agitator.

Pete DeMay, one of the best known French-Canadian lumber camp operators, had a deep fear of government lumber inspectors who kept track of illegal cuttings, and he established the same fear in his men. He told them that they, as well as he, would be sent to a U. S. prison for stealing timber if they were caught at it. He instructed his men to be on the lookout for strangers coming down the skidding roads and to grab their tools and hide them to cover up the evidence.

One day in late spring while the men were cutting beyond the "line" DeMay sent out word that the inspectors were coming in: "Run for your lives if you don't want to go to jail," his foremen shouted through the woods.

The jacks hid their tools and ran back to the bunkhouse, packed their "turkeys" and fled through the woods for town. Some never came back to collect their pay.

This gave DeMay an idea. Each winter toward the end of the cutting season he tried the same trick until word spread around through the lumber camp grapevine that this was merely a device to cheat the men out of their pay. Thereafter the men stayed in camp and let DeMay take the consequences.

DeMay was walking down a skidding road late one dark night when he heard an eerie cry:

"Whoo— Whoo— Whoo."

He answered back:

"Don' you know me? I'm Pete DeMay, the bigges' damn timber jobber in the U. P."

Back came the cry:

"Whoo— Whoo— Whoo."

Frightened, he ran all the way back to the bunkhouse to tell the men

The Road Sprinkler

Prize Load of Pine Headed for the Rollway

of his narrow escape from some wild animal. Wide-eyed, he reported:

" 'E so big 'is hass was on da groun' and 'is face was in a big pine tree."

It was long after that he learned his questioner was a big horned owl which inhabited the woods. This became a standing joke among the men and whenever he appeared the men would call: "Whoo—Whoo—Whoo," until DeMay's big fists silenced them.

DeMay never did learn to read or write or count. One summer and fall his crew cut cedar posts and railroad ties before the big woods operations opened. The men doing this work were called "piece-makers", for they cut the posts and ties by the piece. To count each man's work, Pete would put small pieces of twigs in his mackinaw pockets—in the right pocket for posts and in the left pocket for ties. When he took his mackinaw off and laid it on a stump the men would slip extra twigs into the pockets to swell their count. For weeks Pete could not account for the fact that when he sold the posts and ties, his count was always higher than the buyers'. Then one day he caught one of the "piece-makers" stuffing sticks into his mackinaw pockets. He gave the man a black eye and kicked him off the cutting. Thereafter he used buckshot for the count, since it was harder to obtain.

On one of his trips to town, Pete met the comely wife of one of the men working at his camp. When he greeted her, she asked him how her husband was, saying she was lonesome for him.

Pete replied, "Bee jeez, my good woman, you don' 'ave to be lon'som'. You always got me."

"Oh, I couldn't do that. My husband would be very jealous and he would kill me," she said with a smile.

"Ho, Hi can fix dat," said the lumberman. " 'E will nevair know. You know, Hi ham Pete DeMay, the great lovair! Beside, it is wort' fifty dollar to you, my fine laidee."

So one thing led to another and that led to the inevitable for a lonesome lady and a "big lover."

The next spring when Pete paid the husband his wages he deducted fifty dollars from his check.

"How is that, Pete? You take fifty dollars off my check?" asked the man.

"Well," replied Pete. "It is dis way. Las' winter I meet your woman on the street in town. She short of money. She ask me for fifty dollar. I give it to da poor laidee. Shame on you. Why for you don' send her some money before? You ask 'er if I don' give 'er da fifty. I bet she say 'Sure.' "

What else could the poor, lonesome laidee say?

The most notorious timber steal in the Upper Peninsula was committed in Iron County by the Canal Company which in 1886 had built a canal in New York state in exchange for timber rights granted by the U. S. Land Office in the western end of the Peninsula. The Company was to cut pine on every odd numbered section of land, on much of which stood a million feet per forty acres. The company staked out the odd sections and many adjoining even numbered sections as well.

The even sections had been previously opened to homesteaders who had staked their claims. As the company proceeded to cut their own sections and encroached upon the homesteaders' land, long drawn out lawsuits resulted. Many of the individual claims had been taken by old time lumberjacks who did not easily give up their rights.

While the court trials were in process at Marquette, company lawyers plied the claimants with liquor, so that many of them were not in condition to testify accurately in court. One lumberjack became so confused that he swore he farmed his claim and planted potatoes in February when the snow was four feet deep. With a court on the side of the financial interests, the majority of the homesteaders lost their suits. However, many of the homesteaders stayed on their claims and fought the Company for years.

The Canal Company engaged the Metropolitan Lumber Company to build a mill on the Paint River in the heart of the land in controversy. The mill town of Atkinson was established to house and cater to the mill workers and lumberjacks. When the lumber company started cutting and hauling the pine off the disputed territory, the homesteaders organized. Jack Enright, a tough foreman, was supervising the loading of logs on flat cars when George Cunningham, a homesteader, appeared on the scene and advised Enright not to load or haul any more logs as they did not belong to the company. Cunningham leaned against a flat car. Enright shouted to the teamster:

"Load logs, damn you!"

When the first log was half way up the skid, several rifles cracked from out of the bush and both horses fell to the ground with bullets in them. Cunningham shoved his hands into his pants pockets and walked off. Enright ordered another team brought up, had the dead horses hauled off into the woods and the loading went on. As the loading was resumed, four more horses were shot by the enraged homesteaders who hid in the woods. No arrests were made at the time. The loading crew was ordered to make skids with sharp spikes in them and to load the logs up the cars by hand. Since the homesteaders had no grudge with the men, who were merely trying to make a living in the pine, they withdrew for the day, but that night they loosened the stakes on the flat cars and let the logs roll back onto the ground.

On the third day the men started loading with teams again when a group of homesteaders appeared with rifles on their arms and told Enright they would shoot every horse he had.

"I've got lots of horses," countered Enright.

"Yes," replied one of the homesteaders. "And we've got a bullet for every horse!"

Here Jim Summers entered the feud. A crack shot with a rifle, Jim had drifted into the tall timber with a reputation as a bad man to cross. It was rumored that he had killed another in a quarrel in a town "down below" and had escaped to the north woods and a safe place to hide out.

According to Jim's own telling:

"When I left my last town, I was escorted to the county line by a committee of citizens. They called it a posse. They told me not to come back. In fact they dared me to. But I must have had some friends there, for I had several letters from some of the business men asking me to come back and 'settle.' "

Summers bore a grudge against the company because of Enright's high handed treatment of his men and strangers who came to his camps looking for work. Enright ruled with an iron hand. He ordered his camp cook to feed no one who came into the camp nor to give anyone a bed for the night—an unheard of thing at the time, for every old time lumber camp fed and bedded down, without charge, anyone who came along.

When Jim Summers first hit the country he and a friend came into the company's camp and asked for a lunch. The cook had just baked a battery of apple pies and had them cooling on the window sill.

"I had orders," said the cook, "not to feed any tramp lumberjacks or homesteaders. Orders is orders."

Jim looked at the cooling pies, fingered his rifle trigger, and said to his chum:

"Toss up a few of those pies and we'll see if they are good."

His friend tossed up three pies in succession. Three shots rang out and down came the pies. When the cook cleaned up the mess he found a dead-center hole in each pie tin.

Jim had no homestead to fight over and no timber to cut. But with a feeling for the underdog, he joined the homesteaders and used his rifle to good effect. When the timber crew started cutting "over the line" Jim stood behind a tree with his rifle muzzle in full view, and told the boss not to skid the logs out.

The boss said, "You wouldn't dare to shoot."

"Just drive over the line and see," yelled Jim and felled the first team which appeared.

Sheriff Mansville Waite of Iron County was called in to arrest Jim, but the rifleman held his place behind the tree and chipped bark off the tree behind which the sheriff had taken refuge.

When darkness came, Jim got away through the woods. When he heard that the law wanted him for attempted manslaughter, he drove to the county seat at Crystal Falls and gave himself up. A sympathetic jury recommended leniency and Jim was given a short jail sentence, then released. Soon afterward he gave up the unequal struggle and left the country.

Mrs. Patterson, a widow who lived on Patterson Creek on a home-stead claim which her late husband had filed before the Canal Company moved in, took matters into her own hands without waiting for male assistance. When the timber crew approached her land, she stood them off for weeks with her rifle. She was finally arrested, jailed and fined. On her release she returned to her homestead and used a more subtle method of obstructing the lumber operations. The main log hauling road crossed in front of her little home. The sprinkler sleigh iced the road every night but every morning the teamsters' big loads got stuck on the ashes Mrs. Patterson had sprinkled on the sleigh tracks. The sheriff couldn't arrest an old lady for cleaning out her stove and throwing out the ashes in front of her own property. The company, frustrated and embarrassed by this female saboteur, finally gave up the struggle and built a by-pass around her homestead.

The Canal Company stayed on to clean up all the merchantable pine in the area. Scores of homesteaders were dispossessed of their timber claims and turned to other means of making a livelihood. Once the timber was cut and the profits taken out for the enrichment of the lumber camp and mill owners, Atkinson, like hundreds of other towns, was abandoned, leaving ghosts in the shape of deserted frame houses, tumbledown stores, rotting mills and grass-grown streets where caulked boots and big woods horses once stirred up the dust. A few families remained behind to live off little patches of farm land, fishing, hunting and trapping. Big pine timber was a thing of history, with only tall pine stumps, burned-over slashings and rotted dams to bring back memories of the roaring nineties.

Men of the Red Underground

Chapter III

THE IRON

Chapter III

THE IRON

The First White Explorers

While the lumber bosses and their men periodically filled the town with their repercussions of hot justice and cold injustice, the stuff which gave Iron River its name also became part of our life, and its story began a long time before our town had a life.

It was back in 1847 that the first white men entered the valley of the Iron River, then to be called Maple Creek. Two U. S. Government surveyors, Harvey Mellen and Guy Cartell, packed in their food, equipment and surveyors' instruments from the end of the railroad at Florence, Wisconsin, over a trail of thirty-five miles which Indian moccasins had traversed for centuries.

The two reported in their little notebooks that outcroppings of iron ore had appeared on the bank of the little stream and on a hillside beyond. The soil, they said, was good for agriculture and the white pine stood high and thick on the hills and in the valleys.

It was not until 1873 that J. C. Morse filed a claim on the land the surveyors reported held iron ore deposits. Morse was followed in 1878 by another iron hunter, Richard L. Selden, who made similar exciting discoveries along the Brule and Iron Rivers. Selden had surveyed the right-of-way for the Chicago & Northwestern Railroad from Escanaba to Florence and had heard tales of great fortunes in iron awaiting the venturesome.

On his second trip Selden took along his son, William H. Selden, the father of William H. Selden, Jr., who later inherited his developments. Dan C. MacKinnon also accompanied the men. While travelling the uncharted wilderness, the elder Selden became ill and returned to Quinnesec to await the outcome of the search for the red stuff. At Chicaugon Lake, William H. Selden offered an Indian a sum of money to help him locate the original outcropping marked on the surveyors' map.

"Nisish-Be-Wa-Bic," grunted the Indian, meaning "red rock."

Taking an old Indian trail, the red man brought them to an outcropping which appeared to be a granite boulder. There was a small showing of iron rock in the boulder but Selden, fearing trickery, refused to pay the Indian, whereupon the buck became angry and struck his tomahawk into a hemlock tree. The tan bark showed red on the ax and the Indian grunted in disgust at the white man's ignorance:

"Nisish-Be-Wa-Bic!"

Returning later Selden and some friends bought the land which had been taken up by Morse in 1873. The same year the Seldens and three MacKinnon brothers staked out homesteads on nearby lands. In 1879 the MacKinnons found ore on their claim and started to sink test pits. Three years later they platted the village of Iron River, then just a cluster of log houses and stables. The same year the Seldens laid out the village of Stambaugh on a high, rolling wooded plateau a mile from Iron River. The Beta and Nanaaimo mines were opened on the MacKinnon holdings. The Chicago & Northwestern Railroad extended its tracks from Florence to Iron River. The three MacKinnon brothers built the first saw mill on the river bank and supplied lumber for the building of homes, and timber to brace up the mines.

Up to that time the miners and their families lived in crude log cabins along the river. Mansville B. Waite, who later served as county sheriff for many terms, erected the first large dwelling house with timber cut at the new mill. After that other houses sprung up thick and fast to shelter the influx of miners, lumbermen and business men who came from southern Michigan and Wisconsin.

Denny Haggerty, an engineer, came to Iron River on October 15, 1879 and worked at the new Riverton mine. The first train entered Iron River in 1882. The first trainload of iron ore left for the new ore docks at Escanaba in the fall of the same year. Bill Scott was the first train engineer to make the run. Haggerty, a son of a Civil War volunteer, claimed that he shook the hand of Abraham Lincoln twice. He bought his first cow from my father while my family lived in Stambaugh. He later went into the logging business and also served as the engineer at MacKinnon's saw mill.

The iron and logging boom lasted until the depression of 1893. Mills, mines and camps closed tight. Practically everyone was thrown out of work. According to Denny, "no one knew where the people slept or what they ate. There was no relief organized. There was no welfare. The camps left what supplies were on hand when the depression struck, and gave them out to needy lumberjacks and their families. The camp foremen gave the men seed potatoes and the ground on which to plant them. The people killed deer for meat and fished the streams. Lucky were the men who could find work at fifty cents a day."

1893 was the year of the great dispersion. Finding no work, families scattered far and wide to places where they could find work and a new beginning. There was greater migration out of the iron and lumber district than out of any other region. Perhaps Iron County was "too far from any place to ever amount to anything." Perhaps those pioneers who were caught between the iron and the pine were crushed beyond recovery.

But gradually the demand for lumber and iron revived. A few mines were pumped out again and began shipping a trickle of ore. Small crews were again sent into the timber. Those stores which survived the long credit drought kept their doors open.

Andrew J. Boynton built the first hotel, only to have it burn down. Undaunted, he found credit to rebuild bigger and better. The Presbyterian Church was the first house of worship built, soon to be followed by the erection of the Catholic Church. Father Dowser was followed in turn by Fr. Cleary, Fr. Zimmerman, Fr. Van Stratton, Fr. Manning and Fr. Lenhart.

Now provided with churches, the citizens demanded a place for education. A log school-house was erected and Thomas H. Flanagan was the first school teacher in this rough pioneer community.

In 1884 Marquette County had been split to make room fro Iron County. There were no county buildings for five years and the records were kept in the home of one of the county officials in Iron River. There was a hot debate over the permanent location of the county seat until in dead of a cold, stormy winter's night the books were stolen and removed to Crystal Falls, a small but courageous village fifteen miles distant. For five more years the inter-village political war waged back and forth until a red-hot election in the county settled the matter by selecting, by a few votes, Crystal Falls as the permanent seat of county government.

While the red ore was being hoisted out of the rich ground and smelted in local charcoal furnaces or hauled by rail to the ore docks at Escanaba for re-shipment to the steel mills on the Great Lakes, the green gold of the woods in the shape of the white pine was, as we have seen, not overlooked. Crews of lumberjacks imported from Saginaw and Bay City and as far as the depleted forests of Maine were recruited for the big camps on the Brule, Paint and Iron Rivers and other smaller streams. Paul Minckler built another big sawmill into whose hungry maw went millions of great pine logs, to come out in the shape of wide pine boards and timbers to help build Chicago, Milwaukee and other young Midwestern cities. In 1909 the sawmills of the region cut better than 45 million feet of lumber, an all-time peak, never to be reached again. The white pine of Michigan, which was to have lasted forever, was on the wane. The shanty boys of the Iron River district cut their share.

With the coming of the sawmills, the logging camps and the half-wild lumberjacks, the complexion of the village changed. The fortune of the town had its ups and downs. The depression of 1893 took its toll, but the village life went on. The little people who lived between the iron and the pine weathered hard times and prosperity, raised their children, passed on, to be succeeded by their children.

Each spring at the breakup of the lumber camps, hordes of town-hungry lumberjacks flooded the village. Saloons had sprung up, several in every block of the red-ored main street, and bawdy houses crept in to the side streets. Until their winter's stake had been "blown in" on whiskey and wild women, the plank sidewalks were crowded with mackinawed, caulk-shod drunks. Fights were a common occurrence. The local women and children kept off the streets at night until the 'jacks had either left town for other parts or had drunk up their last dime and sobered up until they went back into the woods in the fall.

The first newspaper, a weekly, was published in 1885. It was "The Iron County Reporter", to be later succeeded by "The Iron River-Stambaugh Reporter" under the ownership of Pat O'Brien, erstwhile pillar of the Methodist Church and later state representative at Lansing. A rival paper was published by a Rev. Donald McDonald, called "The American", a short-lived but controversial sheet which kept the town in a turmoil while it lasted.

A succession of mines and lumber camps and mills added to the

local prosperity. To keep up with the procession and to encourage other
enterprises, the Iron River Business Men's Association was organized
in 1887 and free business and mill sites were offered to any courageous
entrepreneur with a few dollars in his jeans. The Northwestern Cooperage and Lumber Company, known as "The Buckeye" because of its Ohio
origin, opened a great plant and was fed for many years by the elm,
basswood and hemlock that was left after the cream of the pine had been
stripped off.

At the turn of the Century a few telephones were installed. The population, exclusive of itinerant lumberjacks, had reached 2,380. The
first automobile was driven into Iron River in 1905 by Circuit Judge
Flanagan of Norway, Michigan. The Iron Inn, a modern, steam-heated
hotel, was built by Ed Sensiba in 1906. The first electric lights were
turned on in 1908. A bank was established by E. S. Coe, to become the
rival of the one in the little town of Stambaugh on the hill. From that
time on Iron River became a "metropolis" with the Business Association title of "The Home of Opportunity." Churches, home, industry,
business and population multiplied. Bakeries, a theatre, a flour mill,
a second bank, a fairgrounds and other signs of progress were added
in rapid succession.

Red Underground

One of the first and most lasting impressions a newcomer had of the
Iron District was of its red roadbeds. Waste iron rock dumped out in
great stockpiles at the mines was used for road-building. While there
was an abundance of gravel in the hills, it was easier and cheaper to
use the loose red rock from the mines to build roads and streets.

Teams of horses with dumpboard wagons hauled the rock and spread
red ribbons of highways which radiated in all directions from town and
crossed the landscape like spider webs. As the rock became ground
under wagon and buggy traffic it became powdery in dry weather. When
the wind blew it painted the trees, bush and grass with fine red dust for
rods from the road. Every buggy and wagon was coated with the wine-
colored mist. Horses' bellies and legs took on the same hue. Women
were careful to avoid dry, windy days when hanging out their washing.
Houses were covered with a thin reddish coating. The wearing apparel
of even those who did not work at the mines took on a reddish tinge.
After a soaking rain the powdered rock on the roads became a mire of
red mud. Red ore dust was taken for granted and inevitable in that district, as is coal dust in the coal mining regions or lime dust where cement or lime kilns operated.

The men working in the mines came to work in ordinary clothes and
changed into mining clothes in the "dry" or locker-rooms before de-
scending underground. Oilskin pants and jackets were worn over wool-
en underwear to ward off the dampness. Most miners preferred underground work because there the temperature was constant the year
around. Professional miners scorned surface work.

As the men started down the "skip" or elevator cage, they fastened lighted candles or carbide lamps to their waterproof miner's hats. The big hoist in the engine house lowered the "skip" by a steel cable to the "level" where the men were assigned to work. The top of the "skip" was covered to prevent rock and debris from dropping on the men as they went down. "Drifts" or tunnels were drilled and dug out from the shaft to the main body of ore. At the end of these drifts were great rooms from which the ore had been blasted and hauled to the skip, hoisted to the surface, dumped into little handcars and thrown onto the "stock-pile." In winter the ore was piled high to await shipment in ore cars and in summer it was dumped directly into the cars and shipped to the ore docks at Escanaba, then loaded into great ore freighters for the steel mills in Illinois, northern Indiana, southern Michigan, Ohio and Pennsylvania.

Next to coal mining, the work in the deep iron ore mines presented the greatest hazard of the time. The crude tools and methods in the early mines made for an even greater risk. The handling of explosive detonation caps by hand often resulted in the loss of a hand, an arm or a head. The explosion of dynamite loosened unseen overhead rock which would be jarred free when the ore was being loaded into the tram cars. Bluish-green powder marks on the miners' faces and hands and bodies were hallmarks of lucky escapes from serious or fatal injuries. Every mine had its tragic accidents and cave-ins and its quota of widowed and orphaned families.

In the early mines hand-drilling was the only method used for boring holes into the hard ore or the rock overlaying the ore. Two men worked at this operation, one holding the steel drill while the other struck the drill with a sledge hammer, the drill being turned after each blow. Water was poured into the hole as the men worked to keep the drill cool and to wash out the powdered rock. When the hole was drilled to the desired depth, it was plugged with cotton waste and the drillers moved to another part of the rock. At the end of the day the miners placed sticks of dynamite into the holes with fuse and dynamite caps attached. When all the holes were "charged", word was shouted to all men in the mine to "clear out." At a set time all the fuses were lighted and the miners ran out to the shaft. Each man carefully checked to see that his partner was with him and in a safe position. Great explosions sounded throughout the mine, echoed and reverberated and rumbled to the surface until they could be heard for a mile or more around the vicinity. Before the next shift was allowed to enter the "stope" or room where the dynamite had been set off, a few men were sent in to trim the walls and loosen any rock that might fall and injure or kill a miner. Despite such precautions, many were maimed or killed each year. Mining laws to protect the men were few and seldom enforced. "Get out the ore, damn you. Never mind the risks."

When accidents happened the mining companies paid the hospital bills or the funeral expenses and gave the widow and the children a month's or two pay. There was no other compensation, no union to press demands for better conditions or laws. It was the common

practice of the mining officials, with the cooperation of the company lawyer, to try to persuade the widow or the dead man's survivors to sign an
agreement absolving the corporation from further responsibility or
damage suit. This, however, did not prevent long litigation in some
cases. Company attorneys, backed by almost unlimited funds against
the meager resources of the bereaved families, invariably carried the
cases to the higher courts, there finally to have the litigation thrown out.

The mining companies took options on possible iron deposits, drilled
from the surface with steam power drills tipped with black diamonds to
cut into the rock and bring up cores of samples which were tested for
iron content in the mine laboratories by chemists. The process of lo-
cating bodies of ore was an expensive one but the over-all average of
lucky strikes was high and huge mining fortunes were made. Individual
owners of the land were paid a "royalty" on each ton of ore mined and
shipped. Occasionally a company found a good body of ore on a property,
then abandoned it in an attempt to "freeze out" the landowner until such
a time when he was ready to settle for a smaller royalty. Many mines
were worked for many years, then abandoned when the market was low
or when the rich ore was exhausted. The landscape was filled with old
stockpiles of rock, mine shafts and buildings going to decay and with
open pits now filled with green-scummed, stagnant water—a menace to
livestock and small children. Many families which owned iron ore
properties left for more pleasant surroundings or milder climes, to
live at their ease and to pass on to their heirs the continuing royalties.
It was always the dream of landowners there that a rich strike would be
made on their property. Many a poor farmer, who had grubbed a precarious living out between the big pine stumps, woke on a cold winter
morning with the thermometer registering thirty-five below zero, to
learn that he was a potentially rich man and went to sleep at night with
visions of a softer life for himself and his family in Florida or California. But our forty in Bates township never was developed as an iron
ore producer, as much as we dreamed about it.

When the iron rock came close to the surface of the ground, "test
pits" were dug with pick and shovel and dynamite to learn whether good
ore was nearby. The country was pocked with these pits, abandoned
and filled with water, a continual menace to all living things. Drownings occurred and lawsuits were instigated as a result, but the power
of the mining companies was too great for anyone to recover damages.
My father's horses and cattle were turned out into the fields and woods
to forage for themselves. One day one of his valuable workhorses
stumbled into one of these open test pits and was drowned, nearly
breaking my father's heart over the loss.

There was a great deal of sulphur in the rock that was brought to
the surface and dumped on huge stockpiles as waste. Spontaneous combustion set the sulphur afire and burned for months, despite efforts to
quench it. The fumes were blown over the landscape and disintegrated
and peeled the paint off the homes and business places of the town.
Damage suits against the companies failed, for the courts ruled that
this was the risk run by anyone who lived in a mining community.

In this district it was either work in the mines or in the lumber camps. Some nationalities were "naturals" for mining, while others abhorred the underground work and the danger involved. While mining involved certain hazards, it also offered steadier work than did the woods. After all, it was worth the extra risk to be assured that the yearly income would be enough to support the family in comfort. Work in the woods involved dangers to life and limb but it was seasonal, dependent upon the weather and required a man to live away from home and family. So the trend for a married man was away from the woods and toward the steadier employment offered at the mines. Wages ranged from $1.50 to $1.75 a day without board and room, equalling the wages in the woods, where board and room were included.

Mining On The Iron Range

During the time that the big pine was being cut and lumbered off in the Iron River district, the iron ore lying under the entire region was discovered and exploited. Outside capital was brought in to develop mines and smelt or ship the ore. By 1900 the hills around were dotted by mine shafts, great stockpiles of red ore and even greater piles of ore rock which overlay the mineral. The shipping was done by ore trains, which hauled long strings of cars from the mines to Escanaba's giant ore docks. Here Great Lakes steamers loaded their red stuff and carried it to the steel mills which dotted the shores of this inland lake empire.

Most of the underground miners were recruited from among recent immigrants from Europe and the British Isles. "Cousin Jacks" from the copper mines of Cornwall, England, first came to the copper mines around Calumet and Houghton, then drifted to the iron mines as the copper mines became depleted or were closed by the low price of their ore. "Cousin Jacks" disdained any other work but mining. "Once a miner, always a miner" was their gospel. Italians, Austrians, Hungarians, Poles and Finns were the backbone of the labor supply. Since "Cousin Jacks" were natural miners, sober, industrious and dependable and able to converse in English, they held most of the official positions underground. They were captains, shift bosses, mechanics, "dry" superintendents, pumpmen and "powder monkeys." Religious, music lovers and nationality-conscious, they were a loyal, closed group. The "Cousin Jack" boss favored men of his own nationality and gave them preference when jobs were scarce.

Some of the typical Cornish names were Trevitich, Tregenoun, Trevarrow, Polglaze, Penberthy, Panalligan and Penzance. There was a rhyme which went:

"Tre, Poll, and Pen, all begin the names of Cornishmen."

Many are the stories told at the expense of men from Cornwall.

Lester Penalligan hired out to Captain Jim Wall at the Dober mine. The Captain asked him:

"How do you spell your name?"

Lester replied: "My brother helps me."

When Lester saw his first grapefruit he thought they were lemons. He remarked to his friend John Polglaze:

"It wouldn't take many of they to make a dozen."

He bragged how well his son was getting along in the British army:

"I just got a letter from 'im sayin' 'e wuz just made ha court marshall. 'E's makin' 'eadway with royalty!"

Lester and John applied for jobs at the Dober mine where Captain Looney and shift boss Ben Battey hired miners. They entered the office and asked the man at the desk:

"Are you Looney?"

"No," replied the official. "I'm Battey. The fellow in the next office is Looney."

"Do you need any men for underground?" asked John.

Captain Looney said, "I don't know if I need any men. Just a minute and I'll tell you."

He stepped out of the office and looked down toward the mine shaft. Coming back, he said, "No, I haven't any jobs today. But come back tomorrow. Maybe I'll have work for you then."

"Why did you look down to the shaft?" asked Lester. "What has that to do with a job?"

"Well," replied the Captain, "we kill two or three men in the mine every day. I don't see anyone being brought up dead, so come back tomorrow. Maybe you'll have better luck."

Running out of the office, Lester yelled back, "To 'ell with your bloody job!"

Captain Campbell's crew wasn't sinking a shaft fast enough to suit Captain Duff, a tiny Cousin Jack with a terrible temper and a caustic tongue.

Duff yelled at Campbell, "Why, if I paid you fifty dollars a day, you couldn't sink it fast enough to suit me."

"Yes," shot back Campbell, "and if I threw you down that shaft, you'd never reach the bottom. You'd explode before you got there."

Josh May was captain in the new Naniamo mine when he heard that some of the big mine officials were coming down to inspect his operations. Josh decided to make a big show of work. He started his Cornish crew at digging and blasting out a "drift" or tunnel, which was ordinarily made horizontal to the shaft. In his hurry he neglected to use the usual surveying instruments. When the officials arrived and inspected the drift they found that it had been driven in a complete circle and came back to the original starting point at the shaft. When the officials complained about such poor mining, Captain May replied:

"That just shows you can't trust those dumb Finns."

The two greatest hazards in mining were premature explosions of dynamite and flooding of the mine by underground waters.

Dynamite was tricky to handle. If it did not explode after the fuse was ignited, some "greenhorn" miner might try to poke it with a stick to see why. Serious crippling or death frequently resulted. Dynamite was kept in a cold place and was not dangerous of itself. It contained sawdust saturated with nitroglycerin and each stick was the size of an eight-inch firecracker. Usually cached in a "powderhouse" a quarter of a mile from the mine buildings, it froze hard in the cold weather. In this condition it did not easily explode. At one of the mines a whole case of frozen dynamite fell several hundred feet down the shaft and did not explode. It took a heavy jar to set it off, such as is given by the detonation or explosive cap.

To thaw out frozen dynamite, the sticks are placed in a sort of double boiler with hot water in the outside container to warm it until it is soft enough to insert the fuse. It is sometimes placed near an open fire to thaw. The greatest danger is from the explosive cap. In preparing a charge the miner pokes a hole into the end of the stick, the size of a lead pencil. Next he cuts off a fuse, which is a thin cylinder of insulated and waterproofed cloth or paper to cover its load of black powder. The fuse is inserted into the open end of a small shell like a rifle cartridge, at the bottom of which is the explosive element. When the fuse is inserted, the miner either pinches the open end of the cap with a pair of pliers or more often with his teeth, to clinch the fuse and cap together.

The assembly is now placed into the drilled hole in the rock as far as it will go. Dirt or mud is then packed about the top of the hole around the fuse. The fuse is lit with match or miner's candle. The men allow enough fuse to give them time to reach a place of safety before the powder burns down to the cap. When a large hole in the rock is wanted, several sticks are placed in the hole, but only one stick has its explosive cap, for the shock from one of the exploding sticks is enough to set off all the dynamite in the hole.

Flooding of the mine is an ever-present danger. Great pumps are placed on the lower levels under ground and operated day and night to pump the seeping water to the surface where it flows in a blood-colored stream to creeks and rivers, polluting them and killing or driving the fish out of their natural habitats. Should a pump stop for any reason, an alarm is sent to all parts of the mine to warn the men to vacate or be on the alert to do so. Underground streams or small rivers are not unusual and some mines have had to be abandoned after great expense because of the impossibility of keeping them dry.

The Mansfield mine near Crystal Falls lay under the Paint River, which circled the town. In the early Nineties the company had considerable trouble in keeping the water pumped out. Extra pumps were installed and the water level at the bottom of the main shaft was carefully watched by each pump man.

Tom White, a miner at the Mansfield, was sick that one morning and stayed at home a few blocks away. The regular shift had gone down at seven that day. The pumps were working smoothly and everything seemed safe. The men spread out to the various parts of the mine to work. Skips full of ore rose to the surface. Timber was being let down to shore up the stopes. Teams of horses were hauling rock away from the stockpile. The underground pumps poured out red, ore-stained water onto the surface. Then, at nine-thirty, without warning there was a terrific noise like that of a tornado sucking up water. The entire

surface of the Paint River sank and poured into a great hole into the
mine. By ten o'clock the entire mine was filled with water. A stream
came up the shaft and poured out over the surface of the ground, carrying with it debris, miners' jackets and hats, dinner buckets and pieces
of broken timber.

The underground pumpman and Jim McGraw, a shift boss, had heard
the roar of the inrushing water and made a run for the escape ladder
and reached the surface just as the water lapped their boots. Tom White
heard the sucking noise and ran toward the mine. He heard the screams
and cries of the women and children gathered at the shaft. Twenty-six
men were drowned like rats in a rain barrel before they had even a
warning or a chance to escape. Their bodies were never recovered.

The mining company went into bankruptcy and none of the bereaved
families received compensation. Years later another company bought
the property and mineral rights, diverted the river and opened the mine.
When the water was pumped out again a few human bones were found
caught up in the timbers near the roofs of the drifts.

Though iron ore was the chief mineral found underground, a few
hardy prospectors found traces of silver and flecks of "gold" in the
outcroppings in the district. When these small evidences of precious
metal were reported, a fever seized many of the miners who left the
iron diggings to seek the bonanza in the mineral hills.

Civil War veteran Peter Paul had taken up a homestead on the Paint
River northwest of Iron River. Despite his handicap of a wooden leg,
he grubbed out a little farm on the river bank and eked out a slim living
with the aid of his Civil War pension which came through the Iron River
Post Office every three months. One day while he was planting potatoes
near the river his shovel struck an outcropping of black shale which had
streaks of white and yellow between the black layers. Excitedly he
hobbled to his barn for his pick and began digging deeper into his find.
The rock continued to show yellow metal.

Believing that he had a deposit of gold in his homestead, he drove
his little team of trotters and buckboard to Iron River. His pension
checks were awaiting him. He hired two Cousin Jacks miners and together they sunk a deeper shaft with drills and hammers. They worked
the hole, hauled up the rock by windlass and bucket. Piling up the refuse on the river bank, they worked until Peter's pension money ran
out. Peter worked alone and waited for his next check, then brought
out other miners to work his claim. He worked his mine in that fashion
for four or five years. State geologists, who had heard of the "gold
mine" in the northern Michigan woods, assayed the diggings and advised Paul to spend no more money on it. "Fool's gold," they said.
Iron pyrites have a way of fooling an eager prospector.

Undiscouraged and driven by his hopes for riches, the homesteader
kept on by himself until old age stopped him.

Peter's team and buckboard and his tale of gold on the bank of the
Paint River were a familiar topic of conversation in the town. Driving
in to the village, he would stable his horses in Bill Moss' livery barn
and call at the Post Office, buy his grub and supplies, hire more miners,

then drive back home the next day with his eyes sparkling from good
whiskey and his dream of a fortune which would be struck "this time."

The last appearance Peter made in Iron River was the time he came
in, left his horses at the barn and trudged off to the Post Office, dragging his peg-leg along the board sidewalk. Soon he returned to the
stable, a dour, discouraged expression on his face. Bill Moss asked
him what the trouble was and Peter replied that his pension check had
not come. He had hoped, he said, to visit his married daughter in
Menominee but without money he would have to return to his shack on
the Paint.

"Here," said kindly Bill, "I have twenty dollars you can have."

With this money Peter took the train to Menominee where he died
soon after at the home of his daughter and son-in-law.

A few weeks later his daughter and her husband came to Iron River
and drove the team to the scene of the "gold diggings" to dispose of
what little Peter had left. On their return they sold the team and buckboard and gave Bill a shotgun belonging to the old prospector and three
dollars in payment of the loan.

Peter's dream of a gold mine inspired other shackers in the vicinity
to try their luck at discovering gold in the outcroppings but none was
ever found to ease the hard life of those woods pioneers.

The old homestead remained in the old clearing on the river bank, a
favorite rendezvous of fishermen who angled for speckled trout and
witnessed the gradual decay of the shack which had held the dreams of
the little peg-legged Civil War veteran. Fire crossed the uncut grass
and brush that grew up with the passing years. The humble log house
burned down, leaving the old stone fireplace standing like a lone senti-
nel guarding the spot. The pile of black and white slate, still showing
glints of gold-colored ore, remain scattered where it was dumped, to
be disturbed by fishermen seeking souvenirs. The old shaft, the scene
of excited diggings, rotted and sank to decay, leaving only a black hole
overgrown with white birch and willow shrubs—the only evidence of
"what might have been."

What "gold" there was in that rugged country was in the shape of red
ore underground and the dark forests of white pine, to be "dug out" by
the sweat of the brow to offer a meager living for the many and fortunes
for the few.

They Wanted Timber

Mining and lumbering went hand in hand in the Iron River district.
Big timbers and lumber were necessary to safe mining, and the woods
boys in the pine cutting supplied them. The great shafts above the mine
openings were constructed from squared pine trunks forty to sixty feet
long. The sides of the shaft holes were cribbed with eight inch beams
to a depth of from four to twelve hundred feet. Drifts ran out from the
shafts underground in four directions. These tunnels had to be shored
up by heavy planking and timber to keep the ore and rock from caving

in from the ceiling and sides. The pumproom underground was a huge
room with heavy timbers over the roof and sides. Miners could not produce the red stuff without timber from the hills and lumber camps which
radiated out from the town.

Bob Olson was timber trucker in the Bengal mine. It was his job to
take the timber off the cage as it came down from the surface into the
mine and truck it on a little handcar to various parts of the mine to
"brace up the back", as the miners called it, to prevent cave-ins and
accidents.

Bob was a good timber trucker and he kept the miners satisfied, for
he supplied timber in the right quantity and quality at the right places
at the right time. He had to be a good judge of good timber. A mistake
on his part might result in serious accidents.

Drift Number Ten had an extra wide place to timber. Joe Bianci, the
boss timberman below, asked Bob to bring in a fifteen-foot beam for the
night shift.

"Make it a heavy one," yelled Joe as Bob shuffled down the drift in
his heavy miner's clothes and boots. "I don't want any iron ore on my
neck because of a cave-in."

"The timber will be big and tough," Bob called back.

It was Friday afternoon. Bob had supplied all the places with timber
except Number Ten. He had waited until late in the day, for the miners
were not to use the timber until the next shift and it would only clutter
up the dark drift to have it lying there under foot.

Bob went to the shaft and called Rini Maki, the surface timber man,
over the underground telephone system:

"Send me down that fifteen-foot cross beam at the north end of the
timber pile. It is already notched and ready to put in."

Maki grunted "O.K." and waited for the cage which Bob sent up to
the surface to get the beam.

In order to send down a stick of timber, as the miners called it, the
cage had to be raised above the surface of the shaft opening. A heavy
chain hung from the eye-bolt attached to the bottom of the cage. The
squared log was then hung from the chain and lowered carefully into the
shaft to the right level or drift.

Maki and his Finnish partner had the stick selected and moved to the
mouth of the shaft. Up came the cage. Maki stopped it by a hand signal
to the hoist man to about five feet above the surface. The men laid a
heavy plank across the mouth of the shaft and attached the timber to the
chain. Maki signaled the hoist man to raise the cage until the timber
was raised up and over the shaft opening. Then he signaled an easy descent to avoid making the timber sway.

Bob was waiting at the tenth level and the cage slowed up just before
it reached the drift. Bob rang the bell two and two again, to slow up
the cage. As the end of the timber came into view he hooked it with a
timber hook and rang the cage to stop. Then he pulled the end over his
little handcar sitting on the rails in the center of the drift. Bob was
alone—an unusual thing underground, but by giving the hoist man the
right signal he lowered the timber onto the car without too much exertion.

The timber was down for the next shift and the job was done with ease. Bob loosened the chain and dropped the noose on the floor of the drift. It was four o'clock.

"I'll be through early today," thought Bob. "My crew will have to bull that log up to the Tenth by hand."

He reached, gave the bell three quick jerks for the cage to be raised, turned to push the timber around, then down he went on his face. His left leg was jerked from under him and he stood on his head with his feet in the air.

It came to him like a flash. He had stepped into the chain noose and was being hoisted head downward up the shaft. His miner's boots fit loosely and the noose started to slip off the wet rubber. His body began to swing and he threw out his hands to prevent being dashed against the rough sides of the shaft. Up the cage shot. The levels flashed past like a picket fence. He thought of his mother. He lived a century-long nightmare within those few seconds. It was ten levels to the top—a thousand feet. It was seven levels down to the bottom. Maybe they would find him at the bottom if the shift boss remembered to count the men as they came out. God, if that noose only held!

It took only a few seconds. The cage slowed down and went past the surface. Maki, watching, fainted, but his partner ran to the signal button to stop the cage in mid-air, then threw planks across the mine shaft. The hoist man saw what was happening and lowered the cage slowly. The men at the shaft mouth caught Bob in their arms and laid him on the planks. His left boot was cut through and his ankle was bleeding from the chain's grip.

Bob staggered around to get the circulation in his leg going again. Then he sat on the ground to get his breath.

Maki revived when someone threw a pail of red water over him. His partner let out a curse:

"Dose tam Finlanders. You can't kill tam wit' an ax and tay faint ven you need tam mos'."

"You'd better go home, Bob," was the surface boss' only comment.

Bob shook his head:

"No, that gang in Number Ten won't make their five bucks a day if they don't get that timber. Besides, I lost my hat and lamp."

So he jumped into the cage and Maki rang him back down to finish the job on Number Ten.

Fright

The underground in the mines was always gloomy. Carbide lights were used by the miners for a long time after candles were discarded as a means of lighting each miner's way. The carbide lights were composed of the two compartments of a tin holder, one for the carbide particles and the other for water. The water compartment was at the top of the lamp and the carbide below it.

The miner filled his lamp on the surface with water and bits of carbide. When he left the cage or skip for his place of work below ground, he touched a little valve in his lamp and the water dripped onto the carbide, giving off a jet of gas in front of the reflector. He next spun a little flint wheel on the shield and the sparks lit the lamp. The lamp was then fastened to the front of the miner's oilskin hat. The men carried extra carbide in waterproof cans. Water was always available as it seeped through the rock overhead. Old miners always kept extra matches in safety matchboxes and never relied on the flint to light their lamps.

Clyde Ross was not an old timer. In fact, he was fresh from high school. His overalls hadn't quite lost their newness. His lamp didn't have a dent in it, nor had his clothes taken on the color of the red ore in which he worked. He was a "greenhorn" and ignored the voice of experience of the old miners pertaining to safety precautions and rules.

While the company had posted "Safety First" signs on the dry-house and the timber of the shaft, these signs were not to be taken so seriously by the men as to slow up ore production. Ross had been warned by the old miners about the dangers lurking in the dim mine, but his youthful confidence let him to take shortcuts to save time and increase his ore production.

"Never mind how much the bosses tell you to hurry. It's your neck and not theirs," the seasoned miners cautioned the young buck. But Clyde could not understand why the "Safety First" man always preached "Take matches underground; make sure that the back wall is trimmed to prevent cave-ins; make two trips before you blast; carry the dynamite first and the explosive caps second." Wasn't a high school graduate smart enough to take care of himself without all this guff from the bosses and oldtimers?

Clyde cut corners when and wherever he could. When the shift boss wasn't around, he would slip the fuse under his jacket, put a box of dynamite on his shoulder and carry his dangerous load from the underground powderhouse to his place of work, thus saving one trip. The old "powder monkey" who handed out the blasting materials used to refuse to give him all of it at one time, but generally the old man was too busy to notice whether each miner took caps and dynamite at the same time. Clyde would always go back to the end of the line after he had his quota of caps and the "powder monkey" wouldn't be wise when he asked for the dynamite.

Old Tom Waldron, Clyde's partner, didn't like it. He warned him time and again to be careful, and to follow the safety rules.

"Think of me. If you get hurt, I'll lose my job for not teaching you right."

On the first Monday in April the shift changed and Waldron and Clyde went to work on a "raise" between the eighth and ninth levels. A "raise" is a vertical hole drilled and blasted from the floor of one level to the ceiling of the level below. It was after dinner when the drill holes were completed. Tom and Clyde had placed the dynamite in the holes and the fuses were ready to be lighted. Clyde decided he was thirsty. It would be half an hour before the regular blasting time. He set out to walk down the drift toward the water jug. No one was working in that section of the mine but he and old Tom. As he attempted to step over a chunk of ore on the floor of the drift, his foot slipped and he fell headlong on his face in the slimy ore. His hat went rolling ahead of him. As he picked himself up he wondered where his light had gone.

To understand completely the darkness in a mine, you must first experience it. The darkest night has some faint glow. A room or hall has some crack through which some light can filter. But the underground absence of light is so complete that it envelops one with a depressing gloom which has panicked many a sane man.

Clyde's situation was very clear to him now. On his hands and knees he groped for his hat and found it, but his carbide light had rolled away somewhere into the darkness of the drift. He remembered that this drift had many branches, all of which entered many large stopes or dug-out rooms in this region of the mine. There were at least five raises, he recalled, which cut into the drift, down which he might fall to the level one hundred feet below. This was a hair-raising thought in the utter darkness.

A match would have settled the whole difficulty in a few seconds. But Clyde had never carried matches in a waterproof container. He had never needed them until now.

Suddenly he straightened himself up and felt for the wall. His hand hit the wet, slippery side, but his sense of direction was completely lost. To follow the wall to the end of the drift might lead him into a stope or a raise which would be sure death. There was nothing for him to do but wait. Good old Tom would not leave his partner alone in the mine.

Down on the sub-level Tom was getting ready to blast. But where was Clyde? The older partner in a mine was always responsible for his younger helper. Perhaps the youngster had taken a sneak over to the drift where it was drier to smoke. He had done that before. Those young fellows never did care about rules.

When it came time to blast, Tom lighted the fuses and hurried down the ladder to the ninth level. There he met other miners walking toward the shaft to get into the cage at quitting time. Waldron didn't see Clyde at the shaft, but still he didn't worry. Perhaps he had climbed up to the eighth level and taken the cage up to the surface.

It was time to go on top. The blasts began to go off in the various parts of the mine. The ground shook and the explosions echoed and rumbled. Clyde lay on his face to protect it from possible falling rock. He felt the ground tremble. Soon the fumes of the dynamite would begin to pour into the drift from the sub-level below. Matches seemed very important to him now. The necessity for rules was very clear to him— too late. Why had he been so smart when the older men had cautioned him?

He had not yelled before, for he realized that his yells might never be heard. If they were heard, who would know where to look for him? Echoes underground would be more confusing than helpful. Now he screamed! The thick walls threw back his voice in mockery. The drift was cold and damp, but sweat streamed from every pore in his body. He struggled to keep from running. Suddenly a piercing odor struck his nostrils. Fumes from the exploded dynamite burned his lungs and stung his eyes. How long before he became unconscious? Lying face down on the ore, he held his nose as close to the floor as possible to suck up what fresh air there was. The seepage water saturated his clothes but he did not feel it.

When the last cage came up from the eighth level, old Tom told the shift boss that Clyde had not yet come up. Orders flew fast and soon Tom, the shift boss and two other miners, equipped with gas masks, were lowered to the ninth level. The mine was full of fumes and the vision was poor. The shift boss carried a large electric torch. When they reached Tom's place of work, they heard Clyde scream. The subs on the level were searched systematically. This was hard work, for the gas helmets were hot and heavy.

The shift boss led the searchers up the next twenty-five feet and peered into the sub-level. His torch outlined Clyde's body lying on the floor of the smoke-filled drift. He was out but not dead.

Clyde stayed home for three days to recover his poise and self-confidence. His lungs still burned and his sleep was fitful. On the morning of the fourth day he went back to the mine office to get his pay and to collect his red-saturated clothes.

"I suppose I'm fired?" was his first question to Captain Anderson.

"No, damn you," roared the Captain. "Come back to work on the night shift."

Meekly, Clyde replied: "Thank you, Captain," and went home to tell his mother to fill his dinner bucket.

"Why didn't you fire that jackass?" asked the timekeeper.

"Because," replied Captain Anderson, "he'll make a damn good miner from now on. For one thing, he'll never break another safety rule. Those young fellows have to be shown."

A Strange Banquet

The Slavic immigrants who worked in the iron mines were alike in many ways. They looked alike, acted alike and had a stubborn, philosophical way of attacking their problems of making a living and enjoying life which helped them over the rough spots. Generally, they were hard-working, thrifty and home-loving, and although they had their drinking bouts, they saved and kept their money for seasonal lay-offs at the mine.

"Hunkies" they were called by native Americans who lumped all the people whose language and customs they did not understand into one disdained category.

Serbians could understand Croatians; Poles spoke some Austrian; and all seemed to be able to understand Russian. Though they acted and looked alike, each would not let you forget that his nationality was superior to the others. These Slavic immigrants lived in close

proximity in the various mining "locations" and had their own national
celebrations, customs and costumes. Weddings were times of great re-
joicing and celebration. The family of the bride went all out to provide
dowries, wedding gifts and parties which lasted for days on end.

It was a Saturday in June. Steve Borutski was celebrating his marriage to Wanda Zelinski, the comely daughter of Stanislaw and Marie.
The service had been performed at the big Polish Catholic Church at
nine that morning and by noon the Slavic boys were well on their way
to a real old-country "drunk."

A large mining company house had been rented for the wedding reception and celebration and the Poles from far and wide poured into the
"location", so that by supper time the house was packed with sweating
miners and their wives and children from the entire district.

The sound of the "squeeze-box", or accordion, began at full blast.
Couples pounded the floor so vigorously in their dancing that one wondered if he were not in some Polish province. Liquor flowed like water
and the floor of the shed-like summer kitchen off the big room was wet
with beer. Quarter and half-kegs of beer were tapped every few minutes.

Women were dressed in old-country costumes of red, green and blue.
Their hair was plaited with handmade flowers. A few men wore old-
country hats, peaked of crown and decorated with gay feathers.

In front of the "orchestra" was a table on which was placed a dinner
plate. The men who wanted to dance with the bride were required to
throw a silver dollar into the plate. If they broke the plate, they were
rewarded by a free dance with the bride. If the plate was left unbroken,
the dollar went to the bride. Plates were broken frequently and were
replaced by the bride's sister, who picked up the silver and placed it
in a basket. At times several hundred dollars were gathered in to start
the happy couple off in their new home.

The bride was soon in a condition of exhaustion, for she had no sooner made a round of the dance floor with one partner before another Slav
took her away. The dancing continued far into the night, with the bride
being required to participate in every dance.

The regular kitchen was the scene of much bustling and preparation.
The families of the bride and groom had worked for days on the wedding
dinner, to which every one was invited. Huge quantities of food were
prepared for this feast of feasts. Sweating women had worked all day
peeling potatoes, preparing sour cabbage and thrusting enormous roasts
of pork into the ovens of the big kitchen range. What the food may have
lacked in delicacy and refinement was made up in quantity. Home made
breads, sweet rolls, cakes and cookies were stacked on the tables.
Money at Slavic weddings was no obstacle. The Slavs took their weddings seriously. It might mean months of saving before and scanty fare
for weeks after for the bride's family, but it was a custom accepted by
all.

By ten o'clock the stove was covered with pots and pans containing
the favorite Slavic dishes from soup to "Kapusta" (Slavic for cabbage).

The noise and hilarity of the dance attracted a group of young Croatian miners returning home from a Saturday night dance at the Caspian

"location." No work tomorrow, so they needed no sleep for the next day. They boldly barged in on the wedding party, and though they were as welcome as a polecat at a picnic, they joined in with the crowd in order to get a few drinks from the fast flowing kegs and a nip from the jugs of not too highly priced liquor.

The Slavs tolerated their Croatian brothers for a while, but with some misgiving. Though they were uninvited guests, they soon took charge of everything. They danced with the bride and the married women. They were lavish with their silver dollars. At several points only the good nature of the happy bride prevented serious fights.

Twelve o'clock drew near, the time for the wedding feast. The cooks were anxious to have the tables drawn out and midnight banquet served. Cold "kapusta" was never appetizing. They went to the bride and asked her to stop the dance, so the men could set up the tables in the dance area.

The music stopped and the bride called out to the young Croatians: "Boys, the dance is over. Now you must go home."

Joe Ravochich, a young Croatian, yelled "Let's have one more dance. I haven't danced with the bride yet."

Up stepped Zigmond Morovich, a square-jawed Slav and roared in heavy Slavic accents: "No! When the lady say 'no more dance' that mean no more dance!"

That was just enough to begin an international war, for immediately things started to happen. Fists flew, women screamed, men cursed in Slavic and Croatian. Chairs over-turned as Croatians and Slavs locked in a real old free-for-all. The invaders were outnumbered, so they were thrown out into the road in a most unceremonious manner, covered with blood and bruises.

Paul Sabalic got separated from his Croatian cronies and instead of being thrown out of the front door he was driven into the kitchen. He had no chance to escape because several big Slavs were coming in through the back door. Paul was shoved up against the hot kitchen range from which there was no retreat.

Paul was a big man, six feet tall, two hundred pounds of iron-conditioned muscle, and he was quick as a cat and as fearless as a cornered tiger when he had "a few under his belt." But tonight Paul was there for fun. He was one of those good-natured Croats who always laughed off a serious situation. Now he was fighting for existence. Gladly would he have been thrown out of doors with the others. The exits were blocked by Slavs spoiling for revenge—fighting mad. He could hear his more fortunate brothers out in the road raining rocks against the house.

He fought with the savagery of a cornered wolf and as fairly as a Y.M.C.A. boxer for a while, but now the time came when he could take no more beating from his hard-fisted antagonists. He was desperate. He must either escape or end up in the Stambaugh hospital.

He reached back and grasped a pot of steaming "Kapusta." With a great heave he threw it at the assailants crowding in on him. Screams and Slavic curses arose from the mob, but the front ranks gave way, only to be replaced by a fresher and more formidable line. "Kapusta", boiling soup, hot water, turnips and every pot on the stove he could grasp were sailed at the opposition.

Paul finally thinned out the ranks, but he had used up his ammunition. The Slavs rushed in for the kill. In a flash Paul turned and grasped two stove-lifters from the stove rail. Picking up two red-hot stove lids, he used them as a shield and plunged through the Slavs, who stampeded over each other to get out of the way.

The nearest opening was a window. Paul went through it with a crash of flying glass, carrying part of the sash with him and landed out in the yard on all fours. He had hardly landed before he was up on his cat-like feet and away to join his laughing, vanquished comrades of the fight.

The following Monday the Croatian boys were arrested. Their fine was two dollars and fifty cents and costs, which amounted to a total of three dollars and seventy-five cents apiece.

Thereafter Paul was nicknamed "The Waiter", for the boys all agreed that he could "dish it out" at a banquet.

Big Fritz

Number Five drift in the Dober mine was a man-killer. The miners who were employed there worked on a tonnage basis. The amount of ore blasted, shovelled and trammed out was paid for by the ton. Each miner who worked in that drift shared equally in the total. They were paced by a select crew who could out-drill, out-blast and out-shovel two ordinary men each. The men hated the speeded-up work but their pay was tops.

The trammer boss was an exception to the rest of the bosses. Instead of the men doing all the work and having the boss look on, this trammer boss did it all himself, or nearly all. Big Fritz was six feet, three inches tall, and weighed two hundred and fifty-five pounds, all bone and muscle. He never "knew his own strength." He continually roared at his men who knew that his bite was softer than his bark, and they loved him for all his bluster. Should a stranger ever come underground he would have thought Simon Legree had risen from the dead and had gone mining.

Fritz did the work of three men. He kept the ore rolling into the dump cars. If one of the cars loaded with ore went off the rails, he heaved it back on himself without calling for help. The men working with him made money and so did the company. That crew with Big Fritz as their boss was the envy of the whole mining district. No crew ever came near to equalling their record for tons per hour. The men's savings accounts rose in proportion.

Prohibition came. Fritz thought he saw his opportunity and left his crew and the good pay. With his savings he opened a speak-easy in Stambaugh and started to sell moonshine in a wide-open fashion. Money poured into his hands as never before and poured through them again with equal rapidity. Where his money went, few knew. Tales were told

of some young man being sent on to college by some mysterious bene-
factor or hospital bills for indigent families being paid without anyone
knowing the source. Should a drunk ask for credit in the establishment,
Fritz threw him out. When the local football team needed money for
equipment or a trip, the means would appear. Children never passed
Fritz on the street without coming away with a large bill in their hands.

In the back of his place, Fritz cooked his own meals. He slept upstairs in a hall-like room. The whole establishment smelled with an
unholy odor—rotgut, cooking and unscrubbed floors. The place was
filthy, but there wasn't a miner or lumberjack in the whole Upper Peninsula who didn't know about Fritz's place. His income ran into seven
hundred a month on the average.

But things were going too well to last. One day the state enforcement agents appeared and Fritz became a "student" in one of the "colleges of tough characters." He served six months. He did it with a
smile, but somehow he never got over the jolt, despite his smile and
witty remarks. He came back a wiser man and much more law-abiding.

Prison life made him much heavier. He had lost his spark of ambition. He started in at the old stand but this time it was just a pool hall.
He cleaned out the place, but before long it was the same mire of a
place as his speak-easy, but he never broke the law again. The old
friends came around again to see him but he was a changed man.

Fritz now weighed three hundred and sixty-seven and was exactly
six feet around the waist. But still he was as active as a cat for short
spaces of time. He could stage a jig and dance with ease but his wind
gave out quickly. One day he came back from helping a friend move
his furniture and complained to the boys:

"I must be getting soft. I carried out the kitchen stove alone but I
nearly had to drop it."

He spent most of his time playing "Pedro" and "Smear" with the
habitues of the poolroom and roaring at everyone in a Swedish accent
which brought gales of laughter in turn from everyone in the place.

Prohibition was repealed. Michigan went wet again. Fritz took out
a liquor license and sold beer in his former pool hall. He was in the
money again. But easy life and the prison sentence had taken their toll.
He went to Rochester for a check-up. In his own words, this was the
result:

"Firs' dey feel my pulse. Den dey feel my pocketbook. Den dey
say: 'Vot's de matter vit chew, Anderson?' I tole dem: 'I don't know.
Dat's vy Aye come har yust to fin' out.'"

Fritz died soon after his return. The town stopped. Everyone went
to the funeral. The Swedish minister whose church door Fritz had
never darkened offered his services.

A salesman from the Delta Hardware Company of Escanaba stopped
a native on his way to the funeral:

"What happened in Stambaugh? All the stores are closed."

"Why, don't you know about the funeral?" replied the native.

"No. Who died? The mayor?"

"I guess you wouldn't know. The man was just an ex-blind-pigger."

"But why the big fuss over a lawbreaker?"

"Well, I'll tell you. Big Fritz Anderson sold moonshine. He never went to church. He just lived in this town and this town is loyal to him."

"But," said the salesman, "I was here last year when the general manager of the mining company died and I didn't see many at his funeral."

"No, you didn't, even though he was the president of two banks and the richest man in the district. You see, Fritz never kept books and half of the people of this town owe him money and the other half is grateful because of what he did for some of their friends."

"You don't mean that everyone had drunk that much moonshine?"

"Well, the fact is that Fritz didn't sell drinks on the cuff," said the local man. "He gave his money to poor widows who wanted to dress their kids. He sent sick people to clinics and hospitals and bought food and clothing and furniture for burned-out families. He'd kick a bum out of his place for asking for a dime for a drink, then give fifty bucks to some young fellow to pay his tuition in college. We never saw the general manager do that."

"I know," countered the salesman. "Al Capone did some good in order to cover up his crimes."

"A hell of a lot you know. The sad part of it was that Fritz never advertised his charities and he didn't give a damn if anyone ever paid him back. I've heard him deny a hundred times that he ever helped anyone. His insurance will bury him and that's all there will be left."

"Who are you that you know so much about Fritz Anderson?" asked the stranger.

"Well, I'm mayor of this town. But I'll have to be hurrying now. I'm one of the honorary pall-bearers."

Chapter IV

HOME OF THE BRAVE

Little Sweden
Semi-Pioneer Life
Our Finnish Friends
Irish Neighbors
Cousin Jack Tales
Kentucky Moonshiners
Celebrating the Fourth
Choose Your Partners

Chapter IV

HOME OF THE BRAVE

Little Sweden

It took great courage for those European immigrants to leave the
stable life in the "old country" and quit their native shores for the promise of a better life in the wilderness of Northern Michigan, there to
hew out their homesteads in an almost pathless forest. It was still a
land of Indians and a few venturesome settlers. No roads traversed the
regions when they first came. Pine, hemlock and maples stood dark and
thick to block their coming. Bear, wolves and other wildlife were
numerous. What neighbors had preceded them were often miles away
and all communication was over Indian moccasin trails, dimly dis-
cernible in the deep woods.

August Krans, his wife and two children left the rugged shores of
their native Sweden to seek a home in this new land beyond the Great
Lakes. Krans had the promise of work in the recently opened iron ore
mine at Vulcan in the Upper Peninsula of Michigan. Here he found
wages low and seasonal lay-off frequent. Life there was harder than
they had been led to expect.

One day Krans heard of the new government lands which had just
been opened to homesteaders up north. On a May morning of 1881 he
gathered his three mining partners in his little rented home and told
them of the great opportunity awaiting men of courage and industry in
the land beyond. There were Charles Gustafson, Gottfried Norden and
Ole Benson, each of whom had preceded Krans out of Sweden and had
each experienced disappointment with their small incomes at the Vulcan
mine.

Pooling their meager cash resources, the four men engaged a
government surveyor, packed a few provisions and a blanket each, bid
goodbye to their wives and children and set off on foot to explore the
possibilities in that new promised land.

They covered the thirty-five miles from Vulcan to Chicaugon Lake
in Bates Township, then still a part of Marquette County. Here on the
pine and birch-covered shore they made camp the second afternoon.
Krans acted as cook and walked down to the lake for a pail of water to
brew tea. As he dipped his bucket in the water his eyes fell on an old
Indian birchbark canoe tied to a tree. Being of an inquisitive nature, he
approached it and saw that it was covered by a ragged woolen blanket.
He raised the blanket to find the body of a dead white man lying on the
bottom of the craft. He ran back to the camping spot and reported his
find to the other three. Not knowing the meaning of Krans' upsetting
discovery, they held a brief council. Fearing what their own fate
might be in this unknown Indian Country, they decided to move on.
They picked up their packs and hiked hurriedly west to Stambaugh, a

settlement of a few log houses, where they felt safe again.

A few days later, after being assured by the Stambaugh people that the Indians in that territory were friendly and harmless, unless they were under the influence of firewater, the four men walked back to Bates Township and with the assistance of the surveyor staked out a section of 640 acres of timber land, each taking 160 acres to clear and build a house upon. This was Section 23, later to become known as Little Sweden.

In order to prevent anyone else "jumping" their claim, the homesteaders decided to stay a month to make a small clearing and erect a log cabin. They located a spring in the middle of the section and cut trails from it to their own cabins. Then together they trekked back to Vulcan, gathered their families, packed their belongings and walked all the way back to their new homes. Krans carried a small cookstove on his back the thirty-five miles, assisted by his wife and two children who had heavy packs of their own. Here they hacked out the pine and hardwoods to make a small clearing between the stumps. Edible game, deer, partridge, bear and fish were abundant, and close at hand for the shooting or angling. Their lives were hard and their work endless, but they made progress and their hopes were ever high.

An outcropping of iron ore was discovered in the neighborhood and explorers began to stake out new claims. One day while Krans was on a trip to Stambaugh for supplies, a man named Boardman came to his home and ordered Mrs. Krans off the land, stating that it was his claim. The woman comprehended little English but got the gist of his remarks. Unfamiliar with the land laws, Krans made three trips to the Land Office at Lansing to protect his rights. Each time the land agent assured him that his claim was valid. On the third visit the agent asked him:

"How far is your house from the property line?"

"About 500 yards," replied Krans.

"Then, here, take this shotgun with you and when Boardman comes again, give him five minutes to get off your property. If he isn't off by that time, use the shotgun on him."

The next time Boardman appeared, Krans was home. He gave the claim-jumper five minutes to get to the property line. Telling about it later, Krans said:

"By yimminy, dat feller made it in t'ree."

Within two years Krans bought a horse which he used on the farm and to haul stovewood into town in the winter time. The four homesteaders each bought a cow and walked them over the Indian trail from Stambaugh to their farms. When one cow went dry, the other animals supplied the milk for the four families.

In the meantime iron ore was discovered in the Iron River district and the Isabella mine was the first to dig and ship ore to the docks at Escanaba over the newly extended Chicago & Northwestern Railroad. Krans secured work at the new mine at a wage of one dollar a day for a twelve-hour day, six days a week. He walked the distance of ten miles to the mine and ten miles back each day. In his "spare time" he

cleared the land, planted his crops, harvested, cut wood and logs to
sell to the mills. Deer ate their crops, for no fence could be built high
enough to keep them out. Although their chief source of meat supply
was venison, they could not shoot enough deer to protect their vegetables
and grain. Bear broke into their pigpen and carried off their young pigs.
The young stock had to be kept close to the clearing during the day and
locked up in the barn at night to prevent them from falling victims of
bear and wolves.

The greatest hardship was borne by Mrs. Krans. She arose at four
in the morning to prepare her husband's breakfast and pack his pail
before he set off, while it was still dark, for his work at the mine. The
family gradually grew from the original two who had walked in from
Vulcan to a total of thirteen—seven boys and six girls. Their mother
was never attended by a doctor at child-birth and was up and at work
within two or three days after the new arrival, tending her household
duties and caring for the rest of her brood. Krans had a doctor only
once in his life in the wilderness, when he had an attack of pneumonia
and was attended by Dr. Fred Bond, the husband of Carrie Jacobs Bond.

Mrs. Krans, in addition to caring for her children and working in the
field and kitchen, found it necessary to carry water from the spring a
quarter of a mile down the hill. Not trusting the wandering bands of
Indians, and fearing the more savage packs of timber wolves which
ranged the forests, she carried one or two younger children to and from
the spring while weighted down by a shoulder-yoke loaded with heavy
pails of water.

As though life in the wilderness was not hard enough and six days of
work at the mines at $1.00 a day for twelve hours a day not discour-
aging enough to this courageous family, the depression of 1893 added
even greater burdens. The mines closed and families were thrown
almost completely on the land. Shouldering the rifles, the men brought
in deer, rabbits and occasionally a bear to feed the hungry mouths in
the little log cabins in Bates township. Krans and his neighbors found
occasional work cutting four-foot hardwood at sixty-five cents a cord
for the charcoal kilns near the Mansville Waite farm, earning from
fifty to seventy-five cents a day, which began before daylight and ended
after dark. The struggle to keep the breadbox filled was bitter and long.
Families living on homesteads were more fortunate than those living
in town, for they were sure of at least potato soup with a bit of venison
or saltpork.

As the children grew, each one had his specific duties on the farm,
even while attending the little log school. The boys helped their father
with the farm work, cutting wood, caring for the stock and clearing the
land. The girls assisted their mother in the house and with cooking,
washing, ironing and scrubbing. When that work was done, they worked
in the field with the men. The most prosperous time the family enjoyed
in the early days was one winter when they cut, sawed and split and
sold to people in town a total of three hundred cords of stovewood.

Mr. and Mrs. Krans knew just how long it should take the children
to return from school in the afternoon and outlined in advance the field

or housework each must accomplish, according to their size, sex and strength, and woe to any slacker on the assignment!

As new neighbors took up claims and homesteads, life became easier. Roads were built and a Swedish Lutheran Church was erected. Practically all the inhabitants in Bates were Swedish immigrants. The Swedish language was practically the only language spoken except in school and in town. Most children had never heard a word of English until they entered the first grade. Anyone not a Swede in the township was considered a "foreigner", even though his parents were native Americans. Non-Swedes could not find employment on any of the farms or the woods owned by the Swedes. First generation Americans in this community spoke with a decided Swedish accent their entire lives.

Despite their hardships, or perhaps because of them, eleven of the Krans children survived, all were married and all but one continued to live in the Iron River district. Over forty grand-children attested to the ruggedness of this hardy pioneer stock which migrated from Sweden to join their neighbors in building a little Sweden in the wilds of this unknown country, and to carve out a home, a living and an enviable reputation with their bare hands.

Semi-Pioneer Life

The majority of the inhabitants in our town and surrounding district had migrated from Europe and the British Isles to enjoy the freedom and the new opportunities our semi-pioneer country afforded. The early settlers "took up" homesteads comprising from 160 acres to a section of land comprising 640 acres. The entire area was very heavily wooded, even the swamps, with white pine, hemlock, maple, birch, elm, basswood and cedar. Whole families, husbands, wives and children big enough to swing an ax or pull a crosscut saw helped to carve their clearings and cut wood.

The timber from the homesteads was sold at the local sawmills to bring in a few dollars to buy equipment and food which could not be raised on the land. Tree tops, limbs and brush were burned on the spot to make potash, which was used as fertilizer. The soil was virgin, rich, deep and productive. General farming was the rule. All crops which could be consumed by the family and their livestock were raised in these little patches of clearing—potatoes, turnips, rutabagas, carrots, some corn, oats, timothy hay and some barley and wheat.

These early settlers bought or homesteaded land along the winding dirt roads which radiated from town in all directions. Each nationality tended to settle in a territory where others of their nationality had taken up land. Up one road was a settlement of Germans, up another Swedes, another Scotch, another Polish and another Finnish. Each settlement became a tight, compact group with its own social activities, typical of their homeland, its own schools and its own customs. Each group was loyal to its own nationality and to a degree to its "old country."

Most of the homesteaders farmed in the summer and worked in the lumber camps or mines in the winter to supplement their meager income. The early homes and barns were built of native logs, usually pine or cedar, for this material could be most easily shaped with an ax and gotten off their own land. The Finnish excelled in the beauty and utility of their log constructions. The logs of their homes and barns were smoothed with a broadax and the corners were beautifully dovetailed. Plank floors with wooden dowels were made of pine. The roof was usually of handmade "shakes" of cedar, split from short sections of logs with a heavy knife and hammer.

The immigrants from southern Europe were mainly Italians, Sicilians, Hungarians and Austrians. The majority of these worked in or around the mines. A few worked as section hands on the railroads. Few southern Europeans worked in the lumber camps, for they were unskilled in the use of an ax or saw. Most of them had worked in mines before coming to America. They were hard workers, dependable, thrifty and sociable among their own nationality.

The mines were located all around the edge of town and the district wherever workable bodies of iron ore were discovered by test-pitting or drilling. Small communities or "locations" were built around mines by the mining companies to house their families of workers. These houses were rented to the employees at a small rental. They could be occupied only as long as the family breadwinner worked for the company. The practice of operating "company stores", as was done in the coal regions, was not followed in the iron country. Each family had a small plot of company land on which to raise a garden. Other food and supplies were delivered to them by the town stores.

Mining officials, engineers, superintendents, captains and chemists lived in more elegant company houses and were the aristocracy of the community. These gentry were either highly respected or greatly feared by the miners, whose livelihood was dependent upon keeping in their good graces by being cooperative, submissive and industrious.

Even though the town and the mining "locations" were well supplied with saloons, home brew was common. "Dago Red" was made by practically every Italian family, who brought the recipe from Sunny Italy. Each fall several freight carloads of California grapes appeared on the railroad sidings. Wagonloads of grapes were hauled home in a holiday spirit. Children skipped school to be on hand to steal handfuls of the fruit. Sidewalks and streets were spotted with crushed grapes for weeks at a time. It was estimated that 1200 tons of wine grapes were unloaded each fall.

Most of the Italian families did their own wine processing. The grapes were tramped down into great hogshead barrels by means of a stomper made from a section of a tree trunk or, it was rumored, children employed their feet in the process. Within a few weeks the red brew began to work. It was carefully watched and when it had reached a certain degree of tanginess, it was strained through cheesecloth bags and poured into tall wine bottles or jugs, carefully corked and sealed over with wax of candles "borrowed" at the mines. Cellars were lined with bottles and jugs. "Dago red" was used as a beverage at meals and for treating guests. No one ever entered an Italian home without being offered a glass. It was mildly intoxicating for the un-initiated but on the average Italian it had no effect.

The home of one Italian family living in one of the mining locations caught fire. Fire fighting equipment was not available and the water supply came from a deep well and had to be pulled up by a windlass and bucket. The family and neighbors fought the fire with "dago red" from the cellar until it was quenched and the house liberally splashed with the red liquor, inside and out. When the repairs were completed, friendly neighbors replenished the wine supply from their own re-serves.

Saturday nights were times of Italian celebration. With no drudgery in the mines on the morrow, families gathered friends into their homes and the wine flowed freely. Long sticks of "Vienna" bread and strong mouldy cheeses—"Gorgonzola", pecovena and romano—were placed on the table to be broken off by hand and washed down with the red wine. While the older men played "Morra", an ancient Italian finger-guessing game, the accordion was brought out and native music and songs added to the gaiety far into the night. There was little drunkenness at these week-end parties, for most Italians could consume great quantities of wine without much surface effect. Occasionally a fight broke out over Italian politics or a too-ardent lover, but these incidents were rare, for these immigrants loved fun and friendship too much to allow high feeling to result in disagreeable scenes. The next morning found them at mass and confession. Their church had their loyalty and support.

Rev. Poisseur, the Episcopal minister who preached at the local church once a month, called on some of his parishioners in the Caspian location which was populated almost entirely by Italians. As he walked down the street an Italian kid, thinking the reverend was a priest, tipped his cap to him. His Episcopalian chum asked him:

" What did you tip your cap at him for?"

" Well, he's a priest, ain't he? I gotta tip my cap to a priest."

" Aw, he's no priest," responded the Protestant boy. "He's got three kids of his own!"

Our Finnish Friends

The Finns who worked in our lumber camps and mines came from their homeland near the Arctic Circle and were born woodsmen. Much of the big timber in the Upper Peninsula of Michigan was cut by them. They also dug their share of the iron ore in the Iron District. Their early homes there were made of beautifully squared logs cut from the surrounding forest. Most of their furniture was handmade from cedar and pine, carved and waxed to a glowing finish. I am told that our Pil-grim fathers built their early American homes from stone, mud and brick and that it was not until the Scandinavians came to American that the first log houses were built.

The Finns were a clannish race and were divided into two categories by the rest of our population. There were Swedish Finns and the Russian Finns. The former were known for their sober habits, their industry and their devotion to their church and religion. They were friendly, hospitable and open-handed. They were more easily assimilated in the melting pot. Their doors were always open to friends. When neighbors dropped in at mealtime, they were always welcome. Should the housewife be washing or ironing or housecleaning, the women guests pitched in to help her. It was the accepted custom and they visited while they worked. Finnish sweet-cakes were always piled high on the table and the coffee pot was never empty. Their homes and hearts were open to their friends and neighbors.

The Russian Finns were called "Drunken Finns." They were savage in their love-making, their revenge and their loyalty to their own kind. They were violent in whatever they did. They drank hard, fought hard and often died hard. The average Russian Finn carried a small, razor-sharp knife, called a "baku", with a carved handle, in his belt or boot-top, for "social purposes." In a fight he used his knife viciously and furiously. He felt little remorse over his acts of violence and cared little about the results of his acts on himself. A jail sentence for a knifing merely whetted his appetite for revenge and he awaited impatiently the day of his release to wreak vengeance on his adversary.

Eno Huttennen, a Russian Finn, worked underground at one of the mines. He married Elma Heikkilla and they lived rather happily for a few months in their little squared-log house on the hill near the Hiawatha mine. At one of the Finnish skiing tournaments Elma became acquainted with Illmori Nurmi, a handsome young Finlander who worked on the surface at the mine and had a flair for women. They chanced to meet again at a tavern operated by Toivo Sarrkennen. From that time on she acquired a taste for hard liquor and was frequently seen in the company of Illmori when Eno was working in the mine.

Eno learned about his wife's absences and tried to persuade her to stay home, but she preferred the companionship of the well-dressed Illmori to the sweating Eno who came home in his dirty, smelly mining clothes and worked in his garden until dark.

One day Eno came home from the night shift and found the house empty and Elma's clothes gone. He searched the neighborhood and learned that she had left early that morning with Illmori. He apparently gave her up and batched it at home for several weeks. Gossip had it that she was living with her lover in a rented house in another "location."

Early one morning Eno appeared at Illmori's door during the latter's absence and demanded that Elma go back home with him. Eno seemed in good humor and Elma invited him into the house. She was baking bread and the odor of a roast pervaded the house.

Eno placed his arm around Elma's waist and said in Finnish:
"You will go home with me now?"

Elma pushed him away and ran into the bedroom. Furious, Eno grabbed her by the arms and dragged her out of the house and down a

trail leading into the woods. Behind a clump of trees he threw her onto
the ground and sat on her. She fought him like a demon, for a strange
smile on her husband's face warned her that she was now dealing with a
madman. Straddling her, he calmly pulled a stick of dynamite from his
overall pocket, attached a fuse to an explosive cap, inserted the fuse
into the stick and lit a match to it. Elma watched him in horror, shriek-
ing terrible Finnish oaths at her now insane husband. Eno placed
the dynamite under the struggling Elma and still sitting on her, awaited
the result. The dynamite blew them both to bits. Bob Pelo, the undertaker and coroner, filled his basket from the fragments he found in the
trees and bushes.

The foreman of one of the lumber camps berated a Finnish lumberjack for carrying a bottle of pure alcohol into the woods and getting
drunk on the job. In a drunken rage the Finn raised his double-bitted ax
and about to bring it down on the timber boss head. The foreman,
facing sure death, looked the drunken man square in the eye and said
coolly:

"Swanti, that means state's prison for life if you split my head
open."

Swanti slowly lowered his ax and without a word walked back to the
timekeeper's office for his pay check.

Paavo Sukaniivala worked in the mines and was having woman
trouble. He kept brooding over his situation at home and became very
gloomy and morose. It was the practice of the mining bosses to dole
out just enough dynamite to the miners to get their work done each day
and not enough to enable them to store up a reserve of the explosive to
create a hazard in the mine. Paavo and Hjalmer Kiromaki were partners working in a drift. They had drilled into the rock and were ready
to set the blast. Paavo had been depressed all day and spoke only in
short grunts. Hjalmer sent Paavo for a box of dynamite from the underground "powder house" while he himself cleaned out the drill holes.
He waited half an hour and no Paavo appeared. This was unusual underground, where partners kept close together and reported to each other
every few minutes. Suddenly he heard a great blast and felt a strong
puff of air coming up the drift. Hurrying in the direction where Paavo
had gone for the dynamite, his progress was stopped by a great pile of
loose ore on the bottom of the tunnel. In the dim light he found one of
Paavo's mangled hands sticking out of the top of the pile—a suicide
over his woman. Telling about it casually later, Hjalmer remarked:

"Dat Paavo, he 'ploded vun hell of a hole. Det jung feller he like det
dynamite like hell!"

"Black Jack" Rondon, a Finnish miner, was late for work one
morning and half drunk as he stumbled into his work clothes in the
"dry house." The first shift had already gone down and was sending up
skips full of ore onto the stockpile. "Black Jack" watched his chance
and when the skip started the down trip, he jumped into it and stood on
the bottom. When he reached the lower level, the trammers were there
with a load of ore which they promptly dumped into the skip on top of
the hidden Jack. The two tons of ore knocked him flat. The skip shot up

again and he was dumped through the chute onto the stockpile with the
load of ore. Shaking the red ore off, he went home without a scratch,
cursing out loud at "tose tam Finn miners" who couldn't wait for a man
to get down to work.

Finns were among the best lumberjacks, for they were clever with
an ax and saw, a skill which they had learned from boyhood in the fir
woods of their native land. They were able to take an enormous amount
of abuse from the woods and were docile and willing to follow a foreman's instructions, if they understood them. Their skill with a broadax
in the squaring of logs for building construction was outstanding. It was
said that a Finn could prepare a tooth for filling with his broadax. They
were seldom given horses to drive, for they were notoriously poor
teamsters. They could never get a pair of horses to pull together and
they always managed to place the bulk of the load over the back runners
of the sleigh which made the load pull twice as hard as if it were
equally distributed.

I had reason to know what poor horsemen the Finns were. During
my first summer vacation at the University I sought a good, hard outdoor job to earn tuition money and to get in condition for football in the
fall. I hired out to Andrew Autio, a Finnish contractor, to drive his big
team of greys hauling dirt scrapers, building an inter-urban street car
line running from Iron River to Spring Valley and connecting several
mining locations. The team was wild and practically unmanageable.
When I gave the signal, one would plunge ahead while the other lunged
back. When the second one jumped into the collar, the first one sat back
in the breeching. They nearly pulled my arms out of their sockets. I
was utterly discouraged at the end of the first day and was ready to turn
those "wildcats" back to Autio. They were a wonderfully powerful pair
but had been badly mismanaged.

One day I was directed to drive to the town waterworks to get a load
of pipe. I hitched the greys to the wagon and drove down the road to the
pumping station at the edge of town just over the "Buckeye" bridge. I
had just gotten off the wagon and laid the reins down on the ground to go
into the station to learn where the pipe was when the twelve o clock
whistle blew right over the horses' heads. At the first blast my beautiful team made a wide lunge and took off through the gate. Up the main
street toward town they went at a dead, frightened gallop, with me
running and shouting after them. They crossed the bridge and the railroad tracks at the Buckeye mill; then I could see them no longer.

Still running for fear the horses would run over someone in their
mad rush, I reached the top of the hill to see Autio come running toward me, more concerned over my safety than that of his horses. We
ran up the street together. A house was being moved and was standing
in the middle of the street, blocking the onward plunging of the
horses. They did not stop, but with the wagon bouncing up and down
over the rough road, they swung to the left and wedged the wagon between two other houses so tightly that they could not move. Andrew
never mentioned the incident beyond his concern for my safety. Thereafter the reins were never out of my hands an instant. I kept on the job

until college opened and steadied the team down until they were unbeatable on the job. Thereafter it was a pleasure to drive them and I was proud of my horses and my own horsemanship.

The sauna or Finnish steam bath was an institution which those rugged people brought from the old country. Almost every Finnish homesteader and miner built his own sauna as soon as their square-log house was completed. It was a small log structure about ten by twelve feet, chinked with moss and mud, with a "shake" or handmade shingle roof. It had one door and two small windows to let in the light. Within was placed a sheet-iron stove on a bed of field stone. Around and over the stove were piled other field stone to completely cover it. Around the sides of the room were wooden benches built in tiers reaching to the roof. Once or twice a week a roaring fire was built in the stove to heat the surrounding stones red-hot. Disrobing in the home, the entire family and such visitors as they had at the time ran into the sauna where they splashed water onto the heated stones to create a hot steam which enveloped the entire room and rolled up to the roof. Seated on the benches, the occupants rubbed themselves to bring out the perspiration. A bundle of birch switches were used by the bathers to beat themselves until the skin was beet-red. As the steam mounted they stepped up to the higher benches until their heads reached the roof. Here they sat until the steam and perspiration rolled off their bodies. Then dashing outside they jumped into a pool of water, lake or creek in the summer or into a snowbank in the winter to cool off. At a signal they all ran back into the home to dry off and rub their frankly naked bodies with rough towels—scrubbed and clean to the depths of their pores.

Finns often attribute their ability to outrun and outski other nationalities to the beneficial cleaning of their bodies in their sauna. It is said to have another value. A young Finn, before calling on his intended to ask the all-important question, will take a cleansing in his superheated sauna.

A few commercial saunas were operated by Finnish women. The pay guests disrobed in the home in the same manner as the family and got steamed up in the sauna. At the proper time a Finnish woman came in and belabored their bare bodies with birch switches. Then they cooled off in the water or snow outside. The Finns believed in the "body beautiful." There was no embarrassment over the mixing of unclothed men, women and children. It was a part of their ritual of keeping clean.

In later years it was noticed by physicians that the Finnish people who practiced this method of body cleanliness were more subject to tuberculosis than other members of the community. This was due undoubtedly, they explained, to the scalding of the lungs by the superheated steam in their saunas.

Finnish children were quick at book-learning and the ability to repeat what they had read but they had difficulty in applying this knowledge in a practical way. Being an outdoor people, they readily acquired great skill with an ax, saw and farm and woods tools. Finnish women and older girls would wield an ax and pull a crosscut saw as skillfully and as long as their men. They worked along with their husbands and older brothers in clearing the woods, cultivating the fields and harvesting crops. Women could build a haystack or tie bundles of grain as cleverly and as rapidly as the men.

The Finns were said to lose their teeth early due to some lack in their diet or to excess of sweets which were always on their tables. While drinking their steaming coffee, they half-filled their cups with sugar and then sucked the coffee through lumps of loaf sugar held between their teeth.

The immigrants had difficulty mastering the English language. They invariably dropped some letters and placed others in the wrong position —like " s " before "St." as in Stewart, which became "Tewart." A bottle of pop became a "pottle of bop." Their names had an abundance of double vowels and double consonants—Aaltonen, Sukaniivala, Heikkinen, Waakala and Haapaoja. Male given names were Sulo, Loivo, Toivo, Paava, Arvey, Waino, Into and Onni. Girls were blessed with Signi, Ina, Alma, Elma, Serii, Aaila, Imppi, Lempi and Hildur.

Finnish people were as violent and as durable in their games as they were in other activities. They excelled in long races, on foot, or on skis. Several times each winter they organized ski races over the hills with courses from ten to twenty miles long. Their skis were long, narrow and bowed up in the middle to give them spring. They fashioned their own skiing equipment. With two light-weight hand-made poles they hitched themselves along at a speed swifter than that of the fastest racehorse. Few other natives ever entered these long distance runs, for the Finns invariably outdistanced everyone. Their ability at ski jumps equalled their skill at ski racing. They erected long ski jumps on the hills and held state and national tournaments. Some of our national champion ski jumpers were Finns from the Upper Peninsula of Michigan.

Hardy miners and crack woodsmen, our U. P. Finns assisted in exploiting the riches of our Michigan forests and mines and deserve a place in the development of the great "Northern Empire."

Irish Neighbors

We had our share of Irish families who helped make history in our town and give it color in those early days. Most of them lived just off main street but were always in the center of town politics, leadership, and controversy. The majority had come over from the old sod during the Potato Famine but did not lose time in adjusting themselves to life in this new country. Contentious, ambitious and self-confident, they soon made their impression on the community.

There was Paddy O' Toole, a few years removed from County Cork, who lived a few blocks from us with his wife and two or three children. Like most Irishmen, he was continually mixed up in politics and received various political appointments, which seldom were very important and which he embellished by his flair for showmanship.

Paddy was town marshal and poundmaster at times. After an ordinance was passed by the village fathers to keep cows and horses off the streets, Paddy, as pound keeper, became very energetic at catching stray animals and placing them within a pound of barbed wire on a vacant lot near his home, to be repossessed by the owners upon the payment of a small fine. He was continually involved in arguments and fist fights over his right to take cattle which were on their way through town to the common pasture in the hills in the morning, or on their way home at night. Often when he had captured a number of cows and horses and was out rounding up more, the owners opened the gate and let their animals stray back home. His brother Mike, his assistant, was a quiet, peace-loving individual and could easily be persuaded to cooperate with the cattle owners seeking to release their impounded animals without paying a fine. It is doubtful if Paddy ever collected many fines for his labors but he did receive a variety of black eyes for his pains.

Paddy in his cups was a mean actor. On his wedding day, which he celebrated vigorously with his male chums in a saloon, he took his bride home and gave her her first beating—not that he did not love her, he explained; it was just to keep her disciplined and to show her who "wore the breeches" in his house. On one occasion he led his cow into the house and drove his wife out. He told her he preferred the cow's company to hers. Another time he turned on the water faucet in the kitchen sink and refused to let her turn it off until the house was flooded.

Paddy had a telephone installed when the line was first put into the town. He was talking on the phone during an electric storm and received a nasty electric shock. Taking an ax he chopped the box off the wall, shouting:

"Be Jasus, thim puttin' in a machine like that and try to kill people, then charge thim for it!"

When property taxes were first instituted to pay for village services, many of the local merchants refused to pay them. The village president appointed Paddy to collect them. He drove his horse and dray to the front of the stores and went in to present the tax bill to the proprietors. When they refused to pay, Paddy took merchandise off their shelves and loaded it onto his dray. He backed his dray up to the front of Morrison's general store and took an armload of rifles from their cases and loaded them on his wagon. When Finley Morrison protested, Paddy replied:

"Just pay your taxes! Pay your taxes and say nawthin'!"

Even though he was not a good fighter, he always made a good show of fierceness. One day he heard that a certain tough individual was looking for him to give him a thrashing. Paddy, armed with a big Spanish-American War sword, appeared in Joe Lawrence's saloon swinging the murderous looking weapon.

Joe asked him:

" Paddy, what in the name of high heaven are you going to do with that big sword? "

"Nothin' at all, at all, just cut his bloody head off."

Paddy was caught stealing some of Ed Scott's stovewood and when Ed accused him of stealing, Paddy remarked innocently:

"Sure and I wasn't stealing your damn wood. I was jest takin' it."

Mike O'Toole, the brother, green from Ireland, was given the job of driving Paddy's team on the dray. He was so inexperienced at driving horses that when he wanted to turn the team around he had to drive around a whole town block.

Paddy ran up a grocery bill at Pat Kelly's store and there seemed to be little prospect of his ever paying it. Paddy and Tom Flanagan, the first school teacher in Iron River, entered the store one evening and Paddy gave Kelly a big order of groceries to pack up. When that was done, the storekeeper added up the bill and said:

" That will be $5.94, Paddy. "

" Charge it, me boy, " said Paddy. " Just charge it this time. "

" No more credit, Paddy, until you pay up your whole bill. "

Paddy left the store with Tom and said to Tom:

" Pat Kelly isn't the man he used to be, at all, at all. "

" No, " agreed Tom sympathetically. " And I tell you, Paddy, he never was, be Jasus. "

Whenever there was a difference of opinion on local politics and town affairs, the line was sharply drawn between the Irish and the rest of the population. There was no sewer system in the community in the Nineties and the spring thaws flooded the streets and vacant lots and isolated whole blocks of business and residential sections. One spring there was a particularly bad flood and the west end of main street was completely under water. The only areas which remained above the flood were the high plank sidewalks over which the natives had to walk gingerly.

Our boarding house and John Airey's butcher shop across the street had water up to the doors. Extra planks had to be laid to get in and out of these buildings. The situation was serious. My father and Airey organized a crew of friends and dug a ditch with pick and shovels to let the water off the street. But the released stream happened to run in a torrent toward the homes and property where the Irish lived. Within a few minutes Paddy O'Toole and his neighbors came charging at the ditchers, took away their tools and drove them back. From that time on there was continual bad blood between them.

Another Irishman operated a lumber camp " on a shoestring" and did various kinds of teaming and contracting. He got into a one-sided argument with his tiny, browbeaten wife over an alleged oversight on her part of which she was entirely innocent. At the climax of the quarrel he struck her and gave her a black eye. Despite his alcoholic daze, he realized that he had made a serious mistake. He went to his horse stable and brought in a bottle of " Sloan's Liniment" to treat the eye. Had he applied it, she would have lost her sight completely. " Sloan's Liniment" was a sort of liquid cure-all to be used "externally only" on horses, cattle and humans.

The Lalleys ran a rather " respectable " saloon which was patronized by the elite tipplers of the town. Lalley and Pat O'Brien, the editor and publisher of the local weekly "Reporter" were continually feuding over inconsequential matters but Pat had the advantage of always having the last word through his newspaper. He ribbed Lalley over dyeing his white mustache black and Lalley retaliated by circulating a story about Pat being secretary-treasurer of the Methodist Sunday School on Sunday morning, then playing cards in the back room of Boynton's saloon on Sunday afternoons.

Pat O'Brien ran for the office of district representative in the state legislature and his campaign expense was alleged to have been paid by one of the mining companies. While in the legislature he was known for two outstanding acts. One was that he voted against a bill reducing the hours of work in the iron mines from ten to eight. The other was sponsoring a bill to protect sunfish.

Cousin Jack Tales

Walter F. Gries, superintendent of the Welfare Department for the Cleveland-Cliffs Iron Company at Ishpeming, is the U. P.'s champion "Cousin Jack" story-teller. Walter has lived with these Cornishmen for many years and has had close contact with them, their habits, peculiarities and the folklore. He is a sought-after speaker and toastmaster at meetings and banquets where mining men gather.

"I like to tell the story of the two Cornish lads who came to the Iron Country about fifty years ago, from Cornwall," says Walter.

" They had no formal education and they knew little of our currency value. Soon after they arrived at Ishpeming, they went to work in an iron mine. They were contract miners, and were paid for the ore they were able to produce. Wages were not high in those days, and on payday the paymaster came through the mine and handed one of them, Henry, an envelope which contained the pay of his partner, Dick, and himself.

" Henry opened the envelope and took out of it three five-dollar bills. He looked at his partner and said:

" 'Look 'ere, pardner, three bills; any bloody fool do knaw you can't 'alf up three!'

" 'That's right, 'Enery ,' replied Dick. 'What shall us do h'about hit?'

" 'We'll lev it go until the boss do come. 'E 'ave been working 'ere for ten years; 'e'll knaw what to do.'

"When the boss appeared, Henry said to him:

" 'Look 'ere , Captain—we 'ave our pay 'ere. We got they three bills. Anybody do knaw you can't 'alf up three. What shall we do now?'

"The Captain said, 'Let me see the bills.'

"Henry gave him the envelope.

"The Captain looked over the three bills, gave one to Henry, another to Dick and placed the third bill in the top of his boot and walked away.

"There was a moment of silence. Dick looked at Henry and commented:

" 'Damme, pardner, esn't it grand to 'ave a h'education.'

" 'Yes, it is grand to 'ave an h'education, if you can make use of it.' "

The Cornish miners brought with them from their homeland their favorite dish, called "pasties." Traveling deep underground to do the hard physical labor of drilling, blasting and shoveling the red ore, they carried with them these delicious turnovers. Filled with "mayt, turmit, taty, h'onyon and parsley," they were a nourishing meal— easy to pick up in grimy, red-soiled hand and easy to heat on a shovel over a miner's lamp.

This dish served at a bridge table, picnic or a church supper is guaranteed to bring out the "Ohs and Ahs" and requests for the recipe. One Chicago visitor remarked in his brash way:

"They are better when they are made for love then when they are made for money."

I like them either way.

Walter gives us his best recipe, which he has tried and found not wanting. Here it is; if you don't like it, you haven't made it according to Walter's directions:

The pasty is a whole meal in a jacket and when made by a real "Cousin Jenny" (or by my wife or mother) is a delicious food. Moreover, a pasty is a substantial type of food and stays by you in grand fashion. Many a mine in the Northern Peninsula of Michigan owes its development to the good old Cornish pasty.

Here's a recipe which I have given to many of my friends throughout the state. The making of a pasty is somewhat of an art. I have made them but I do not claim that they are the best that I have eaten. I do claim, however, that they are good and therefore I am glad to give this recipe to friends who may request it.

RECIPE

3 c. flour	$\frac{1}{2}$ # diced or cubed pork,
1 c. suet ground fine	good quality
$\frac{1}{4}$ c. lard	potatoes
1 tsp. salt	turnips
6 - 7 tbsp. cold water	onions
1# diced or cubed beef, good	butter
quality	

Work or blend the lard into the flour, preferably with a pastry blender. Then add the suet which has been ground through a food chopper, using the finest cutter. Work in thoroughly with the flour mixture. (The suet is important because it gives the crust a rich flavor and a flaky texture.) Add cold water to make a soft dough, just a little bit more moist than ordinary pastry dough but not as soft as biscuit dough

Divide the dough into four pieces and roll each piece out to about the size of a dinner plate and on one half of the rolled out dough build up the ingredients as follows: A half-inch layer of finely chipped potatoes; season these with salt and pepper. Then follow with a thin layer of sliced turnips, then a very thin layer of chopped onion. Cover this with about one fourth of the mixed cubed beef and pork and season once more. Now add a piece of butter about the size of a walnut to the top of the built-up ingredients. Now fold the uncovered portion of the dough over the filled portion and crimp the edges. Your pasty is now somewhat in the shape of a half moon.

" Make a one-inch slit in the top of the dough and place prepared pasty on a greased cooky sheet or a pie pan and put in the oven. Bake at about 400° for an hour. This recipe will make four nice size pasties.

You will love pasties for outdoor picnics or for buffet suppers. They can be kept hot for several hours by being wrapped in several coverings of paper and placed in a basket.

Pasties are rich and very substantial and it is always a good plan to have a good salad of greens with them. Some people like sliced tomatoes, others prefer to have a Jello dessert to follow the pasty. Of course, a real Cornishman will want his Crosse and Blackwell chow chow with his pasty. Either tea or coffee go well with pasties.

This little poem will give you another slant on the pasty:

> I dearly love a pasty;
> A 'ot leaky one,
> With mayt, turmit and taty,
> H'onyon and parsley in 'un.
>
> The crus' be made weth suet,
> Shaped like a 'alf moon,
> Crinkly h'edges, freshly baked
> 'E es always gone too soon.

mayt   — meat
turmit   — turnip
taty   — potatoes
h'onyon — onion

Kentucky Moonshiners

About the turn of the century federal agents made heavy and repeated raids on the moonshine stills in the mountain country of Kentucky, with the result that many of the moonshiners scattered to what they thought would be more favorable parts of the country in which to continue their chief source of livelihood. Many of these came to the wooded area which straddled Iron County of Michigan and Vilas County, Wisconsin, with the Brule River between. Here they bought up cut-over and second-growth timber land and cleared small farms and built little log cabins and barns. Some of them had decided to reform their ways and did well by working on their little farms in the spring and summer, then working in the lumber camps in the winter. Others made good use of their early training. Using the grain and corn they raised on their lands, they began their illicit business again. For a time

Michigan went dry under local option and the Kentuckians did a flourishing business.

Most of these migrants were typically shiftless hillbillies and lived a very meager and precarious life, raising large families of children who did the hard work on the farm and in the woods, while the men pursued their previous trade or spent their time at hunting and fishing. It was risky for anyone not known to them to show in their neighborhood. Crack shots with a rifle, these men were dangerous to encounter. Those who knew them were in no danger. One could leave a silver dollar on a stump near a Kentuckian's farm and come back an hour later to find a jug of clear white "moonshine" in its place.

The Kentuckians lived largely off the land, raised a few potatoes and vegetables between the stumps and obtained their meat from the woods. Game wardens seldom molested them. It was too dangerous. The woods and what was in them belonged to these migrants. Frequently reports would come out in the hard winters that some of these families were on the verge of starvation for lack of a balanced diet or that some of their children went without shoes or socks. Relief expeditions were organized by local women to send them food to supplement their steady diet of venison and rabbits and castoff clothing for the children. Those who took the supplies to them would find a quarter of venison hanging up in their own woodsheds a few weeks later. Schools in those sections were few and far between, with the result that not many of the children had even an elementary education. Growing up wild in the backwoods, the children took up the same life their parents lived. One boy was said to have been sixteen years old before he was caught and had shoes put on him. They were a hardy and independent lot and multiplied rapidly, but they would not accept charity and always returned with some gift from the woods for their benefactors.

Tall, angular and bony, they somehow withstood the rigorous winters in their log shacks. The only time the men shaved was when they came to town two or three times a year with their tough ponies and buckboards to lay in a few supplies. The women and children seldom appeared in town and when they did they were as shy as deer and stayed in the wagon or buckboard while the men did the buying. Even the female dresses and dressgoods were purchased by the men, who sometimes bought whole bolts of cloth for the mother to fashion dresses for herself and her daughters. At one time a Kentuckian's family of seven girls appeared in town, all wearing dresses all made alike out of the same bolt of cloth.

"Barefoot" Charlie was a holdover from the early Kentucky migration. He was a giant of six feet six, shoulders like an ox, big handed and feet which called for a size fourteen. He earned his nickname from going barefoot most of the year, except in below zero weather when he compromised on shoepacs, which could stretch to any size when wet. He loved the woods and would be seen traveling miles barefooted over the trails and dusty roads. He seldom came to town, for, he said:

" If you want to find the biggest fool on earth, go to the city. You 'll always find him to be the man who moved in from the country. " He claimed to be a Yale graduate to please his mother and became a moonshiner to please himself.

The Kentuckians learned from the wandering Indians to gather and raise another woods product which brought them an income with little expenditure or labor. It was ginseng, a medicinal root found growing in a wild state in the deep woods. The Indians had used it for medicine for generations and carefully guarded the secret of gathering it. They dried the roots in the sun and sold it to the local drug stores which shipped it to pharmaceutical companies in Chicago. It brought fifteen dollars a pound dried. The Indians learned that by drilling holes in the green roots and filling them with lead shot the ginseng would bring them more per pound, like the country woman who hid a large rutabaga in her jar of butter and sold it to Pat Kelly.

Our Kentuckians, who spent much of their time roaming the woods, soon learned about ginseng and did a good business each fall gathering it. Several of them transplanted the roots onto their own property and grew it under sheds covered with tree branches, simulating natural conditions.

One Kentucky family lived near the lumber and mill village of Atkinson where the husband cultivated ginseng on a large scale. His neighbor was a Polish family who were a quarrelsome lot. The Kentuckian had a well on the edge of his clearing, which the Polish family had to use. One day the small son of the Polish family was drawing water from the well with his pail and forked stick, when the Kentuckian's dog started to attack him viciously. The boy threw a stick and hit the dog which went yelping back home. The Kentuckian came out of his house with his deer rifle and called on his neighbor for revenge, not knowing it was only a small boy who had struck his dog. The boy's mother came out and started to berate the Kentuckian and all his ancestors. The homesteader promptly sent a bullet through her thigh.

The sheriff came out to investigate the shooting. The whole area was astir over the affair. The officers made careful inquiries and learned that the Polish woman had gotten what she deserved. They made no arrest. Thereafter the Polish family dug its own well on the far side of their farm.

On the first day of school near one of the Kentuckian settlements, one of the boys, dressed in overalls slick with grease and grime, brought his new teacher a big red apple. When she thanked him for it, she remarked:

"My, isn't it bright and shiny! "

"It should be," replied the boy. " All the way to school I spit on it and rubbed it on my pants."

"Well, thank you. What does your father do, Sonny?" she asked him.

"My pappy doesn't do anything. He doesn't like to work."

"What do you do for food?"

"My mom sold her chickens last week and bought some salt pork and cornmeal."

" That didn't last long. What did she do then?"

" Well, she sold her wash machine."

" What will she do now? " pursued the teacher.

" That's what my mom wonders! " replied the boy, hanging his head.

The Kentuckians knew where the deer trails were and were often engaged as hunting guides in the fall. A hunter from "down below" hired Zeke Montgomery to show him where he could get his vension. They hunted all morning without success. When noon came the hillbilly invited him to have dinner with him.

"I don't know what the woman's got to eat," he said, "but we'll make out. "

When they sat down at the handmade kitchen table, there were only a few slices of sowbelly and three small boiled potatoes in the dishes. The hunter took a slice of the pork and the Kentuckian, with true mountain hospitality, passed him the potatoes, saying:

" Here, have some potatoes. Take two. Here, take dang nigh all of 'em."

One of the Kentuckians had done right well with his moonshine business and decided to go to town and buy up his winter's supplies and extra treats for his large family. In Barney Krom's store he bought a bolt of dress goods for his wife and daughters and a pair of shoes for his fourteen year old son who had worn nothing but shoe-pacs all his life.

As he was loading up with his food supply at Pat Kelly's general store, Pat asked the moonshiner why he did not buy an outfit for himself while he had money and needed clothes. The Kentuckian decided he would spend the balance of his money on himself. He bought a suit of long woolen, red underwear, a pair of shoes, a blue serge suit, a white shirt and a felt hat.

Pat wrapped up the clothes in a brown paper and tied a string around the package. Together the men placed the purchases in the wagon box behind the spring seat.

On the way home the Kentuckian drove his team through a ford in the Brule River and let his horses drink.

Taking off his clothes down to his skin, he threw them into the river piece by piece and watched them float out of sight, remarking to his horses:

" We'll surprise Zeldie. "

When the last garment disappeared around the bend of the stream he reached around to pick up the package and dress himself in his new outfit. The package was gone, evidently having been bounced out on the rough road.

Scratching his grizzly beard, he picked up the reins, clucked to his horses and said to them:

" Git up, you nags. We'll surprise Zeldie anyway."

Choose Your Partners

Every nationality brought their native dances from the land of its birth and in their national social groups danced them with an abandon in their new American homes. Schottiches, waltzes, two steps, gavottes, Irish jigs, Scottish flings, Polish Rounds and a great variety of other steps from European lands enlivened the parties and weddings of the time. However, the American square dances were the most popular and were interspersed with the other dances brought from abroad.

Every Friday night a regular square dance was held in the town hall or in a grange hall and was open to all. In between informal square dances were held in homes in the country or town. Neighbors visiting neighbors organized spontaneous dances in the course of an evening. When a dance was suggested on these visits between families someone was sent out to invite other couples and to round up musicians for the evening and the dancing often continued far into the morning hours, then broke up to allow the participants to reach home, snatch an hour or two of sleep before the work of the day began.

The music was furnished by men and sometimes women who played a variety of instruments—mouth organ, dulcimer, jews harp, guitar, banjo, bull fiddle, ordinary fiddles, pump organ, zither, accordion, and sometimes a piano. At times one lone mouth organist furnished the tunes for a home parlor dance. From two to five musicians made up an orchestra, who played from eight in the evening to three and four o'clock in the morning with no intermission except a midnight lunch or a glass of beer between dances. Professional orchestras, of which there were few, played all night for ten dollars, then went home to breakfast and off to their regular work in sawmill or mine or store.

By seven-thirty of a Friday evening sleigh bells sounded in the distance over the crisp, frosty air, to become louder and louder by the second until a cutter discharged a young couple swathed in heavy robes and fur coats. The young man escorted his lady to the door and then turned back to drive his steaming horse under the shed back of the grange hall. Other couples came in rapid succession and traipsed into the buildings amid shouts of glee over the prospects of a happy evening. Two horse teams raced down the road pulling sleighfuls of men and women and unloaded into the place.

The hall was ablaze with high-hanging kerosene lamps and the big horizontal wood stove in the corner was red with heat. The cold couples hovered around the heater to thaw out. Heaps of fur coats, fur caps and overcoats were piled high on the tables in the back of the room. The orchestra of three musicians with fiddle, accordion and mouth organ was tuning up and stomping its feet in cadence with the music they were preparing.

The official caller stepped upon a raised platform and surveyed the hall. Then raising his voice above the babble he shouted:

" Choose your Partners
    One and all;
    Fill up the floor and
    We'll dance some more."

The men whirled their ladies around and with their arms about their waists took their places in the four sets of eight dancers in the four corners of the floor.

The orchestra stuck up for the first square dance. The caller sang in tune with the music:

" First change.

" Commence your honor and the corner the same.
 (Bow to your partner, next couple the same)
 First four right and left;
 Balance across;
 Two ladies change.

" Half promenade, half right and left;
 All men left.
 Side four right and left;
 Two ladies change.

" Half promenade, half right and left;
 All men left.
 Right hand to your partner;
 Grand right and left.

" Second change.

" First couple lead to the right;
 Take your lady by the wrist;
 Round that lady with a grapevine twist;
 Back to the center and cut a figure eight;
 Go round the gent with the same old gait;
 Join your hands and circle four;
 Break with your right;

" Lead to the next;
 Round that lady with a grapevine twist;
 Back to the center and cut a figure eight;
 Around that gent with the same old gait;
 Join hands and circle six;
 Break with your right and lead to the next;
 Round that lady with a grapevine twist.

" Back to the center and cut a figure eight;
 Go round the gent with the same old gait;
 Join your hands and circle eight;
 Places all and all men left.

" All men left;
 Right hand to your partner;
 Grand right and left.
 Watch your partner and watch her close
 And when you meet her you'll double the dose.
 Your right foot up and your left foot down,
 If you don't hurry, you'll never get around.

" Third change.

"First two couples lead up to the right;
When you get there you'll balance and swing;
And while you're swinging remember the call;
All men left and promenade all.

"First couple lead down to the right;
Stay until I find you.
Pass right through and balance too
And swing with the girl behind you.

"Take that lady and lead to the next
And stay until I find you.
Pass right through and balance too,
And swing with the girl behind you.
Take that lady and lead to the next;
Etc.

"All men left,
Right hand to your partner,
And grand right and left.
Swing with the opposite;
Swing her alone.

"Swing with the one you call your own;
Finish your swing and take her home."

At the close of the square dance all couples left the floor and the orchestra struck up a Strauss waltz in which the older couples excelled, sweeping the floor in wide, circling turns.

Immediately after the waltz, the orchestra, with a minute or two rest swung into the second square dance. Between the square dances schottiches, two steps and other couple dances took place.

With flushed faces the dancers kept on throughout the evening and into the morning, with nearly everyone dancing all the dances. As twelve o'clock drew near the refreshment committee poured out steaming hot coffee at a table drawn out of the kitchen and spread out plates of sandwiches, doughnuts and cakes.

Some of the boys were seen leaving the hall at frequent intervals for their own refreshments hidden in their cutters. As the excitement grew and a few became too boisterous, the caller stopped the dance while strongarm members of the committee ejected the alcoholic celebrators, with the warning not to return until they had cooled off.

As the early morning hours came the couples and sleighloads left the hall until one set remained. These danced to the end of the last set and sought their blanketed horses and lap-robed cutters to find their way home for a few hours of sleep. The seven o'clock whistle at the sawmill and mines saw them in their work clothes and dinner buckets, ready for another day's work.

The square dance of the Nineties had its place in bringing our mixed nationalities into common touch and helped to unite us in a feeling of belonging in the community. That it has come down through the years with increased popularity is evidence that there was something fundamental in its amalgamating influence.

It was at these happy, carefree dances and social affairs that the children of European immigrants mixed and accepted each other as equals. It was there that Josephina Narretti, the dark, comely Italian maid, met and fell in love with blonde Oscar Olson of Swedish descent and later married him. There Wanda Zelinski, the daughter of an old country Polish couple, danced with John Pengelly, the son of a Cornish miner, and together started on their way to happy family life. Nationality met nationality, courted, married and began a new generation of Americans. Herein lies the secret of a New American solidarity, an interwoven chain of relationships between descendents of once foreign races. The melting pot which was the Upper Peninsula became a loom which knitted and wove all races and nationalities into one new race—an All-American nation.

Celebrating The Fourth

Though we were in a sense a polyglot community, with many European tongues still spoken in our midst, the Fourth of July was celebrated by our town with great fervor by all. This was a time when our population gave expression to their gratefulness for being in a land of freedom and opportunity.

For us kids it was almost as important, and even more exciting, than Christmas. We looked forward to its coming and planned for it weeks ahead. Early in June individual and community plans for its celebration were under way. Kids saved their money and families set their plans for the day in motion. A village committee of merchants and professional men arranged a gala program for the Fourth which would bring in prospective customers from miles around to spend their money and do their shopping while all the stores were open.

We youngsters earned spending money or begged it from our parents to buy firecrackers, lemonade, candy and homemade ice cream. The whole day from daybreak on into the night was spent in celebrations of various kinds and degrees of enthusiasm.

Enterprising individuals and organizations set up booths called "boweries", consisting of raised platforms of rough lumber from the local mills and surrounded by railings and small trees in their heavy foliage, with red, white and blue bunting tacked around the bottom. Here were held dances at ten cents a round—square dances, two steps, quadrilles, waltzes and schottisches. Music was furnished by a number of two and three piece orchestras with fiddles, accordions, sometimes a piano or guitars. Each "bowery" had a caller who continued until his voice gave out, to be relieved by another as the dancing continued late into the night.

Swains and their girl friends from miles around came in for the dancing and the fun. Couples made the rounds of the "boweries", then repeated. The dancing and merrymaking continued through the night and until the first pink rays of the morning sun appeared. Refreshment stands did a flourishing business. Gallons of strong coffee kept the celebrators awake. Mountains of sandwiches were consumed. Whiskey bottles kept in the waiting buggies and wagons added to the riotousness.

Churches set up temporary eating places under tents on the vacant lots to make money for their missionary work among even more primitive peoples over the earth. Lemonade and ice cream stands dispensed homemade products and were always crowded. Money was "no object." We spent it in "riotous living."

There was no limit on the quantity or size of firecrackers, bombs or torpedoes, which were exploded everywhere. One never knew when a giant firecracker would explode at his feet. Casualties were frequent and the town doctor had a busy day. Many accidents occurred when firecrackers set set off under the feet of horses drawing buggies, buckboards and wagons. Horses in from the quiet country were particularly unmanageable and run-aways were common on the Fourth.

Races and contests of all kinds were staged—shotputs with big lumberjacks and miners using large rocks for the shot; hop-skip-and-jump, sack races, horse races, team races with husbands and wives running against other couples, miners' rock drilling matches, tug-o'-war, greased pig and greased pole events. Darius Faulkner, the colored teamster, usually won the greased pig contests, for he had a technique of diving onto the hog's back and catching it by the front legs. There were cash prizes for all events, although often the prize money offered by the merchants ran out before the races were completed.

In addition to the "boweries" set up for dancing and booths dispensing refreshments and meals, the entire main street was lined with small trees cut down in full leaf, stuck into the ground and fastened to the outer edge of the wooden sidewalks, making a green lane for the celebrators to walk along. The otherwise bare street became a tree-lined thoroughfare. The green leaves and the fresh smell of the newly-cut maples, birch and poplars mingled with the acrid odors of exploded firecrackers and horsemanure added to the holiday atmosphere.

The night before the Fourth was a nightmare of explosions of dynamite stolen by the miners from the powder houses at the mines. The dynamite was set off outside the village and the detonation rocked the houses and stores all over town. The Farley boys set off a charge of dynamite in a stump at the edge of the town one night before the Fourth and a chunk of the stump crashed through Mrs. Berghini's bedroom window.

Three of the young men of the village decided one year to make it a real celebration by stealing a box of dynamite, fuse and detonation caps that would "blow the top of Weimer Hill" on the outskirts. They pried open the back window of a powder house at the Hiawatha mine. Propping up the window with a stick, they sent the smallest of their number in to hand out the explosives. He found the dynamite and a long roll of fuse and handed it through the window to the others. He then located a box of explosive caps and put them into his back pants pocket. As he crawled back through the opening his foot knocked out the prop. The window sash fell, striking the box of caps. The caps exploded. The others

carried him to the local hospital, then called the town doctor at his
home. The next morning the boys called at the hospital to inquire about
their comrade who was " wounded in action." When they asked the
doctor how the boy was, the medicine man replied:

"I don't know how he feels this morning. I expect's he's pretty sore.
I spent all last night picking copper out of his backside."

At mid-noon the town orators mounted second balcony of the Boynton
Hotel and impressed their listeners with the great privileges they enjoyed in this land of freedom and opportunity and to remind them that
" the merchants of this city made this celebration possible for you. Be
sure to show your appreciation by patronizing our local stores instead
of sending your orders off to Sears, Roebuck or Montgomery, Ward"
We kids were bored by this long-haired patriotism and sneaked off to
find some deviltry which was more to our liking.

The money dealt out to the small fry by their parents was soon
squandered on lemonade, ice cream, stick candy and firecrackers. Wise
parents doled out their change carefully in order to make it last out
the long day. Families with several children had to do this surreptitiously to avoid jealousy among their brood.

The most fun of all for some of us were the " calithumpian " parades,
when individuals, stores and organizations dressed in costumes, built
floats and competed for prizes. Where the word " calithumpian " originated is lost to dim history but to us it was a word of magic, fun and
adventure. It was an early and small version of the Mardi Gras in our
pioneer town. Whole families and neighborhoods combined to vie with
each other in the construction of floats, clown costumes and commercial exhibits mounted on wagons for the prizes offered.

One of out prize-winning floats was erected on a lumber wagon
whose " reach " was extended to make it twice as long as the average
wagon. On this we constructed a long animal cage with wooden slats
" borrowed " from the cooperage mill for " iron bars." In the cage were
placed the "wildman from Borneo" (my brother Ed), a cross-eyed
wildcat (our own tomcat striped with paint), a snake charmer (one of
the boys holding a two inch rope painted green), a two-headed calf (one
of the heads made from a defunct calfskin), and tied behind the wagon
was an elk (our blue roan cow with deer horns tied to her head). Perched on top of the high cage was one of the older boys dressed in a homemade ballet costume and I, in a ringmaster's uniform (a Spanish
officer's suit captured in the Spanish-American War), swung a great
blacksnake whip and drove the four-horse team along the route of the
" calithumpian " parade.

On another Fourth we collected all the ponies we could find and
painted them up to resemble Indian war-ponies. The riders were
dressed in dyed loincloths, our faces, arms and chests painted in red,
blue and yellow war paint, carrying bows and arrows and tomahawks.
This entry "stole the show" for, coincidentally, a tribe of Chippewa
Indians had come into town to celebrate the Fourth and were dressed
like white men of the day. Upon seeing our " Indian " float, they fell in
behind us in the parade and made a ludicrous contrast to the white
"Indians."

To country folks, homesteaders living at a distance in the woods and to the idle lumberjacks in town, our Fourth of Julys were banner occasions, long to be looked forward to and long to be the topics of conversation during the balance of the year. Whole families appeared in town in wagons and buckboards early on the Fourth. Wide-eyed youngsters in motley dress stared at the parades, witnessed the races and crowded the refreshment stands. Mothers took the opportunity to buy clothing and supplies for the whole family. Fathers frequented the wide-open saloons and celebrated in the fashion they liked best. One family came on the scene at daybreak, with their six daughters and five sons. The mother and the girls were all dressed alike, in clothes of the same color and pattern, the result of a previous shopping trip by the father who bought a whole bolt of dress goods which was tailored for the girls by their mother. Wherever they appeared they were the center of attention because of their "Ike and Mike, they look alike" dresses.

Irrespective of the language and the native customs which our families had brought from other lands, the new generations returned along the roads that fanned out from the town with a fuller consciousness of who their neighbors were, and how good it was to be among them. The land of the free and the home of the brave? We never called it that, because the land itself never bragged. But perhaps it was and perhaps we were.

Chapter V

LAND OF THE FREE

Growing Our Own
Village Animal Life
A-Berrying We Went
Meat For The Winter
Earning Spending Money
Without Modern Conveniences
Local Color
Playboys Of The Nineties
Six Months of Winter
Our Western Bronchos
My Worst Runaway
Winter Sports
The Fire Fighters
Folklore And Superstitions
Stealing The Courthouse
Our Organized Athletics
School Daze
I'll Never Forget When—
Indian Incidents

Chapter V

LAND OF THE FREE

Growing Our Own

As we have seen in earlier chapters, although money was never easy to acquire, food was usually plentiful, and in the Upper Peninsula with its economic uncertainties so much a factor, all families got some of their living from the land. The price of those services from the land was—effort.

Since nearly every family has its own home garden or little farm where most of their vegetables for the year were raised, little produce was shipped in from "down below", meaning from Wisconsin, Illinois and southern Michigan. In fact southern grown vegetables were unheard of and greenhouses which raised vegetables for the market were unknown.

We raised all of our own potatoes, planted them by hand, hoed them, picked potato bugs and dug the crop. It took over one hundred bushels of potatoes to supply our needs. When the crop was harvested it was either stored in the cellar under our home or placed in a trench in the ground and covered with a layer of straw or hay and a top layer of earth, to be dug up later as needed.

Cabbage for winter use was buried in the same way or placed roots first in the dirt floor in the cellar. A hogshead or two of sauerkraut was made each fall. This process was engaged in by the whole family, taking two or three evenings to do. A great heap of fresh cabbage heads was dumped on the porch outside and brought in a bushel at a time. Some of us cut the heads in two, removed the hearts and the surplus outer leaves. My father sliced the cabbage through a special back-and-forth slicer into a fifty gallon wooden barrel. A layer of cabbage leaves was first placed on the bottom of the barrel, then a six-inch layer of sliced cabbage spread on top the leaves. A liberal handful of salt was thrown over the shredded heads. As each layer of cabbage and salt was placed in the barrel a heavy stomper made of a section of log was used to pound the mixture down until the juice rose to the top. This went on until the hogshead was filled. Some families were accused of stomping it down with their feet. On top of the barrel a layer of leaves was spread, a round barrel head was set on and weighted down with a heavy stone. The barrel was left in a warm room for a few days until the mixture "worked." When bubbles appeared and salt water rose, the juice was taken off and replaced by fresh water. We often had two or three barrels of kraut which lasted us until the fresh crop of cabbage grew. Home killed pork cooked in the kraut was a staple, and a tasty and savory meal. Home made bread, home churned butter, a variety of vegetables, home killed pork, beef and sausage and potatoes made up most of our meals.

There was little fruit used, except apples, for there was little fruit

107

shipped in. Oranges were a rare treat and that at Christmas time only. Dried prunes, raisins and apples were extensively used. These, with quarts of wild blueberries, raspberries, strawberries and cranberries gathered in the summer gave us a variety for the table.

Breakfasts usually consisted of pancakes with maple syrup, our own smoked ham and bacon, oatmeal and cornmeal, with an ample supply of cream and milk from our own cows.

Ice cream was homemade in five gallon freezers. Pure sugar, thick cream with occasional blueberry or raspberry mixture and vanilla flavoring made a dessert which we all loved. Mother had no difficulty getting help to break up the ice or turn the freezer, for she rewarded us by giving us the big ladle to lick when the ice cream became frozen. When served the ice cream was topped with ground hazel nuts which we had gathered in the woods in the fall.

The variety of candy was rather limited. Home made fudge and fondant were made from supplies of sugar and sweets on hand. When we had maple syrup we boiled it down to a soft consistency and poured it on snow to harden into candy. With what few pennies we were given or earned we bought penny stick candy, horehound, licorice, gum drops, hard mints, rock candy, chocolate mounds of a doubtful nature, and sweetwood for chewing. "Yucatan" gum in yellow wrappers and spruce gum made from resin of spruce trees were sold in confectionery and grocery stores. We spent many long minutes before a candy case pricing all the penny candies before buying, much to the disgust of the clerk. It was: "How much of this for a penny? How many of these for a penny?" Quantity was the only consideration.

With the coming of the English, or "Cousin Jack", from the copper mines around Calumet and Houghton, pasties were introduced and became a popular dish to the rest of the population. These pasties were made from a rich bread dough rolled out and filled with pieces of meat, rutabagas, turnips and onions, well seasoned, rolled up and baked in the oven. One or two made a full meal. "Cousin Jack" miners who carried their dinner buckets often had pasties as their main course. A number of housewives went into the business of making and selling pasties for pin money. Every church bazaar sold or served them.

Men who worked in the mines and other pursuits carried big dinner pails for their noon or midnight meal if they worked on night shift. These tin pails or buckets had several compartments containing coffee or tea, meat, sandwiches and dessert. In our boarding house "putting up" dinner pails was a big task which took place after mother and the girls had washed the supper dishes. Preparing and "putting up" from ten to twenty dinner pails an evening was no small undertaking. Each nationality had its preference of food and the way it should be prepared and each one was not hesitant about criticizing what they found in their dinner bucket the day before. The expression, "A Full Dinner Pail", which was used to good effect in political campaigns in the United States, originated from this practice and was the slogan which turned the tide after the depression of 1893. It was during depressions and slack times at the mines that a "full dinner pail" became a serious matter for the workers and their families.

Every farm family and most of those living in town had a big copper or iron kettle which served many purposes from boiling water to scalding a hog at butchering time, cooking apple butter, boiling down maple sap and making soft soap.

For soap making, no scrap of fat was too small to find its way into the big crock which stood in the cellar. Bacon rinds, ham trimmings, tallow and suet and even deer fat were destined to become soft soap before their usefulness was ended.

Lye, which was the other important ingredient of soft soap, was made from hardwood ashes saved from under the firepot of the cookstove. Ashes were leached with water to remove the coarser particles and the liquid strained through a sieve.

The big kettle was set up on a tripod of iron or stone in the back yard and a fire built under it. Into the kettle went the salvaged grease and the leached lye, to be boiled and stirred until it had a soft-cheese consistency. It was then ladled out with a big dipper into flat pans to harden and later cut into squares to be used for washing clothes, scrubbing floors and even washing hands and faces. Some women boiled wild rose leaves in the soap to scent it for toilet use.

Apple butter making followed the gathering of the apple crop in the fall. The whole family participated in this chore, peeling apples, coring them, and cutting the apples into wedges. Just enough water was poured into the kettle to float the sliced apples. A small fire was lighted under the kettle and the mixture was allowed to simmer slowly until the apples were soft. A great wooden spoon three or four feet long with holes in the bowl was used, enabling the stirrer to stand far enough away from the bubbling mass to avoid being burned when the bubbles burst. The one who stirred walked round and round the kettle to keep out of the strong wood smoke, dipping the big spoon in where the air bubbles were biggest and down to the bottom of the kettle to prevent scorching. The girls of the family were persuaded to do the stirring by being told that "smoke follows beauty."

When the mixture had boiled to the proper thickness it was sweetened with brown sugar and maple syrup. Cinnamon and other spices were added. When cool, the dark brown apple butter was ladled into crocks, covered with cheesecloth and stored in the cool cellar under the house or in the root cellar dug into the side hill. All fall, winter and spring a large dish of apple butter found its way to the table for breakfast, dinner and supper. Apple butter and cracklin's from the fall butchering took the place of dairy butter for many families.

Hazel nuts grew wild in the woods around and on the roadsides. When the green, spiny husks began to turn brown, they were ready for the gathering and storing in the attic for the winter. It was necessary to use leather gloves while picking them to protect the fingers from the tiny, sharp needle-pointed prickers on the husks. Long winter evenings were spent in taking off the now dry husks, cracking the nuts and eating the sweet meat. Hazel nut meats were used in making cakes and cookies and as treats in our Christmas stockings.

Harvesting ice was a necessary occupation for farm and some town

families. It was used in iceboxes for refrigeration and cold storage.
In January and February the water in the lakes or ponds had frozen to
a depth of from twenty-five to thirty inches and was ready for harvesting. In preparation for the cutting, the snow was shoveled by hand or
snow-plowed off by team. A spud or sharp pointed crowbar was used
to chop a hole into the ice large enough to admit a crosscut saw. A
series of parallel cuts were made from twenty to thirty inches apart
and from twenty to forty feet long. In the same way, cuts were made
across the first cuts the same distance apart and of the same length.
The result was square cakes of ice which floated on the water. Ice tongs
were used to pull the cubes out of the water and onto low horse-drawn
sleighs. Several teams and sleighs were kept busy hauling the ice to
icehouse or storage sheds where it was stacked up, eight to ten feet
high. The whole pile was covered with sawdust or marsh hay as insulation. When warm weather came the cubes were uncovered as
needed and carried to the icebox. Some families had storage rooms
built in their icehouses and completely covered by the ice on top and
three sides to preserve their winter's meat.

Without this thrifty husbandry on the part of the early people in
growing, gathering and storing their food against long winters and with
layoff in the mines and lumber camps, many families would have fared
very poorly. Necessity was the mother of foresight and thrift.

Village Animal Life

There was no limitation on the animal life which roamed the village
streets and alleys. The majority of families owned one or more milch
cows, plus their annual crop of calves. These were driven to the outlying hills and woods to graze during the day and herded in at milking
time in the morning and evening. Because our family was a large one,
we always had four or five cows and a various number of calves in all
stages of growth. Each boy was required to learn to milk. We chari-
tably taught our eight sisters to milk and sometimes bribed or threatened them into helping us. It was a job I detested, for it interrupted my
busy play life. In fly time it was particularly trying. To have a cow's
dirty, well-manured tail switched across one's face was no fun. I tried
various devices to prevent this and finally hit upon the idea of tying a
brick to their tails. This worked beautifully until one particularly mean
Holstein switched too hard and I came away with a black eye. All milking had to be done by hand. We learned early how to squeeze a cow's
"tits" by pressing the forefingers first, then each finger in succession
until the milk was pressed into the pail between our knees. I tried an
experiment to hurry the process. I cut short pieces of oat-straw and
placed them up two of the "tits" so that the milk flowed through them
while I was working on the other two "tits." This worked out well until
my mother saw my invention. She gave me a sound slap over my ear
and ordered me to return to the slower but more conventional way of
getting milk from a cow.

There were no cattle-pounds until about 1905. The cows and their offspring wandered about town at night and found a resting place wherever they wished. There they lay, chewing their cuds until someone stumbled over them in the dark and drove them away. Our baseball field was on a commons known as Weimer field. This was the cattle's favorite spot to graze and sleep. We kids didn't mind that too much until one day I slid into what I thought was second base. After that it was a problem of either keeping the critters out by building a fence or no baseball grounds. Eventually we got our cattle pound and a safer second base.

The cows and horses wandered far into the fields and woods to find grazing. It sometimes took us hours to find them and drive them home. If they strayed in the morning and we were late for school, we didn't complain, but as grass got scarce during the dry summer they would wander miles off into the woods where we found them only by the tinkle of their bells. This made it necessary for us to use up all our play time after school to search for them. Since most of us boys went barefoot all summer and into the early fall, we often had the pleasure of kicking a cow from her resting place on the grass and warming our cold feet where she lay, as was the boyhood experience which President William McKinley frequently mentioned as he campaigned in the rural areas. My most frustrating experience was stepping on a bumble bee with my bare foot while chasing our horses home. When I got to the barn my father asked me where I had been so long.

"Chasing your damned horses!" I said. "I stepped on a bumble bee. You'll have to get me a new pair of shoes or chase your own nags."

My father always owned from two to four horses for his draying, lumbering and farming operations. He never owned just an ordinary horse. Each animal had to be the best and usually the most expensive he could find. Whenever a new shipment of Indiana draft horses arrived at Billy Hokin's sale stable, my father had to inspect them. Too often he made a trade for a new horse or team and mortgaged the new horses and our cattle as security. It was one of my mother's greatest problems. When we kids needed new shoes or clothes for school the money had already gone to pay for his fancy work horses.

When our family first moved from Racine, Wisconsin to Stambaugh, my father owned a pair of small mules which he used for draying freight from the Chicago & Northwestern Railroad station up the mile-high hill to the village. I didn't remember the mule team but they must have been a fabulous pair judging from the tales he told of their running away and spilling the load, balking halfway up the hill and kicking his hat off when he tried to harness them. Neither did I ever see the buckskin suit he wore for many years while at work. This suit had a long history. It was made by an Indian squaw who probably wore her teeth to the gums chewing the skin to soften it, as was the custom among the Indians. He must have worn it out completely, or otherwise it would have been handed down to one of his five sons, as were most of his other worn clothes.

Every spring a western horse dealer brought a carload of wild, unbroken bronchos from Montana to town to sell. Most of these animals were frightened of human beings and it took considerable skill and know-how to train them for riding or pulling in harness. Two Irishmen, Pat and Mike O'Toole, bought a pair of matched chestnuts from the herd and had the time of their Irish lives breaking them to harness. They smashed sleighs and tore up harness and had no respect for fences. One day when the pair was half broken Mike and Pat decided to take a load of friends on their double bob-sled to Pentoga, a distance of fifteen miles. They were all loaded into the sled and were going past our house when I saw them. The horses were bucking and rearing and jumping from one side of the road to the other. I decided that it would be great sport to hitch a ride on the back end of the sled. I made a run for it as they drove past and caught on. I was leaning over the edge of the sleighbox when the bronchos became frightened and took off across the fields out of control. Before I could disengage myself the sled hit a snow-covered stump and knocked me out completely. When I woke up the party was just a streak of flying snow down the road two miles away.

Of course, nearly every boy in town had a dog. Those were the days when the butcher did not sell his bones and scrap meat, so we could afford to keep dogs. One of the town topers sent his son to John Airey's butcher shop for ten cents worth of dog meat. The boy handed John the dime and said:

"My father wants ten cents worth of dog meat. But you better not put so much fat in it. The last time it made my father sick."

No dog license was required and distemper and rabies were more or less unknown. Our dog Shep was a black and white sheep dog of great size. He was a great help in rounding up our cows and horses. He knew instinctively what we wanted him to do. He would circle the animals and nip the heels of the laggards. They soon learned that our appearance with Shep meant that they were to head for the barn and no fooling. When nipping a horse or cow by the heels, he would bite, then crouch down to avoid a kick. One day he picked on the wrong horse. Harry Sunn's big bay team was grazing in the field when Shep took after them with some urging on our part to see the fun. He nipped one heel, then ducked down. The horse kicked with one foot, then immediately with the other, catching Shep just over the eye with his heavy-shod hoof and knocked him unconscious. That did not discourage Shep from chasing horses but he was most cautious thereafter.

Shep pulled us in a handsled in winter and in an express wagon in summer. What he excelled in was fighting. His method was to run at any size dog and knock him over with his weight and speed, then tie into him while the dog was dazed. No dog in the neighborhood could outfight him. Yet he was gentle to human beings, especially children.

Billy Jobe, the superintendent at one of the mines, had a big white bulldog which followed behind his horse and buggy past our home. It was Shep's delight to rush at the bulldog, knock him over and give him a good chewing. This hurt Billy's pride. One day when Shep made a rush for his dog, Jobe pulled a pistol from his pocket and shot at Shep but missed. That was too close a call and thereafter we called Shep off when the Jobe parade went by.

My youngest brother acquired a billy goat which he trained to pull a sled and wagon. He drove the outfit along the village streets, the envy of the younger fry. All went well until one day a dog chased Billy, who ran away and tipped my brother into the dusty red road. When Billy reached home he climbed to the top of the fence, wagon and all, to get away from the dog. My brother chased after him, filling the air with lumberjack oaths. Mother was standing on the front porch and saw and heard it all. That was the death-knell of the goat. The next day my father slaughtered Billy and he was served up as mutton. None of us relished the stew, for we were too fond of Billy and his cute tricks to eat him.

Our experiences with animal life in the village gave us a deep fondness for livestock even though the work and grief connected with it was not too pleasant at times. It helped to fit us for practical work, taught us patience and made us appreciate more the effort that was necessary to make a living in those early days.

A-Berrying We Went

Blueberries and raspberries grew wild in great abundance for miles around the town. Wherever the land had been lumbered off and fires had burned the "slashings", the berries grew in great profusion and were the chief source of jam and fruit the year round. Every family did its own picking, canning and preserving.

Our family organized several berrying trips every year. These lasted for several days or a week. We took tents, camping and cooking equipment, food, lard pails and baskets and set off by horse and wagon to the blueberry or raspberry plains. These were delightful experiences in which everyone joined heartily. We slept on the ground covered with pine needles and ferns. We scattered around, each in his own direction with a five pound lard pail strapped to our waists to leave both hands free for the picking. Our containers were soon filled and brought back, to be emptied in washtubs and boilers, then off for more. By the end of our stay every possible container was filled to the top and overflowing. When we reached home my mother and sisters spent days cleaning, sorting, canning and preserving the crop. One winter we had over 225 quarts of blueberries canned in addition to a hundred or more quarts of raspberries and strawberries.

On one of these trips my sister Mary was busy picking around a blueberry patch when she came upon a black bear eating berries on the other side. She dropped her pail and ran screaming back to the camp while the bear took off in panic in the opposite direction.

Picking and selling blueberries was one source of cash income for the Indians inhabiting the woods. One August day my brother Bill and I were on a berry-picking expedition of our own across the Brule River in Wisconsin. As we walked through the brush to locate a good patch of berries we spied a tribe of Indians engaged in the same pursuit. This was our first experience with Indians in the wilds. We dropped our pails and ran through the woods to Fred Miller's shack three miles distant. Here we related our narrow escape from a scalping, then started preparations for the twelve mile walk home. Just then the same tribe appeared and told with gales of laughter of the two white boys they had seen running away from them.

Wild raspberries were a choice dessert during the winter months. No berry excels the wild raspberry for flavor, tang and succulence. We always had a great supply of these preserved berries and jam on our cellar shelves. My father bought two or three barrels of eating apples every fall which we could eat down to the bottom of the barrel by spring. Cabbages were buried with their roots in the soil of the cellar. Bins of potatoes, turnips and rutabagas raised on our little farm lined the walls. With a whole beef and two or three hog carcasses hung in the woodshed, frozen solid during the winter months, we were well prepared for the dozen or more hungry mouths clamoring for food three times a day. I don't recall ever going hungry in all my youth, although we must have "scraped the bottom of the barrel" during the depression of 1893, when my father worked for fifty cents a day and was glad to be able to find work. We grew big and strong and healthy, due to my mother's wise feeding and unending thrift and our combined efforts to keep the cellar well stocked.

There was always a crop of wild gooseberries, blackberries and currants to be had on the burned-over land for the picking. Cranberries were luscious and red in the bogs after the first frost. Our summers and falls were busy days when this fruit was ripe. Gathering mushrooms was an activity in the spring and fall after warm rains. Our mother carefully instructed us in the selection of the edible varieties which grew abundantly in the shaded woods. We picked them by the bushels to dry in the sun or can for the winter, to be eaten with the meat meat processed after the winter freeze had set in.

Our garden and small farm supplied us with dill and sweet pickles by the crock. The dill we raised and gathered early, to be hung in bunches in the cellar until pickling time began.

Our family table did not depend upon the food which was shipped in from "down below." We raised and gathered our own. It was simple fare, with meat and potatoes as the center of the diet, supplemented by home grown vegetables, berries and fruit gathered from mother nature's own storehouse in great abundance, free for the picking.

Maple syrup and maple candy making was a spring activity we all looked forward to and we all enjoyed. After a long winter it was a frolic to get out in the sugar bush, to see the first signs of spring in the melting snow, the squirrels frisking in the treetops at the first peep of the sun, the calling of the bright bluejays and the budding of the trees.

Sugaring was no easy task. It required long preparation. It necessitated the construction of a roof or shed under which a long stone fireplace was built to hold the long, wide pan for boiling the sap. Great piles of wood were cut by hand and hauled in. Dozens of sap buckets of every conceivable size, ranging from five pound lard pails to five gallon wooden water pails were saved all year. Holes were bored with brace and bit into the sugar maple tree trunks waist high on the sunny side and the containers hung from grooved spiles driven into the holes, with the groove uppermost to catch the sap as it came from the hole and dropped into the bucket.

It takes about fifty gallons of sap to make a gallon of syrup. A steady, slow heat was required to evaporate it. If the fire was too hot or the amount of the sap in the pan was too thin, the syrup burned and became useless except for stock feed. It took one person's full time to feed and watch the fire and stir the sap, while others carried the sap in buckets hung from neckyokes or hauled it in with a team and sled in barrels. Anyone who complains at the price of maple syrup should spend a spring in the sugar bush to appreciate the amount of work and time it takes to produce one gallon. Perhaps the only reason a person will spend many hours tapping, stirring, firing and processing syrup and then selling it for a few dollars a gallon is that just getting out of doors after a long, dreary winter offers an exhilaration which is part of the compensation.

Sugaring off is the most exciting part of the process. When the sap is boiled down to a certain consistency a spoonful is poured on a patch of clean, white snow. If it hardens to a satisfactory degree it is pronounced ready for canning. It is at that time that the workers gather around for the tasting of the result.

The weather must be watched for successful syrup making. Frosty nights and warm days assure a good run of sap. The frost stops the formation of buds while the warm sun sends the sap up from the roots. Warm nights and warm days spell the end of the run.

The hard work of sugar bushing is forgotten on cold winter mornings when nut brown pancakes come direct from the hot kitchen stove to be drowned with golden maple syrup, or when baking powder biscuits are served at dinner with fresh home made butter and our own maple syrup.

In the spring, woodsmen and farmers tap maple trees and use the sap as a drink in the place of water. The liquid has just enough sugar and maple flavor to make it a delicious and satisfying drink. Men working in the woods usually had a few sap buckets hung from the maple trees around them. The sap was thought to have a medicinal virtue—a sort of spring tonic like sulphur and molasses.

With wild berries, mushrooms and maple syrup and maple sugar to supplement home grown vegetables, home grown meat and wild game to be had if one were willing to do the necessary work connected with securing it, the pioneer and early settler needed only a little additional income to eke out a fair living.

Meat For The Winter

One of the home activities we all enjoyed was the annual fall butchering. We raised all of our own winter meat—pork, veal and beef—in our barn behind the house on the edge of town. My father was skilled at this necessary pioneer art. Butchering took place on Saturdays when all the children were home from school. Mother and the girls scoured all the crocks, pans and jars needed. Early in the morning my father started a fire under a big fifty-gallon iron kettle in the back yard and brought the water to a boil. The fattened hog was pulled out by a rope amid ear-splitting squeals. While we older boys held the hog father struck it on the head with a sledge and slit its throat deep under the breast. The blood was caught in a pan and stirred constantly to prevent it from coagulating.

This done, we filled a barrel with the scalding water and dipped the carcass into the barrel until the skin was thoroughly scalded. Then we drew it out upon a raised platform made from a barn door. Using hog scrapers and knives we scraped off the bristles until the skin became a smooth, delicate pink. The hog was raised hind feet first to a rafter in the woodshed and carefully disemboweled. Then it was cut in two down through the backbone and left to cool. The next day after the meat had become firm it was cut into quarters and smaller pieces. The deep layers of fat were rendered in a big kettle on the kitchen stove and the smaller scraps were ground into sausage. The hams and bacon were saved for smoking over a smouldering fire of hickory bark in a little smokehouse next to the woodshed.

The large and small intestines were thoroughly emptied, washed and soaked in brine and the ground meat, flavored with spices, stuffed into them to be cooked for two hours. There was headcheese, pork sausage and blood sausage made of meat and the blood. The scrapple was cooked with fresh apple slices for a bread spread. Even the bladder was used by us kids as a football.

We also butchered a beef and a calf or two in the fall after the cold weather had set in. It was hung from the rafters in the woodshed and kept frozen. Most farmers and homesteaders had an icehouse where they stored cakes of ice cut on a lake or pond. This served as a refrigerator for the meat during the winter. After butchering they dug a hole between the cakes and cached their surplus meat therein. When they needed meat they dug into the icehouse and brought it out frozen stiff.

We always had venison during hunting season and some in between. Before there was a limit on the shooting of deer, we often had gifts of venison from our hunter and homesteader friends. Rabbits, snowshoes and cottontails, were plentiful and my brother Bill could be depended upon to snare them and hang up a good supply in the woodshed for later consumption. Partridge and wild ducks were frequently on our table, for they could be gotten within a few miles of town. Some backwoods families in that section lived on wild meat exclusively, for it was just a matter of going out with a rifle or shotgun and getting it in the woods or lakes around.

Nearly every boy in his teens owned a shotgun or rifle and became a good marksman. I was never a "Deadeye Dick" with a gun but I got my share of game, although I did not relish shooting deer. The best shooting I ever did was of an accidental nature. Roy Gartland and I were searching for his stray cattle near his farm in Beechwood township and had taken a rifle along "just in case." We had no luck. On our way home through the woods we spotted a flock of crows sitting on a tree top about seventy-five yards away. Roy gave me the gun and urged me to shoot them. As I raised the gun the crows took off. Just for the sake of shooting something, I raised up and pulled the trigger. Down came one of the crows like a rock. Roy's eyes bulged out of his head and he exclaimed:

"That's the best shooting I've ever seen!"

A crack rifle shot himself, Roy told everyone about my shooting ability. I couldn't have done it again in a thousand tries, but I passed it off as if it were an everyday occurrence. To this day Roy believes I could have repeated the feat.

The first time I shot a gun I accompanied my brother Bill on a partridge hunting trip. He had a heavy twelve gauge shotgun and was expert in its use. I was eight years old, so I didn't know better than to ask him to let me try a shot. I placed my feet together and shot at a red squirrel on a limb. When I pulled the trigger the gun knocked me flat on my back. But I got the squirrel.

My first gun was an old 45-90 rifle which I resurrected somewhere. It must have been left at our house by someone who had gotten tired of carrying the big "cannon" around. It weighed about twelve pounds and required big cartridges. I took it to my heart and polished, sanded and oiled it for months before I had the courage to shoot it. I bought a box of the big shells and trained on tin cans and stumps. I shot my first deer with it on Golden Creek when I was fifteen.

Fishing was another source of meat the year around. In the spring, summer and fall we angled in the many streams for brook trout and in the lakes for bass, pike and sunfish. In the winter we fished through the ice. Ice fishing was a rugged sport. Fish shanties were a luxury. I went out ice fishing with one of the old-timers. Our only protection was a blanket which we pulled over us as we lay on the ice waiting for fish to take our bait. The old-timer smoked Peerless tobacco in his rancid pipe and the smoke under the blanket was suffocating. He had difficulty keeping his pipe between his toothless gums. At one stage of the expedition his pipe went out and he asked me to crawl out and fill it and light it for him. I accomplished the feat amid coughing and spitting. Then I crawled back under the blanket and handed him the lighted pipe. Just as he put it in his mouth a big pike came into the hole, attracted by the minnow on the hook. The old-timer became so excited that he dropped his pipe into the water. The fish made a lunge at the pipe as it wriggled down into the water just as my companion jabbed his spear at the pike. The old man jumped up and threw the fish onto the ice. The blanket flew off. When we saw the fish it still had the pipe in its mouth and the tobacco was still smoking.

With low wages in the woods and mines, many of the pioneers eked out a fair living by raising and slaughtering their own meat and getting their wild game in the country round about. Boys of the day early took their part in securing meat for the long winters. Depressions and "slack times" found most of the breadwinners thrown back on their own resources. For those who loved to hunt and fish it was both a necessity and sport.

Since wild game was abundant and easy to secure, nearly every man and almost every boy became a skilled hunter. Deer, rabbits and partridge lived in almost every thicket and could be gotten within a few miles from town with little effort. In fact one of the first bear hunts I knew about occurred within a mile of our home. A she-bear and three half-grown cubs were reported in the woods on top of Weimer Hill, almost within sight of our house. When Dr. Tyler, an enthusiastic hunter and fisherman, learned about their location, he came to get my brother Bill and his bear dogs. Armed with two 30-30 rifles they set out. As they reached the wood the dogs scented the tracks and went off at a swift run, baying and barking, with the ruffs of their necks standing straight up. The dogs treed the cubs and the she-bear stood off the dogs, making ferocious lunges at them, wide-mouthed and claws extended.

The men circled the mother and Dr. Tyler brought her down with a neck shot. Bill dropped two of the cubs. In the excitement the third cub took off through the dense woods and was soon lost to sight and smell.

But bears were not always so easy to contend with. A trapper was walking his trap-line on snowshoes, carrying his rifle by a strap over his shoulder, when he heard a snort behind him. He swung around to see a black she-bear charging for him. He did not have time to unsling his gun but swung it down until it pointed at the bear and shot three times. She came straight for him and dropped dead on the toes of his snowshoes. He dressed her out, then decided to investigate the reason why she had charged him. Most bear are as afraid of a human being as most humans are afraid of bear. He followed her deep tracks in the snow and within fifty feet came upon a stump from under which she had crawled. He reached in and pulled out three cubs a month or two old and as large as half-grown cocker spaniels. He placed the youngsters in his pack and set off to his cabin for a team of horses and sled. He brought the she-bear's carcass and the three cubs to town and gave the cubs to a poolroom operator and divided the pork-like meat of the she-bear among his friends. The poolroom man built a cage of chicken wire in the corner of his place and placed the cubs in it. He bottle-fed the babies until they became weaned. They grew rapidly under his care. People fed them candy and pop.

The game warden learned about the captives and took two of them away, leaving the one as a pet. This cub frequently broke out of his cage and begged the patrons of the poolhall for candy and treats. As he grew he became stronger and harder to keep penned up, and was a minor nuisance and a menace. One day he broke out of his cage and wandered out the door on Main Street. Here he spied a boy walking past holding a sack of candy in his hand. The half-grown cub ran after the boy and placed his two front paws heavily on his shoulders. The boy fell to the ground and dropped the candy. The bruin's only interest was in the sweets and not in harming the lad. He licked up every drop of candy and looked around for the boy to see if he had more.

This was too much for the parents, who complained to the game warden. He took the cub with him and turned him loose in the woods where he was originally found. But once having tasted the sweets of civilization and fearing no man, he became a pest in the neighborhood by raiding pig pens, calf barns and chicken coops. He frequently walked into the kitchens of homesteader families for food and frightened the women and children. The game warden finally organized a posse, tracked down the bear and shot him.

Venison was the most favored wild meat and the most easily got. In fact hunters became very selective in their shooting and attempted to kill only young deer. One hunter came upon a buck deer with an enormous set of antlers. When he shot and inspected his kill he found that the buck was so old that his face was white, his joints enlarged with rheumatism and his ribs showed his emaciation. As the hunter looked at him and realized how tough he would be to eat, he decided that he did not want him, even though the antlers were unusually large and well formed. As he stood there deciding what to do, another hunter from Chicago came up and admired the deer.

"What a wonderful set of horns!" he said. "I'd give anything to shoot a deer like that."

"You can have him," replied the hunter. "Just put your tag on him and he's yours."

"How much do you want for him?" asked the city man.

"I don't know," returned the hunter. "You may be a game warden. Take him if you want him. I'll get another."

The Chicago hunter placed a roll of bills on a stump and then placed his tag around the base of one of the big antlers.

The deer killer picked up the roll of bills and counted out forty dollars. Within an hour he came upon a spikehorn buck and shot him. He had meat that he could eat, plus forty bucks.

Old Oak Swamp was my favorite haunt. It was located three miles from town and was overgrown with giant red swamp oak trees entangled with moss hanging down from the limbs. The swamp was always flooded in the spring and in the fall and was inaccessible on foot. It was a stopping-off place for migrating ducks. I trained my horse to stand when a gun was shot off his back. Since ducks were not frightened by the approach of a horse or cow, I invariably got my limit of ducks within a short time. No one else seemed to know about the Old Oak Swamp and its game, so it was more or less a private reserve of my own.

On the high ground around the swamp grew a great profusion of wild plums, gooseberries and hazel nuts, and it was here that I spent many happy hours gathering the fruit and shooting ducks. The hillsides in June were pink with wild roses. Squirrels frisked up and down the trees and partridge drummed their love calls on fallen logs. No foreign sound entered the swamp. Fragrant flowers scented the air and bumble bees droned there from daylight to dark. It was a haven retreat for a boy in his teens. When the spring flood dried up, a dank odor of decaying moss and black earth rose to my nostrils as my pony carefully treaded his way between the high roots of the oaks. Even my mount seemed to enjoy the scents and the seclusion we found there.

As game laws became more stringent a game warden was appointed to stop the poaching of deer and fish and birds. The natives who had

hunted and fished for years without restriction used every wile to out-
smart the law enforcement officer. Wardens were frequently picked
from among successful poachers, for they knew all the tricks of the
hunters and fishermen in evading the law. These former poachers became especially vigorous in catching violators, once they were appointed. But the warden's life was a hard one. He worked day and night to
lay traps to catch the violators and often when he made an arrest the
case was dismissed by the justice of the peace on the grounds that the
man's family was hungry and needed the venison or fish. One young
warden lived in the home of a local merchant who boasted that he could
shoot partridge out of season and get away with it. He brought in his
illegal game and placed it in his icebox where the warden found it. The
officer promptly served him with a search warrant and had him arrested and fined. The next morning the warden found all of his clothing and
personal belongings thrown out on the front lawn.

One well-known poacher continued to get game illegally for many
years, yet was never caught "red-handed", although the warden hid for
many hours trying to catch him with illegal game in his possession.
One early evening the poacher and his wife were driving home in their
Model "T" with a large mess of undersized speckled trout when they
recognized the warden's car coming toward them from a side road
where he had been hiding. Since the poacher was notorious for his illegal activities, the warden pursued them down the road toward town
as fast as his car would travel. Both cars had about the same amount
of speed and the chase covered several miles. Desperately the poacher
and his wife tried to think of some safe way of getting rid of the trout.
The pursuit car was so close that they did not dare throw the fish out
along the road, for that would be evidence enough to satisfy the law.
Finally as they reached the top of a big hill and their car gained speed
down hill, the distance between the cars lengthened. Just as they were
about to heave the trout into the brush, the warden turned his headlight
on. That wouldn't be safe now. In an inspiration the poacher's wife
stuffed the trout down her ample bosom and pulled up the front of her
dress. As they reached town, the warden overtook them. He made a
thorough search of the car but found no evidence of game law violation.

While no game wardens were ever shot to my knowledge, many shots
were fired in their direction to frighten them away. It was a long time
before the natives developed a respect for game laws.

Virgin streams and lakes abounded. Their pure, unpolluted waters
were filled with speckled trout, bass, pickerel and sunfish. Any boy
with a pole cut from the woods and a string and hook could get a mess
of fish for the family within a short time. Fresh fish graced the tables
of most families every week, Fridays included. Sundays found hundreds
of fishermen off to their favorite streams or lakes, each to his "secret
hole" and they seldom came home with an empty creel.

But some of the lazy citizens used a simpler and more effective
method of getting their fish. Dynamite used in the mines to blast out
iron ore was often stolen and used in fishing. The dynamite stick was
greased and the explosive cap and fuse were insulated the same way to

prevent water from dampening them. Then the fuse was lighted and the
dynamite thrown into a fishing hole or beaver dam. The poacher then
ran down to a narrow place in the stream with a burlap sack in hand to
await the explosion and to gather in the dead fish as they floated down.
This method was frowned upon even by ordinary poachers, for they
realized that soon the fish supply would be depleted. The dynamiters
were usually reported, arrested and heavily fined or given a jail sentence or both. No justice of the peace would countenance such wasteful
violations.

Many deer crossed the small farm which my parents owned three
miles from town and which we brothers helped operate during the summer. Polack Joe was our farmhand who lived in a little log cabin on
the place. He supplemented his food supply by shooting deer. He had
erected a scaffold in the crotch of a big maple and nailed boards up the
side of the trunk for a ladder. Under a nearby tree he placed a quantity
of salt to attract the deer. From his seat in the tree he would watch for
deer which came to the "salt-lick." He got his deer in season and out,
but never shot more than he could use.

This seemed to me an easy and thrilling way to get meat for the
table and I decided to try it. One day I borrowed Joe's rifle without
asking him and made my way up the scaffold. All was still and I listened for the sound of approaching footsteps. I must have been up there for
half an hour clutching my gun tightly, with my finger on the trigger. Suddenly I heard a sound like that of a deer taking a cautious step. Then
another. Then a third. I gripped my gun more tightly. I began to shake-
The more I tried to hold it steady, the more it shook. The steps continued to come in my direction. The gun began to wave, almost out of
control. "Buck fever" had me in her grip. With a desperate effort I
held the rifle tight. Just as I was gaining control again, I looked down
and saw a snowshoe rabbit hopping toward the tree. The steps I heard
were the hops of the rabbit.

On another day as I was walking through the woods back of the cabin
I flushed up a flock of partridge. Scarcely frightened, they rose into a
small evergreen tree and sat there looking at me, ten or a dozen plump
bodies in their brown and grey feather camouflage. I soft-footed it back
to the cabin and borrowed Joe's rifle. Filling the magazine with shells,
I approached the tree. The birds were still sitting there, frozen in position, their necks stretched high and their eyes shining. I aimed at one
on the lowest branch and dropped it. Then I aimed at the next lowest
and I saw him fall. I kept this up until the magazine was empty and the
gun barrel was hot in my hands. I killed six partridge without disturbing the others left in the upper branches.

Bear were rather numerous in the woods and frequented the blueberry plains during the summer and early fall. If left undisturbed they
were never dangerous, for they avoided all possible contact with human
beings. When a bear caught sight or wind of a person he took off quietly through the woods and if suddenly frightened would crash away in full
flight, breaking brush and small saplings by his weight and speed. Even
a she-bear with cubs would try to avoid contact with humans and it was

only when she was surprised at close range that she would first send her babies into a nearby tree, then charge the intruder, more to frighten him than to harm him.

I was baking blueberry pies before a reflector baker at our blueberry camp when two forest rangers stopped for lunch and told me of their experience with a she-bear and her cubs that morning. Jim was walking ahead of Jerry along a trail looking over some timber. Jerry carried a small cruiser's ax. As they came over a small rise of ground they surprised a she-bear and her two cubs walking along the trail toward them. Her first act was to cuff the cubs roughly out of sight into the brush, then she charged at the rangers with her red mouth wide open. The men turned and ran back faster than they had ever travelled on foot. Jim was closest to the bear and kept looking back over his shoulder. The animal was gaining on him and he could almost feel her hot breath at his heels.

Jim yelled: "Stop, Jerry! She's gaining on me. Bring your ax!"

But Jerry kept running. The bear evidently thought she had chased them far enough away from her cubs and turned off into the brush.

When the men finally stopped, Jim puffed:

"Why didn't you stop, Jerry? You had the ax."

"Aw," replied Jerry. "Don't you know you should never run from a bear?"

Manny Krans tracked a bear in the snow to a hollow stump, which evidently was its place of hibernation for the winter. Digging the leaves out of the hole, he pointed his gun into the opening and shot twice. There was a roar and a great thrashing about, then all was quiet. Satisfied that he had killed the bear, Manny laid his rifle against the stump and took a rope from his belt. Crawling carefully into the dark hole he groped around until he found one of the bear's paws. He slipped the rope around the paw and backed out, pulling the bear with him. As they reached the outside of the hole the bear suddenly came to life and made a dash for Manny. They circled the stump three times before he could catch up his rifle and shoot the bear through the breast, killing him for sure.

When Manny brought the bear home and told my brother Bill about his narrow escape, Bill asked him:

"Were you scared, Manny?"

"Vell, I tell you, Bill, it war no foolin'," admitted Manny.

Bear frequented the lumber camps at night to eat the garbage which was tossed out of the cook shanty. Here they gorged themselves to repletion, then retired for the night. Whole families of bear would appear and grew bolder as they found themselves unmolested. They often came in during daylight. The cook at one of the camps decided to catch himself a bear. He took a small barrel and drove long spikes into the sides with the sharp points slanted toward the bottom of the barrel. Then he placed a slab of rusty bacon in the bottom of the keg and rolled it near the garbage heap. That night he was awakened by a great roaring. Running out with a lantern he found a bear with his head wedged in the barrel, held fast by the spikes. He secured a gun from the foreman and shot the bear. The whole camp had roast bear for Sunday dinner.

One of the boys wanted to get a cub bear for his brother in town. At night he gathered an armful of rocks and climbed onto the cook shack to wait for the bear to come for their nightly snack. In the moonlight he saw a she-bear and two cubs approaching. When they came within range he yelled and pelted them with rocks. The she-bear ran off into the woods and the lumberjack climbed down and picked up one of the little cubs. The youngster put up such a battle with his claws and his needle-sharp teeth that he dropped the cub and ran back into the cook shack just in time to escape the mother, which came charging out of the woods to rescue her baby.

Wolves are naturally cowardly creatures despite their alleged reputation for bravery and never attacked a human being unless they smelled blood and were certain their victim was helpless. Most stories told of wolves attacking a person were pure fiction. It is only when they are starving and desperate that they approach a man. Their howl is worse than their bite. In fact, their howling is among the most weird animal sounds in the woods.

One moonlit evening in winter when we were at a woods camp we heard wolves howling in the distance. As we listened we tried to decide how many wolves were howling. I guessed twelve. My pal said twenty. The old woodsman with us smiled and said:

"Let's see how many there are."

We followed him through the soft snow to the top of the hill overlooking a cut-over plain and listened. Down in the valley we heard again the eerie howls of what must have been from a great pack. We were close enough to see their dark forms against the snow and their frosty breath in the moonlight.

"Count them," said the experienced woodsman.

The whole pack which had made that terrible din amounted to just two lone wolves out there under the moon. You can't tell by their howl how many wolves there are.

Early homesteaders who needed meat and had little time to hunt with a rifle reverted to the old Indian method of snaring deer. These timid animals have the habit of traversing the same territory the year around and following the same trails from one area to another on their way to their feeding grounds or to a lake or stream for water. The meat hunter would locate a well-beaten deer trail to set his snare. Finding a slim hardwood tree near the trail, he would bend it over the deer path and fasten it down with a string just strong enough to hold it. To the bent tree he tied a piece of hay baling wire, made a loop two feet in diameter and hung it across the trail at the height which would meet the head of a deer walking along. When a deer made its usual round of the woods and walked its head into the loop, the string gave way at the first tug and the deer was flung into the air by the spring of the tree. There it would hang until the poacher came along to get his meat. This method, like that of setting a gun across a deer trail, presented a real danger to human life and was frowned upon by the natives and promptly reported to the law. However, with the miles of woods to carry on this type of hunting, more poachers operated than were ever caught.

Trapping was one of the profitable pastimes for the boys of the village. Rabbits, weasels, skunks, mink and muskrat were plentiful. Many a lad had a trapline which he followed on Saturdays and Sundays. It was a good source of spending money for us. "Louie", the Jewish junkman, bought all the good pelts we caught at a fair price.

A family of skunks made its home under our barn and my brothers and I set muskrat traps for them. We fastened the trap with a chickenhead for bait to the end of a long pole and shoved it under the barn. As we caught a skunk we lifted it by the pole and drowned it in a big rain barrel under the eaves at the corner of the house. An old pipesmoking crone took the carcasses to her home to skin them for us and rendered the "skunk oil" for her rheumatism. We suspected that she also ate the meat. After we had caught the whole family of eight skunks we innocently dumped the rain barrel over onto the ground. We never smelled such a smell in all our lives. It took several weeks before we could approach the place again.

And speaking of skunks recalls the time the driver of a lumber camp supply team saw a family of skunks walking along the road—a mother and her five black and white striped kits.

"Here," he said to himself, "is my chance to get a present for my children."

Taking a horse blanket off the wagon and frightening the mother skunk away to a safe distance, he threw the blanket over the kits. He placed his catch in the wagon and took them home.

Calling his wife, he said:

"Get the children. I've got a present for them."

As the whole family gathered around in the livingroom to see the wonderful present daddy had brought them, he unrolled the blanket. Those kits were older than he thought. One whiff and his wife drove him and his present out of the house with a broom.

Earning Spending Money

Spending money was hard to get, especially where there were only one or two breadwinners to feed a dozen or more mouths, clothe them and furnish them all with the necessities of life. There were no luxuries. We had no such thing as an allowance. We depended upon handouts from our parents and these were seldom and small. If we did earn some money at odd jobs, part of it had to go into the family exchecquer.

One of the men who worked at the cooperage mill brought his sixteen year old son with him from "down below." The boy lived and ate at our boarding house and earned six dollars a week at the mill. His father drew the boy's pay-check and kept it, doling out only such money as was necessary to feed and clothe him. This went on for several months and the boy was in a virtual state of family slavery until some of the men at the mill learned about it and told the father in no uncertain language, flavored with a few threats, that he had better give the boy an allowance. Thereafter the youngster received fifty cents a week for spending money.

During the summer school vacation, in addition to working on our small farm, we brothers picked up odd jobs, which were few in number, for almost every family was selfcontained and did its own work. We gathered and sold salvageable articles like worn-out rubbers and whiskey bottles thrown away by the innumerable imbibers. We scoured the alleys and yards for castoff brass, iron, copper, tin and zinc. A Jewish junk buyer, known to us only as "Louie, the Jew", came to town periodically with his team and wagon and bought up our collections. He stabled his horses in our barn and slept and ate at our boarding house. He claimed that he paid us boys more than he did others because he knew our parents and we were his friends. We always had a box or gunnysack full of articles which we saved toward his coming. He was a kindly old man who lived in Iron Mountain and drove over two counties buying junk. "Louie" was the victim of one of the first crimes I heard about. On one of his trips over a lonely road near the village of Saunders he was waylaid by two tough Flynn brothers who robbed him of his purse and beat him into insensibility. When he finally reached Iron River a week later he still bore the marks of his terrible beating.

We brothers and sisters picked blueberries, raspberries and strawberries which grew wild in the fields and roadsides and sold them when we could find buyers. I recall hearing my sister Mary tell of her experience selling raspberries to a rich but stingy dowager. The woman crushed the berries in her hand while transferring them from Mary's lard pail to her own measure and packed them down in order to get more for her money.

Oshinsky's drygoods store was always good for odd jobs and a few dollars spending money each month. Oshinsky and his sons, Io, Leo and Nate, ran the establishment with occasional help during their bi-monthly bargain sales. It was my job to distribute sale handbills about town to advertise these "stupendous, record-breaking clearance sales." Goods were advertised as "marked down one-half" and placed in boxes and on the counters. Bankrupt stock was bought by Oshinsky in distant cities and brought in for the big event. I was present one morning when a boxful of long winter underwear was placed on the counter and marked at $1.98. Io picked up one of the suits and said to his father:

"Why, papa, this suit was marked $1.56 before the sale. Why did you put it in the box marked $1.98?"

Giving the boy a resounding slap on the ear, the old man said:

"Mind your own business. How do you ever expect to be a good business man by talking that way when we are having a sale?"

That was Io's first lesson in good business practice.

On the morning of the sale women were lined up for half a block awaiting the opening of the door. When they crowded into the store, it was my responsibility to hold back the crowd outside until those inside had fought, bought and left again. Such shoving and pushing! I earned my fifty cents a day fighting women shoppers!

At the age of fourteen I was eligible to take a vacation job at the cooperage mill, called the "Buckeye" plant. I hired out to stack and bind barrel staves as they came off the cutter. I did not ask "Buckeye"

Joe Kelly, the superintendent, when I hired out how much he would pay me for that backbreaking work. I was a conscientious worker and expected a good daily wage. I put everything I could into the work and came home dog-tired at the end of each day of ten hours labor. When I received my check at the end of the week I found that my wage was sixty-five cents a day—six and a half cents an hour. I protested to "Buckeye" but he laughed and said:

"If you don't like it I can get Polacks to work for me for fifty cents a day."

Then I understood why he had gotten a hundred dollar bonus the year before for running his plant so economically.

When the telephone system was first installed in town, "central" became the chief information source and the chief gossip in the community. She knew more about everyone than anyone knew about himself. She was the best informed person about. She knew more about the weaknesses and foibles of the citizens than the family doctor. Frequently she was called upon to settle arguments and quarrels between neighbors over the telephone. Shortly before noon each day "central" received a call from the engineer at the "Buckeye" cooperage mill asking for the time. This went on every day for several months until she met the engineer on the street.

"I want to thank you," said the engineer, "for giving me the time every day before noon. It is very helpful."

"I'm glad to do it if it is helpful to you," replied "central." "You know, I've been curious about your calling me for the time. Why do you do it every day?"

"Well," said the mill man, "you see I set the whistle by your time."

"Now, that's a coincidence," smiled the operator. "You know, I've been setting my office clock by your whistle."

We sometimes earned pennies holding horses on main street while the owners did their shopping or drinking. I had two steady jobs before and after school the year around. One was working for Dr. Robert Sturgeon, a refined and kindly English physician, who, when he first set up his practice in town, rode a bicycle on his rounds calling on his home patients. Our winters were long, the snow deep and the ground often icy. To make his calls the first few years, Dr. Sturgeon wound cloth around the tires of his bicycle to prevent them from slipping on the frozen surface. Later he bought a fine spirited bay mare and a buggy. It was my duty to feed, water and groom his horse. He also had a cow and a flock of chickens which I cared for in the stable back of the hospital. The doctor lost his life one summer's day when he drove his mare over the Chicago & Northwestern Railroad tracks just as the passenger train was pulling into town. The mare came galloping up Main Street with just the shafts of the buggy striking against her heels. A hundred or more people ran down to the tracks, knowing what must have happened. The good doctor's death was greatly mourned, for half of the children of town had either been delivered by him or had been treated for some childhood disease.

The other steady job was carrying four foot stove wood up stairs for

Lillian Bond and her mother who lived on the second floor of Barney
Krom's drygoods store. These refined ladies were the sister and mother
of Dr. Frank Bond, the husband of Carrie Jacobs Bond, composer and
writer of "A Perfect Day" and over two hundred other nationally sung
songs. My brother Ed and I carried the supply of heavy wood up steep
stairs to feed their long, horizontal heating stove which stood in the
middle of their big livingroom. Coal was scarce and costly. Wood was
plentiful and cheap. Maple and birch gave off an abundance of heat and
green chunks would keep the fire going all night if properly banked on
cold nights when the temperature dropped to thirty and forty degrees
below zero.

The boys of every family had their rounds of chores, some pleasant
and some hard and boring. We learned early how to do practical work.
The job that I hated with all my soul was turning the grindstone when my
father or some hired men wanted to sharpen their axes, scythes or
knives. We turned the crank until our eyes bulged out like cucumbers,
our arms ached and our heads spun, but the implement was never sharp
enough to suit them. To do this turning for my father was hardest of
all, for it was a "must." He seldom complimented us for doing a good
job, but for the hired man it was sometimes more of a pleasure, as he
inspired us by a few flattering remarks about the strength of our arms
or our ability to "take it." Flattery was motivation enough. I could
play at football or other sports until my clothes were wet with perspiration, but when it was "work", I was always insufficiently motivated.

During long summer droughts it was necessary to haul water from
the river in barrels on the wagon. This was a task we had to do in the
evenings after the team was brought home from work and it cut into our
play time. My father always blamed the Democratic administration for
misfortunes and implied that the drought was another evidence of political blundering, which did not make sense to me, when the cattle were
thirsty and bellowing for water.

One summer when our well went dry, a neighbor offered to find a
lasting supply of water on our little farm for a fee of five dollars. We
were desperate for water, so my father agreed to the price. The neighbor went into the woods and brought out a forked branch of hazel brush.
Holding the forks in his hands in a horizontal position, he walked carefully over the ground. Suddenly the point of the stick turned in his hands
with such force that the bark twisted off and pointed straight to the
ground.

"Here," said the diviner. "You can dig and find water."

Sure enough, we spent two days digging and struck water at eighteen
feet. But two days later our next door neighbor struck water at ten feet.
My father was "madder than a wet hen" for spending his five dollars
needlessly.

Girls and young women found it harder than did the boys to earn
spending money. The only jobs open to them was as "hired girls" in
the homes which could afford extra help. Housework was hard work
and underpaid. Hired girls were required to scrub floors with a scrubbing brush on their hands and knees, wash clothes in a tub on a

washboard and rinse the clothes by hand, carry in rainwater from barrels outside, heat it and carry it out after it was used. They baked and
cooked, tended babies and did housecleaning. They had one afternoon
and evening off once a week. Their average pay was one dollar and a
quarter or a dollar and a half a week plus board and room. They were
lucky if the lady they worked for was their size and weight, for they
might get castoff clothes to wear or remake in addition to their wages.

Girls who had graduated from high school could sometimes secure a
job as country school teachers at thirty-five dollars a month, which was
about what a skilled lumberjack could earn. The teacher generally had
to board with families of their pupils, making the rounds each week.
Women cooks in good hotels received a dollar a day. The best ones
were paid two dollars a day if they were exceptional cooks and were
economical.

For both boys and girls, it was necessary to start earning as soon
as work was available. Few of the youth went beyond the eighth grade
and most of them dropped out earlier to find work to supplement the
family income. It was only after the turn of the century and later that
graduation from high school was a common ambition. College was still
the dream of a few.

Without Modern Conveniences

We had heard of this wonderful invention called electric lights and
electric power, which gave illumination and turned wheels, but it was
only in its experimental stages and far removed from our experience
until the turn of the century. Our light was derived from kerosene
lamps and lanterns. While we were grateful for these lamps, they
added work and drudgery to our lot, for they required constant cleaning
and filling as well as being a source of danger. Many home and barn
fires were started by explosions and from careless handling of kerosene. Chicago was not the only place where cows kicked over lanterns.
Mrs. Behnan's and Mrs. Orlonowski's cows kicked just as unexpectedly
and just as hard.

In the early "Nineties" telephones had not yet been installed, so
communication between friends and families and business was conducted
on foot, horseback or by horse and buggy. The tempo of our life was
gauged by the speed of our horses or "shank's mares." Life was perhaps more leisurely but our work days were long. Ten to twelve hours
made up the work day, six days a week and often extended into Sundays.
During the fall, winter and early spring many workmen never saw their
families during the daylight hours except on Sundays, when they were
too tired to do anything but sleep or sit around the house. For months
children did not see their fathers in the light of day. Stores and shops
opened at seven in the morning and closed at six or seven in the evening. Some stayed open until nine and ten o'clock to "catch the late
trade." A shopkeeper was a slave to his business, for if he closed his
place of business at an early hour he feared he would lose a few sales.

"Woman's work was never done." On early Monday mornings, long before daylight, clothes were soaked in soft soap and rain water, rubbed by hand on washboards and hung out to dry. Water was carried from the pump or rainbarrels and was carried out doors again and dumped on the ground. Rainy days presented a problem to the housewife. Freezing weather stiffened the clothes on the line until they were like boards and had to be brought into the house and hung around on the furniture until they were thawed out and dried. Ironing was as tedious as washing. Flat irons were heated on the kitchen stove and because of their uncertain heat frequently scorched and burned the clothes. Floors were scrubbed on hands and knees. Housecleaning occurred in the spring and fall and was a very upsetting routine in which the entire family engaged. But women accepted their daily drudgery as their common lot. Daughters were pressed into household service in their tender years and learned practical housekeeping, cooking, sewing and mending early. If a husband or a boy could be pressed into helping with dishwashing or dish wiping, it was an exceptional occurrence. Women had their work and men and boys had theirs and seldom did the twain meet. There was little sharing of work with the exception that women frequently joined the men in the fields and even in cutting wood, but that was confined largely to the fami- families of recent immigrants.

One summer vacation I worked as a delivery boy for Finley Morrison's grocery and meat market. This required me to be at the stable by seven o'clock to feed, water, groom and harness my team. By seven I was at the store to load my delivery wagon and set out through the town and outlying countryside. After supper I worked at the store "putting up" orders for the next day until nine or ten o'clock before "calling it a day." Wages were just enough to eat and live on. There were no labor unions and no labor laws to protect the worker. Any attempt to organize a union would have been summarily defeated by the employers.

Hardwood was the fuel used for heating and cooking. The wood was cut and hauled into town by horse and sleigh and sold for a dollar a cord. One woodcutter working ten hours a day might cut two cords of wood a day if the trees were easy to cut and split. His pay was fifty cents a cord. Splitting blocks of wood for our stoves was an early and required experience for me. As I grew older and stronger I enjoyed nothing more than using a sharp ax splitting wood or pulling a keen crosscut saw through a log. Because of the long and severe winters and the deep snows it was necessary to haul great stacks of stove wood as soon as the fall roads were covered with snow and ice. To wait longer meant snow-blocked roads and a cold house and no warm breakfast.

Practically all bread, pies, cakes and cookies were baked in the home with wood heat. Maple, birch and beech wood were the chief source of fuel. Cedar, stacked and dried in the woodshed, was used as kindling to start the early morning fires. Large chunks of knotty green wood were placed in the pot-bellied heater the last thing at night to keep the fire going until morning. Frequently water left in pails overnight was found with an inch thick crust of ice on it in the morning.

Baking was done once or twice a week, depending upon the size of the family. Saturday was always a bake day and the time of preparation for the big dinner on Sunday. Perhaps one reason why husbands tell their wives how much better their mother's cooking was is that as children they were always hungry and the quality of their mother's cooking was therefore never questioned. We liked our mother's cooking best because we acquired a taste for it in our childhood. Later cooks may have better balanced and more attractively served meals but mother's cooking and baking always remain in our childhood memories as the finest imaginable.

We had no water heaters as such. Water for bathing on Saturday nights, washing clothes, cleaning hands and face and rinsing was heated in boilers or kettles on the kitchen range or on top of the heating stove in the livingroom. Some kitchen stoves had "reservoirs", a tank-like affair at the end where water was heated and dipped out for all purposes. Since pump or town water supply was "hard", we placed rain barrels under the eaves of the house or woodshed and caught soft rainwater to be used for all purposes but drinking. It was one of my chores to give my numerous sisters weekly hair shampoos in warm rain water.

In our boarding house, chicory was used extensively to "stretch" coffee. It was bitter and black but seemed to satisfy those who drank it. Its use required only half as much coffee bean. The best known coffee was of the Arbuckles Bros. and Four XXXX brand packaged in heavy, highly lithographed paper. "Use our brand and you'll never use any other coffee."

There were many home remedies for the various ailments we children were heir to. Mother treated colds with a spoonful of sugar on which was poured a few drops of kerosene. She had to hold our noses to get it down, but it was the common remedy for the "common cold." Our spring tonic to "thicken our blood" after the long, sunless winter days was a combination of sulphur and blackstrap molasses, which was as bad tasting and as nauseating as the cold cure.

On our camping trips, which were many, we were cautioned to drink water from running springs only for fear of swallowing a pollywog. We were told of a neighbor who was operated on and the doctor found a live frog in his stomach. That was probably the first case of appendicitis in the community but it served a good purpose as far as our parents were concerned.

Before a home was constructed, a hole was dug into the ground for an outdoor privy. "Long Herman" was the semi-official privy-hole digger in town. He was six feet, four inches tall and said he dug the holes only six feet deep, so in case he ever fell into one while he was intoxicated his nose would stick up above the ground. There was no ordinance regulating the construction or location for this necessary building. The spring floods which washed out the vaults played havoc with its contents, but this had to be borne like measles and deep snow. The number of holes required and the width of the building was dependent upon the size of the family and the prospects of its increase.

In summers it was not too unpleasant or too difficult to patronize this convenience but on those sub-zero mornings the pressure had to be great before venturing out to sit in the frosty seat for the required length of time. There were no signs, "His'n" or "Her'n." One door let in both sexes and there were often times of long waiting, to be reduced in length by the throwing of a rock or snowball against the door to hurry the slow occupant. Two-story flats had double decker privies, with the top deck having a long walk leading from the second story. These tall double-deckers were particularly vulnerable on Hallowe'en nights and were usually heavily guarded by the landlord with a shotgun filled with rock salt.

Our preference was for the pulp paper catalogs published and mailed out upon a postcard request by Sears, Roebuck and Montgomery Ward. We preferred these to Spiegel's out of Chicago, for the latter was printed on glazed paper. Two catalogs sufficed for a year.

Most of the homes were erected on cedar blocks, from twelve to twenty-four inches off the ground. The lack of sewers prevented many homes from having cellars which the spring floods would soon have filled. Each fall the man of the house banked his house all around the bottom with barnyard manure or sawdust to keep out the winter winds and the drifting snow. Each spring the manure or sawdust was spread onto the garden or lawn. Cats, dogs and skunks took up residence under the raised buildings and many families turned trappers to rid their places of polecats.

Alleys intersected every block in the village. Horses and buggies and wagons plied through them. Stray cats and dogs nosed through them in search of scraps which were thrown into the alleys by the merchants and householders. Piles of rubbish, manure from the barns, litter of all kinds were allowed to collect and freeze until spring, when a general cleaning was ordered by the village council. Kids searched the rubbish piles to find pieces of scrap metal, castoff rubbers and whiskey bottles to sell when "Louie, the Jew" came around with his junk wagon.

The village had the appearance of a half-organized pioneer settlement with few laws and ordinances, seldom or spasmodically enforced. As the population grew and the town became more prosperous civic pride led to cleanup campaigns, better street beds and more public works. It was a slow process but the more public spirited citizens pressed improvements as the years went by.

Local Color

One source of excitement for us kids each year was the coming of two Italians with their two trained cinnamon bear. They had secured these tawny colored animals from a circus and made a very profitable living by going from town to town exhibiting them and showing off their tricks. They spent two or three days in each community until all the loose pennies and nickels had been drained off, then travelled on foot to the next town.

The bear were safely muzzled and were rather docile for their masters but to us they were as ferocious as Alaskan grizzlies. The Italians made them dance in a circle, turn somersaults, wrestle, climb a pole and beg for food. When the performance was over one of the men passed the hat to the spectators.

Jim Summers, the "gunman" in the Canal Company feud, stood watching bleary-eyed on the edge of the crowd near the Piper House as the bear went through their tricks. He stepped into the circle and ordered the Italians to make their bear dance for him. He was told that it would cost him twenty nickels to see them perform.

"Hell!" said Jim. "I'll make 'em dance for nothing."

He stepped into the Piper House and brought out his 45-90 rifle. Pointing the gun at the bear, he ordered the Italians to make them dance, which they did—for half an hour. Jim then threw a silver dollar in the dust at their feet.

My brother Ed and I gave many performances mimicking the Italians and their trained cinnamons. He was always the Italian and I the bear. He put me through a series of tricks while he sang a chant. We used the stunt at many picnics and family gatherings.

Yearly another Italian made the rounds of the towns and mining "locations" with his pet monkey and a grind organ to garner the children's pennies, then move on to a more fruitful territory.

Two "Cousin Jacks" stood fascinated by their first sight of a monkey. John said to Bill:

"Did ye ever see such a sight, Bill? Ain't 'e human-like?"

"Aw," replied Bill, "'e ain't more human-like nor you or I are."

Wandering bands of Gypsies came through each summer with their strings of horses and wagons, tents and gay costumes. They were chiefly fortune tellers and horse traders, who invariably got the better of a sale or trade. Their animals were spavined, windbroken, heavey or outlaws which they had picked up along the way, to be sold or swapped off to less experienced horsemen. It was "caveat emptor", let the buyer beware. Their women told fortunes for the gullible and superstitious after their palms were crossed with a silver coin. We were warned to be on the lookout for pocket-picking and to keep our chicken coops locked, for they "lived off the land" as they went and could not be trusted with anything lying around loose. The local marshall hovered around their encampment. They were reported to be notorious kidnappers but I never heard of any kids being 'napped by them. My sister told me when I was older that they prevented me from being taken by them because of their fondness for blond babies.

The usual superstitions were prevalent. Ghosts, bad signs, etc. kept us kids on the alert. One superstition which one of the older boys planted in my young mind was that an old man lurked under the high wooden sidewalk near our home on main street and would capture a lone boy who passed that way at night. This spot held great peril for me and if I had to pass that way in the dark I gave it a wide berth.

Everyone but the undertaker seemed to fear dead people. One of the worst frights I ever had was when I went into the undertaker's "parlor" to see an old hermit who had committed suicide by hanging himself by a rope in his woodshed in the cold winter. There I saw him on the

marble slab, frozen stiff, his blue, glassy eyes staring into space, with
the rope still around his neck.

We heard of a queer homesteader who never wore shoes or rubbers
in the dead of winter but encased his feet with several pairs of woolen
socks instead. I decided to try it. So one day when my mother was not
looking I slipped off to school in the below zero weather with three pairs
of woolen socks on my feet but no shoes. Every time my feet hit the
cold snow the frost bit deeply. By the time I reached school I had frost-
bite. It was the practice in my schoolroom for the boys to slip off their
shoes or rubbers or shoepacs and walk about in their stocking feet, so
my teacher was not aware of my experiment. My chilblains did not dis-
turb the teacher but I was worried about how I was going to get back
home at noon without my mother catching me shoeless. I made it successfully but that was the last experiment I attempted to emulate the
queer homesteader.

Our lumbering and mining village had more than its quota of old
fashioned saloons. In fact, there was no limit on the number of drinking places. The demand regulated the supply. Anyone could open a
saloon if he paid the liquor license, which went toward the upkeep of
the volunteer fire department and the streets. It seemed to me that almost every other place on main street was a saloon.

The law required that the front windows of the saloon be curtained
off and swinging front doors blocked the view from the outside. There
was a side entrance "For Ladies Only" but only "fancy ladies" ever
entered. Occasionally a desperate wife would enter a saloon to lead
her drunken husband home or to implore the saloonkeeper not to sell
her man drinks because he spent all his pay check on liquor and the
children were starving and ragged. Some inebriates were "posted" in
the saloons, which meant that their wives or families had requested the
saloon owner not to supply them with liquor. Justices of the peace were
frequently appealed to to serve notices on barkeepers to stop selling
liquor to certain family men. This was effective for only a few days
or few weeks, for saloon operators were a callous lot.

Most of our miners came from southern Europe. The saloon was
their "club" and their yelling, cursing and singing could be heard
blocks away. One Italian stone mason had a particularly excellent
tenor voice and in his youth had sung in Enrico Caruso's Roman chorus.
He frequented Louis Datres' saloon and when filled with a considerable
quantity of "dago red" wine or vermouth he would burst into song, to be
joined by others. The strains of "Il Trovatore" and "Carmen" floated
on the air and many citizens stopped before the saloon to hear these
snatches from Italian operas for the first time.

Our refined town voice teacher came down the plank walk one evening in company with one of her older male pupils when the stone mason
was in fine fettle. They stopped to listen, then went to the open side
"Ladies Entrance" to watch him through the opening and hear him sing.
Her boldness was the topic of town gossip for weeks thereafter.

Since there was little entertainment in town, meeting the daily passenger train was an event which drew many to the little red-painted,

wooden railroad station. When the train whistle blew as it approached
the town, young and old hurried down to see who was coming in and who
was departing. The Boynton Hotel bus with its long parallel seats and
its fringe around the top, drawn by a pair of dejected bays, always met
the train in the hope that some of the passengers were travelling men
who would be guests at the hotel. One could set his watch by the coming
and going of the bus.

George Ennis had the only other "hotel" in town. Having no bus to
transport his guests to the Ennis House, he would appear at the station
with a wheelbarrow and call to the incoming passengers:

"Free ride to the Ennis House. I've a good wheelbarrow to haul
your baggage and a good sidewalk to my place."

Every newcomer was carefully inspected and speculated about. Pat
O'Brien, the editor of the weekly Reporter, was always on hand with his
little note pad and pencil to report in his paper on the next Thursday
"who, what, when and where, and why, if possible." No one ever entered
or left town without being noticed and reported. Their dress, baggage
and manners were carefully noted and sometimes imitated. Lumber
operators, mine officials, travelling salesmen, gamblers, panderers,
four-flushers, "fancy" ladies, workmen, mill owners, fishermen, - all
were noted and classified by the townspeople as they came off the little
yellow passenger coach at the Chicago & Northwestern depot.

Swains and sweethearts made meeting the trains one of their objec-
tives—to linger after the crowd had departed to carve their names and
hearts entwined on the wooden walls of the station. Obscene and sentimental carvings, names and dates scarred the walls until some unsen-
timental railroad official conceived the scheme of throwing sand into
the freshly painted surface to dull the jack-knives used in the art work.
This ended an old, romantic custom.

In the early 'Nineties most boys and girls wore similar kilt-like
skirts until they were five or six years old. There was little distinction
between the dresses of boys and girls except that girls had to be pro-
tected from the tanning and freckling effect of the sun by wearing long
sleeves and sunbonnets. Boys wore wide, ruffled collars which reached
to points at the shoulders. Their hair, like that of girls, was worn long
and curled at the end. Their long, home-knitted black stockings reached just to the bottom of their skirts and were fastened by garters coming down from the waistband under the skirts.

When a boy was emancipated from these "sissy" garments he often
became a changed person, whose mother "could not understand him"
any longer. Wilfred Quirt, who didn't get his first pair of boy's pants
until he was six, came running home from the store with his father,
shouting down the street as he ran:

"I've got pants! I've got pants!"

Diseases of childhood were common and little was known about
germs, preventive medicine and curative doses. Measles, whooping
cough, chicken pox, diphtheria, rheumatic fever (growing pains), and
other afflictions were accepted as unavoidable and had to "run their
course."

Smallpox was the most dreaded disease. We saw evidence of its ravages on the faces of many of the people who had emigrated from Europe, particularly from Russia and Finland. Their faces were deeply pitted and scarred. Vaccination against this disease was used commonly. The family doctor scratched the skin of the bicep with a small quill, put on a smear of vaccine and tied a bandage over it. Our arms were sore and tender for two weeks until the scab dropped off. The kid with a vaccinated arm kept out of games and had a miserable time of it from the punches landed on it by his teasing playmates.

Mother hung a small sack of camphor around our necks to ward off disease. During epidemics every child had such a sack around his neck under his shirt or waist.

Fumigation by burning sulphur was used in a room after convalescence. The fumes were believed to kill all germs in the room. I followed this idea to a practical conclusion. If sulphur fumes would kill imperceptible germs it surely would kill lice on my chickens. I set a pot of burning sulphur in the chicken coop while the chickens were on their roost, and closed the door. All went well until I looked in and saw all my chickens lying on the floor gasping for breath. Dashing in, I pulled them out into the fresh air and applied artificial respiration until they were able to walk again. My mother came out and asked me why the chickens were staggering around and sneezing so. I kept my experiment a secret but never tried it again.

We had forty acres of land three miles from town which we farmed and from which we cut our stove wood for the winter. During a diphtheria epidemic in town mother took us all out there for three weeks where we lived in a small log cabin. Those were among our most carefree days. With ten children of various ages and sizes to help, the hoeing and gardening was soon done. We spent our time chasing squirrels, picking blueberries in the nearby swamp, wild raspberries on the edge of the clearing and along the roadsides, or just knocking around, building shelters and climbing trees.

My father had an old Polish gentlemen working on the farm and cutting wood for our use in town. He was known to us only as "Polack Joe." His pay for cutting wood during the winter was fifty cents a cord. He seldom came to town and depended on me and my brothers to bring out his supplies and his Polish newspaper. How angry he got if we forgot his newspaper! It seemed more important to him than food.

Polack Joe had a history which many local people had forgotten. Years before we knew him he was passing the town postoffice when a bunch of the older boys pelted him with snowballs, knocked off his cap and made him drop a package he was carrying. This enraged him so furiously that he went home and came back with his shotgun. He hid the barrel down his pant leg and the stock under his overcoat. His tormentors had congregated in the barber shop next to the postoffice, laughing over their fun. Joe spotted them, assembled and loaded his shotgun with fineshot, then gave them a blast through the barber shop window. He hit one of them in the abdomen. Ed Scott, the town marshall, attempted to arrest him and Joe shot him through the wrist.

Men were deputized and set out to arrest him. They found him barricaded in his house. Paul Minckler, who wasn't afraid of the devil in
person, broke into a back door, captured him and took him to the county
jail. A posse gathered and threatened to storm the jail and hang him.
The sheriff rushed him to Florence, Wisconsin, by train for safe-keeping. After the hot-heads cooled off, Joe was tried and sentenced to
state prison at Marquette for a long term. It was several years after
his release that my father hired Joe to work on our farm. He became
a recluse and avoided strangers. It was only great necessity that could
bring Joe to Iron River again.

Playboys Of The 'Nineties

While the life of a boy in the 'Nineties was a busy one with many
home and farm chores, still he found time between for wholesome fun
and recreation. We had the freedom of the village streets before the
curfew whistle blew, the fields, the woods and the lakes and streams
which were our playground.

In summer there was the old swimming hole below the sawmill. It
was small but deep and well screened from public view by willows and
firs. On warm days in the early spring we stampeded from school to
see who would be "first in." Yelling like Indians we raced for the hole,
undressing on the way, then plunged into the cold water. On hot summer
days, divested of all habiliments of civilization, we spent many hours
diving into the cool water, climbing out, drying ourselves in the sun,
playing "stump the leader", then going through the whole routine again,
sans bathing suits. Older boys hazed the younger fry by stealing our
clothes, dunking them into the water, then tying them in knots so tightly
that it sometimes took us an hour to untie them with our teeth, while
they sat upon the opposite bank of the stream singing:

"Chaw raw beef. The beef was tough. The poor little sucker could-
n't get enough."

Because of my larger size I tried to keep up with the older boys and
got into difficulty. Before I had learned to swim, I followed them in
"running logs" on the mill pond. These logs had been dumped into the
river previously to be carried up into the mill for cutting into lumber.
To run these logs was a thrilling experience and we often sank waist-
deep into the water when we stepped upon a small log which could not
bear our weight. One day I was following the older boys across the logs
at Arthur Quirt's shingle mill when I suddenly found myself thrown into
the water by a rolling log. I yelled to the others for help but they were
so far ahead of me that they could not hear my cries. I was on my own.
It was either swim or drown. So I struck out as best I could across the
open water to the opposite bank. As I struggled and made my arms and
feet go, I found that I could swim when I had to. Thereafter I had confidence in my swimming ability and joined the other more daring boys
without fear.

Log running was dangerous sport for those boys who could not swim.

Even experienced swimmers were in peril of being caught between logs and once under a log boom found it difficult to find an opening through which to escape.

"Broken-Ass" Wagner, so called because of a hip deformation which caused him to walk with a peculiar twist of his rear end, lived in "Frenchtown" with his wife and two sons, Henry and Tony, "across the tracks" from us. His was a hard-working but always indigent family. Tony, about ten, was running logs on Arthur Quirt's millpond when he fell beneath the close-packed logs and was drowned. The gates of the dam were raised to let the high water out. The mill closed down and the entire crew searched for the body with pike poles and grappling equipment, without success. Someone suggested that dynamite be used to raise the body to the surface, without results. Finally a deep sea diver was brought up from Green Bay to explore the river bottom. He found Tony's remains wedged under a deadhead at the bottom of the stream. During the dynamiting great numbers of speckled trout were killed and floated on the surface. Some of the searchers took the trout home to eat, as did Henry and his father, but they reported that when Mrs. Wagner placed the fried trout on the table none of them could eat them.

Games of our own contriving were our greatest source of play. Whenever a group gathered of an evening, games went into operation spontaneously.

There was "Aunty-Aunty-I-Over", where two sides were chosen up and each group was on opposite sides of a barn and threw a ball over the roof. If it was caught, the catcher ran around the barn and tried to hit a member of the other team with the ball. The one struck with the ball went over to the other side. This went on until all the players were on one team.

"Pump, pump, pull away" consisted of two teams, each lined up on opposite sides of a field or playground. At the signal, "Pump-pump-pullaway — Come away or I'll pull you away", one side attempted to run through their opponents and reach the opposite end of the field without being tagged by the defending side. Players tagged joined the opponent's team. Each side took turns at running through the opposition until all players were on one side.

"Duck-on-the-rock" was a dangerous game which the older boys played. Each player found a small rock which he could handily toss. The boy who was "It" placed his rock on a boulder and at a signal the others threw their rocks underhanded and tried to dislodge the rock off the boulder. When someone had succeeded in knocking the rock off, "It" had to replace it on the boulder and tag one of the throwers while he was retrieving his rock from the place where he had thrown it. The one tagged before he got back to the restraining line was the new "It." Many smashed fingers was the result.

"Shinny-on-your-own side" was also played by two teams, each member having a stick, similar to a hockey club. The puck was a tin can which was placed in a hole in the middle of the playfield. Two players in the middle would batter at the tin can to get it started over

the ground or ice. Then there was a free-for-all in an endeavor to
drive the can over the opposing goal.

Among the most exciting games we played was outwitting the town
marshall after the 8:30 curfew whistle at the waterworks blew. Mike
was a genial Irishman but he was slow of foot. It was his duty to clear
the streets of kids under fourteen. We kids had other ideas. It was not
a question of defying the law. It was merely a friendly game of wits.
Our gang would divide into two groups. One group took the back street
to one end of main street while the other waited in plain sight at the
other end, six blocks away. When the whistle blew one group would
start catcalling and yelling. Mike would soon appear and make a dash
for the noise makers. He no sooner started for them than the others
would let out a blast and duck between buildings. Mike never did catch
us, although he made many valiant efforts to corner us.

One sub-zero evening after curfew we were standing around on the
wooden sidewalk on main street wondering what had happened to Mike,
when suddenly he appeared on the run between two buildings and started
for us. We scattered like sheep, everyone streaking for home. The last
sight we had of the town marshall was of him pulling off his bulky overcoat, throwing it on the snow and making a dash for the nearest boy.
Early the next day we each made carefully casual inquiries to learn if
any of the boys had been captured. Everyone was "present and account-
ed for." Although he knew every boy in town and everyone in our parti-
cular gang, Mike never bore a grudge or mentioned our teasing to us or
our parents. Whenever he met us on the street he was as friendly as
ever. It appeared to be just a part of a game with him, as it was with
us. Years later Mike was appointed superintendent of streets and he
hired me during my high school vacation. There never was a finer boss
or friend. We became close friends and that friendship continued throughout his life.

Every kid looked forward to Hallowe'en night in the village. That was
in the days of Chic Sales plumbing, when backhouses were the target of
most of our depredations. We younger kids usually joined forces with
the older boys and young men. What we lacked in courage they supplied.
We went along more for the thrill of being with daring older boys than
for the damage we could do. In fact, if left to our own resources, our
celebrations would have consisted merely of knocking on doors and tip-
ping over garbage cans.

It was the practice of the village president to appoint several deputy
marshalls on Hallowe'en to keep us kids in check, so it became a game
of push over, run and hide. One night we pushed over a Chic Sale establishment. The owner was waiting for us and gave chase. We finally ran
to the other end of town and rested on the benches in front of Bill Moss'
livery stable with two lookouts posted. Suddenly one lookout whistled
and off we went, chased by a deputy marshall who fired his pistol into
the air. We took off through back lots and lit out into the country,
scared stiff, we smaller kids trailing the older and faster boys, expecting at any moment to be grabbed by the deputy and led off to the
town lockup. We didn't stop until we reached the Hiawatha mine, three

miles from town, completely exhausted. It was late at night when we sneaked back home singly and to bed. The next day we made circuitous rounds to consult with the other members of our party. But everything was quiet on the Chic Sales front, although we saw several evidences of our celebration of the night before. No one was ever caught or punished for these escapades, which seemed to be taken for granted once a year.

On one such Hallowe'en night, while some of us smaller boys were prowling around to see what we could do to make village life interesting, we passed the home of Tom Webb, a special deputy for the evening. As we went by Tom came out of his house and we made a run for it, with Tom following in hot pursuit. We dashed into a back yard and under a string of clothes lines, Tom close on our heels. We could almost feel his hot breath on our young necks. We ducked under the clotheslines but one line caught Tom just under the chin and threw him flat on his back. Luckily none of us was recognized and we heard nothing more about the incident. But Tom appeared for work the next morning with a red streak across his neck.

One disagreeable farmer left a wagonload of grain out in his barn-yard. The next morning when he harnessed his team and started to hitch the horses to his wagon, it wasn't there. He soon found it perched on the roof of his barn, loaded with grain. The same morning a "hell-fire and damnation" preacher of a small country church found a heifer tied to the organ of his Sunday School room.

"Sparking" was the term used to indicate that a young swain was courting a girl. Bundling had already passed out in the early eighties but there were other means whereby boys and girls became intimately acquainted.

Many families had their buggy horses and fancy rigs with which a young man could take the girl of his choice out for an evening or Sunday afternoon spin out into the country where they could have privacy. Work horses from the family team were often pressed into unwilling service to promote "sparking." Those dudes who were fortunate to have a good buggy horse were popular and their horses were overworked. With a fancy flynet over the horse, gay tassels at the bridle or ear nets, long red and yellow tassels dangling down at the sides, an open or closed buggy with bright fringes, shined up for the occasion, these dudes would pull up before their sweetheart's home and whistle while they held their restless steed. It was part of the "sparking" technique for the girls to keep their beaus waiting and play hard to get. Off they would go over the dusty, rutty roads to some nearby lake for a swim, a picnic lunch, a walk through the woods, then home by dark. The dude with the fastest horse usually got the choicest girl.

Bicycles were at their height as a means of enjoyment. The 1900 "bonebreakers" or "scorchers" had evolved from the funny old "ordinary" bicycles with their high front wheel and their small back wheel, which appeared as antiques in Fourth of July parades. There was an infinite variety of designs to the bicycles. Men's singles and girl's singles. The latter had no running bar from the steering handles to the back seat to enable the girls to get on and off their vehicle more gracefully. Tandems were popular and used by couples. Three-seaters were rare. Some had multiple seats, carrying three and four riders. These required a good sense of balance and close cooperation by the riders. Spills were frequent, resulting in scuffed hands and faces and soiled clothes or the showing of laced petticoats.

Girl bicycle riders wore split skirts with one or more petticoats, wasp waists, wide leg o'mutton sleeves, a blouse with a bright bowtie and small hats decorated with bird feathers or fancy ribbons, fastened down with several long hat pins. High-top button shoes were in vogue and were a good protection to tender ankles from the gears of the bicycle or spills. Men wore caps, knee-length breeches or trousers with a steel clip around the ankles to prevent them from catching in the gears, high button shoes and high starched collars. The men's knickers were usually white for extra fancy style, requiring the wearer to tie a hand-kerchief over the bicycle seat to prevent their "lemonade" pants from becoming soiled from dust and perspiration.

These "scorchers" were the bane of those who drove horses and buggies. Coming along a dozen or more at a time down the road at the terrific speed of ten or twelve miles an hour, stirring up the dust and yelling at each other, they caused many a runaway.

Women still rode their horses side-saddle. It was highly unlady-like and undignified for a woman to ride astride. Those who did were not "ladies." It was always a mystery to my young mind why this should be the case and led me to much speculation as to the physiological differ-ence between the sexes. The daughter of a local minister taught a coun-try school and rode her own horse side-saddle out of town and back, coming through the town at a dead gallop to the amazement of the more sedate women, especially the leaders of the local female "aristocracy."

A young Jewish lad joined his uncle's sales force in a local furniture store. His pay was a few dollars a week plus board and room in the back end of the store. He started "sparking" the daughter of another merchant. A friend met him on the street one evening and asked:

"Where are you going, Abe, all dressed up in your Sunday suit?"

"I'm going to meet my girl inside the show at the town hall," he replied.

"Why are you meeting her inside the show? Why don't you meet her outside the hall and go in with her?"

"Well," said the young clerk, "it's cheaper that way."

After the show they took a walk up one side of main street and down the other. When they reached the store where the clerk slept, he said to his sweetheart:

"I'm going in now," and left her to go home alone.

In discussing the nether extremities of a female, one never said "legs." It was "limbs." Skirts were worn to reach below the high tops of the button shoes. To expose an ankle was disgraceful and set the offending female down as a "hussy." Women teachers in high school held a meeting of all the girls at the beginning of the school term and coached them carefully about exposing their "limbs" and cautioned them against crossing their legs (limbs) in the presence of boys or men.

Dad and Mother with Joe Ellis Piloting the Two Horse Open Sleigh

Author's Sisters
Clara and Anna in Their Christmas Finery

Despite this training a few girls dropped out of school because they had "gotten into trouble." When a local citizen was tried and sentenced for raping one of the girls, skeptical women speculated that "she must have cooperated", for wasn't a hatpin a "woman's best protection"?

The ticket taker at the town hall when shows appeared was at his post of duty when one of the town belles handed him her ticket. As she ascended the stairs he watched her climb. She drew her skirts tightly around her ankles and gave him a "dirty look."

"Go right up, lady," he admonished. "I've been here on this job a long time. Legs is no treat to me!"

Six Months of Winter

Winters started early in October and lasted into late April. Once the snows came they continued without a break until the spring thaws. Some towns had ordinances prohibiting the residents from shovelling the snow from their walks into the street, as this would completely block team traffic. The snow on the streets and roads lay there until it was packed down by horses and sleighs, and offered the only means of foot travel. Tunnels were sometimes dug from the front doors of homes to the street. Drifts piled up from five to eight feet high, so that a passing team could be heard by the jingle of trace chains but could not be seen. Snowshoes and skis were the only means of travel immediately after a blizzard. Farms and homesteads were isolated for days at a time. Stock left to wander for forage in the woods and fields were stranded and had to be rescued by snow shovels.

Fur coats of buffalo skin, goat skin and bear skin were worn by most men when on trips in the open, except when working. Caps of bearskin and muskrat were fashioned for the men by the women. Home knitted mufflers were worn around the neck and spread over the chest to ward off colds. One or two pairs of knitted woolen mittens were worn inside horsehide mittens and were drawn tight at the wrists to keep out the snow and cold. To protect the more sensitive parts of their anatomy, woodsmen sometimes resorted to the use of weasel skins, which gave rise to the rhyme:

"Bye Baby bunting,
Peter's gone a-hunting,
To get a little weasel skin
To wrap his little Peter in."

One Christmas vacation the teachers who had been left stranded in town by a blizzard organized a sleigh-ride party for high school boys and girls. Their destination was a grange hall ten miles from town. The road had been packed down by traffic and the day was clear and bright. The team of horses easily drew the sleigh full of twenty bundled pupils and teachers. They reached the grange hall and had a dance and refreshments. At ten o'clock the party started for home. A great, blinding blizzard had sprung up and completely blocked the road and all visibility. By the time they had gone three miles the horses were exhausted and could go no farther.

One of the boys reported having seen a light in a farmhouse a short distance back. The whole party fought its way back on foot to the farmhouse, with the horses pulling the empty sleigh. Ice and sleet froze on their faces. At times their eyelids were stuck shut with ice. Girls cried and the boys tugged them to the farmhouse where they were taken in by the surprised farmer and his wife. The boys stabled the tired horses and brought blankets from the sleigh. The girls bedded down on the parlor floor while the boys slept in the kitchen. Luckily the farmer had killed a beef a few days before and had a good store of vegetables and canned fruit in the cellar. There the party stayed two nights and two days until the anxious fathers of town organized a rescue crew, shovelled out the road and brought them home.

The open abandoned mining pits about the town and the deep snow of our long winters presented many thrilling hazards. The snow drifted level across the mouths of these pits and we kids would make a running jump down into the snow to see who could sink the farthest. One day when I was alone I made such a jump from a high point of the pit's edge. I kept going down and down through the light snow and finally found myself in total darkness. The snow was packed all around my body and over my head. I couldn't move my hands or arms. Frantically, I kicked my feet and found that they were free below my knees. Not knowing what was below me, I struggled and kicked until I found myself falling through the darkness. I landed on my feet and looked around me. On all sides were gray walls and a ceiling of snow. The ground under my feet was hard and dry. As I looked around my cold prison for a means of escape, I spied a tiny streak of light in the distance. As I stumbled in fright toward the light, I found an opening under the snow leading to the end of the hole and out into daylight. As I emerged from my confinement, I realized that I was in a ditch which had been dug into the side of the hill to let the water out of an abandoned test pit. The snow had drifted across the mouth of the pit but did not fill it, making an under-snow tunnel out of which I walked safe and unharmed.

When I told my father about my experience, he looked at me with a half smile. I had a hard time even convincing my buddies until I took them over and showed them how I had done it. Then they all tried it and believed my tale.

My experience was like that of a Cornish miner who reported:

"I stepped on the plank and the plank wasn't there, - then down I went, plank and all!"

One of the most popular winter indoor sports of my teen years was at girl and boy parties playing "postoffice." The one such party that stands out most vividly was held at the home of Captain Duff, a little snappy Cousin Jack mining official, living in one of the company houses on Carnegie Avenue. He had three attractive daughters who made the arrangements. About twenty boys and girls arrived there about 7:30 of a Friday evening. The first game the Duff girls proposed was "postoffice" which received unanimous support. The elder Duffs had retired to their bedroom upstairs, so we had the run of the downstairs as the game started. A girl was sent out into the dark hall from which the stairs led to the second floor. A boy was sent out to "collect a two-cent stamp." That meant he had the privilege of giving and the girl had the opportunity of collecting two kisses in the dark. A postcard was a mere hug. Stamps of larger denomination gave extra privileges. The game went on for two hours without a change of variety, and without a sign of boredom on the part of the kids. When my turn came around again, I went out into the hall and started "collecting" from a girl of whom I was particularly fond. Suddenly Captain Duff appeared in his long nightshirt at the top of the stairs. Evidently he had listened to the unvaried pro-ceedings long enough. Just as I was about to complete my osculation, he yelled in his mine boss' voice:

"Can't you kids think of anything but kissing? Get home, all of you."

I bolted for the front door and home and didn't even stop for my cap.

Every anniversary was the occasion for a party at the home of friends. Birthdays and holidays saw us gathered somewhere for an evening of fun. On one occasion when a party was held at the home of my first sweetheart, I had a case of mumps. I went to the party never-theless and passed my affliction around liberally. I couldn't stay away from my girl's house with so many other rivals there, especially if "postoffice" were to be played!

Weddings were an excuse for entering the home where the marriage celebration was held in order to get in on the refreshments. After we had our fill of food and lemonade and candy, we would gather outdoors and conduct a "charivari", which meant a "belling" of the couple—ring-ing cowbells, pounding on tin pans, banging kettles and making an unholy racket until the groom came out to give us money for an extra treat at the candy store. The groom at one such wedding was Jim O'Brien, the town marshal, who naturally did not enjoy our popularity. "Rorie" Ellis, a town character, joined in the celebration by bringing along his deer rifle and shooting it off under the window of the bridal chamber. Jim promptly came out in his long underwear and confiscated the rifle while we kids scampered home for fear he would use it on us.

Some of our other recreation consisted of making life unbearable for some of the villagers we did not like. One crusty old spinster was for-ever complaining to the marshal that we kids disturbed her. The mar-shal never did anything about it but we decided to give her good cause for complaint. First we took a thread spool and cut notches on the edges, then put a nail through the hole in the spool. One of our brave number placed the spool against the window of the spinster's house and pulled the thread, making a buzzing rattle which sent shivers up her straight back. She came bursting out of the door to give us a tongue lashing, but, naturally, there was no one to be seen. Next we took two tomato cans, filled them with water and tied a string between them. These we stretched across the walk in front of her door. One of the boys played his "Tick-tack-toe" on her window again and ran for dear life. This time the old witch came out with a broom and gave chase. She got as far as the string stretched between the tomato cans. Her foot hit the string and both cans of water cascaded up her legs (limbs, that is). We carefully avoided that part of town and kept clear of the marshal for days after.

We were making a disturbance in John Airey's butcher shop and grocery one day and were promptly ushered out none too gently by John and
his ever-handy cleaver. To get even that night we rigged a string to the
top of his screen door and stretched it across the street between two
buildings. From that vantage point one of the boys pulled the string to
open the screen door whenever a customer came along and then let the
door close after him. The customer's eyes would bug out to see the
door open without hands touching it and close without assistance. This
was the first door ever operated by an "electric eye." When there were
no customers in the shop we kept banging the door back and forth to
harass John for his lack of hospitality to us.

The town hall was the scene of a few travelling vaudeville and black-
face shows during the winter months. On one occasion a mesmerist
came for a three-night stand. Before the show began the mesmerist's
assistant asked some of us who were gathered outside to become "victims" in exchange for a free pass. It was necessary, he explained, for
us to be very cooperative while we were placed under a "spell." Sure,
we'd cooperate if it meant getting into the show for free. When the
other victims and I came into the hall the place was filled to the walls
with adults and children, all eager to see the performance. The stage
curtains were down and painted with brightly colored advertisements
telling the bargains to be obtained at Barney Krom's Emporium, John
Airey's Meat Market, Smith's Bargain Store and Oshinsky's Chicago
Store.

When the curtain rose the mesmerist appeared in a dress suit, his
long hair combed high over his head and his waxed mustache pointed up
toward his ears. He called for "volunteers" and a dozen of us who had
been given passes walked up on the little stage. He proceeded to put
Mike Monahan to sleep and told him that he was a farmer milking a cow.
Mike got on his knees and proceeded to milk the legs of his chair. Milton Hopkins, the son of a furniture dealer, was next persuaded that he
was a blacksmith and was shoeing a mule. I was the mule. I did not
like Milton and here was my chance to show my dislike for him. When
he took hold of my leg to put a shoe on, I kicked hell out of him and
woke him out of his "spell." I followed him about the stage, kicking
him until he escaped into the audience.

Two Chinese laundrymen occupied a small, one-story building where
they quietly and unobtrusively carried on their business of washing and
ironing the clothes of the bachelors of town. I learned that they were
well supplied with a variety of Chinese delicacies, nuts and sweetmeats.
Each week I visited them and helped them to read simple words for
which they gave me a handful of treats. The building was always filled
with steam and smelled of hot ironing. Packages of wrapped laundry
were piled on the shelves with only Chinese characters on them for
identification. How they knew which package belonged to whom, we
could not guess, but as customers came in to claim their laundry, the
front man always was able to associate the bundles with the faces of
his clients. They shuffled back and forth in the heelless slippers and
their shirts which draped over their embroidered trousers. Where

they came from and where they went no one seemed to know. They were friendly in their place of business but never mixed with the rest of the population. Most of the food was imported and they were seldom seen on the village streets. Their life was a mystery to all of us. One day they disappeared, leaving their little laundry empty.

Our Western Bronchos

From early boyhood I was a lover of horses. Our stable always held from two to six horses and I soon learned their care and use. One of my first saddle horses was a four year old broncho which was part of a string brought in with a carload from a ranch in Montana. My father had promised to buy me a saddle horse and I liked the appearance of the little brown gelding with a star in his forehead. The price was forty dollars as he was roped and handed over to me in the corral.

I had Ned until he died of old age and he was my inseparable companion for years. I soon gained his confidence and a week after I had him I was able to ride him with only a halter. I trained him to do a number of tricks I had read about, such as kneeling, shaking hands, running at full speed while I picked a handkerchief off the ground and standing alone when the reins were on the ground.

Ned had an unusual amount of speed and loved to run. Others had bought bronchos out of the same herd and trained them to the saddle. We organized many races and on every holiday, like the Fourth of July, labor day and other community days, we had spirited competition with our mounts. Ned won most of these races to the disgust of red-faced Paddy O'Toole, who had bought and trained a beautiful black broncho.

One day Paddy wagered me twenty-five dollars that he had a faster horse than I had. That was more money than I had ever possessed but my brothers and sisters and my father pooled their resources with mine and the challenge was accepted. We met on a Sunday afternoon on wide Carnegie Avenue for the race. A big crowd had gathered for this long-heralded event. It was to be two heats out of three. I mounted Ned and started to warm him up. However, I had not counted on George Bisbee, my Sunday School teacher and spiritual advisor. He appeared just before the first heat was to be run and persuaded me that it was wrong to race horses on Sunday. But I had already committed myself to enter my horse, so I let my brother Bill ride Ned. No one had ever ridden him but myself and we understood each other. I had confidence in him and he had confidence in me. In the first heat the horses came thundering down the mile stretch. At the halfway mark Ned took a dive sideways and refused to finish the race. That was too much for me. By this time my Sunday School teacher had left. The Irishman had won the first heat with ease and Ned had to take the other two coming up. I took Ned in hand and won the next two heats and the money.

This incensed O'Toole who gave his horse a whipping with a black-snake whip. Then and there he announced to the crowd that he would race me again for the same stake within two weeks. For the next two weeks Paddy was out every day training his horse for the coming event. His horse seemed to pick up speed every day and I didn't feel so confident. I didn't have twenty-five dollars to lose. The winnings from the first race were already divided among the family who had staked me. But Ned and I were not idle. I ran him in practice heats over the same track in the cool of each evening and he loved it.

My brother Ed had a brown mare which was fast for the first half mile but was windbroken, so she could never go the entire mile at full speed. I negotiated a deal with Paddy for a three horse race, which he accepted. I instructed Ed how to handle his mare. I was to try to take the first heat. In the second he was to push his horse for all she was worth while I held Ned back, letting the Irishman take the second heat. The third heat I was to try to take with Ned, after his slow pace in the second. It was two heats out of three again.

We lined up at the line drawn in the red road dust. At the crack of a pistol we were off with Ned taking the lead and holding it all the way. Paddy, flailing his racer with a big whip the full length of the race, came in second, two lengths behind me. We walked our horses back to the starting line.

"Now," I instructed Ed again. "You do as I told you. Give that Irishman the ride of his life. I'll jog in and give Ned a rest while Paddy's black gets tired and winded."

Off we started, with Ed's mare six lengths ahead of the black for the first half mile until her wind came out and let the other horse pass to win the second heat. Ned came in a late third.

Paddy was elated. Shaking his big blacksnake whip at me, he shouted so all could hear:

"Bejabers, I told you your horse wouldn't last."

We lined up at the starting line for the third time. Ed's mare and Paddy's gelding were puffing and wet, while Ned was calm and in prime condition after his slow run. At the signal Ned plunged to an easy lead and kept it, reaching the finish line five lengths ahead of Paddy's tired broncho. The money was mine and Paddy never figured out how he was foxed out of the prize.

While the hazards of the automobile are great, we had our horse-power risks too. Anyone who had handled horses on the farm, in the woods or in buggies and wagons is familiar with the dangers involved. Wild bronchos from the western plains are an even greater source of injury for the handler. The training of an unbroken colt to draw a wagon or to ride is always an adventure coupled with danger. Until the trainer, be he a farm lad, a woods "horseskinner" or a jockey, has gained the confidence of his horse and has overcome the animal's fear of him and of unfamiliar objects, he never knows when there will be a runaway or other serious accident.

We bought a beautiful bay mare, Topsy, from Olaf Benson in Bates township and used her as a buggy and saddle horse. She performed well unless she got her tail over the reins. She was known as a "switcher", for she kept switching her tail from side to side, even in winter, hoping, no doubt, to catch the reins under her tail and put on an act.

When she was hitched to the buggy and caught the reins under her tail, she would either kick, back up or run. It took a strong and brave man to reach forward and lift her tail off the reins.

My mother was coming home from a visit with Topsy hitched to the buggy and was passing a big, open mine pit, unfenced and full of water to a depth of a hundred feet or more. Topsy switched her tail and caught the reins tightly. She started to back the buggy toward the open pit. This was mother's first experience with the switcher. She whipped frantically but Topsy kept backing closer and closer to the hole with its sheer drop. Just as the back wheels were about to drop into the pit, mother jumped over the front wheel to the ground and took hold of the bridle. Before she could stop the mare, one of the back wheels hung over the lip of the hole. Two miners coming along from work in their iron-red clothes saw her predicament and helped drag Topsy forward to safe ground. They tied the mare's tail to the breeching with a heavy string and sent mother home, still shaking from her narrow escape.

My father was hauling a load of lumber from a mill near Beechwood with Tom and Jerry, a fine pair of chestnuts, when the horses evidently smelled a bear or wolf and ran away. Father was sitting on the smooth, slippery, freshly-sawed lumber and had nothing to support his feet. As he pulled on the reins, his shoes slipped forward, throwing him between the galloping horses and onto the wagon tongue. Here he hung until the wagon wheel struck a rut. He was bounced off and under the wagon while the team ran on to smash the wagon and spill the lumber into a ditch. He had lain there unconscious for an unknown length of time, when Mrs. John Gartland came along with her horse and buggy and found him. She brought him to town, a distance of ten miles. His scalp was hanging down the side of his head and bleeding profusely. The doctor took forty-four stitches to sew up his wound and he was disabled for over two months.

"Never trust a horseman" was the caution passed around in those days when there were almost as many horses in the district as there were human beings. Let the buyer or trader beware! One had to be a good judge of horseflesh to make a good deal. One horse dealer mentioned elsewhere in this saga sold a pacer with the guarantee that the animal could pace a mile in three minutes. The buyer tried him out on the track against a stop watch and found that the best he could do was a mile in four minutes. He brought the horse back to the dealer and said:

"I want my money back. You said this horse could pace a mile in three minutes. He can't do it in less than four."

"Well, a man must be in a damn hurry if he can't wait a minute," replied the horseman.

This same dealer sold lottery tickets at a dollar each on a horse which had died in his barn. He collected over a hundred dollars before he announced the lucky winner. The ticket holder appeared at the stable to claim his horse and the dealer showed him the dead animal.

"I'm sorry about the horse. There is nothing I can do about it, but I'll give you your dollar back."

The dealer was showing off a team—a gelding and a mare.

"Which is the best horse?" asked the prospective buyer.

"Well, I'll tell you. The mare is the best of the horses of the two, especially for the breeding purposes."

My Worst Runaway

For days after, the hair on the back of my neck rose from fear of what might have happened. I'll never forget that runaway team.

Most boys of seven or eight could harness a team of horses, drive them in a wagon, use them on the hayrake and do various jobs with a team. When we were too short to reach the harness over a horse's back, we stood on the manger and slipped the big collars around the neck. Then we mounted a box beside the horses to push the harness over his back, fastened the hame strap and slid the breeching over his rump and under his tail. The bridle came next. On frosty mornings when the steel bit was cold, we held it in our hands until it was warmed up enough to take the frost out, then slipped it into the horse's mouth, taking care that he did not close his broad teeth on our fingers.

Carefully backing the team out of their stalls so they would not step on our feet, we snapped on the double reins and drove them to the wagon. The neckyoke was buckled into the neckyoke strap and the ring slipped over the end of the wagon tongue. Calling the horses to "back up", we hitched the tugs or trace chains into the whiffle trees, so many links from the "D." Then gathering the reins carefully and holding them tightly in our hands, we got into the wagon or hayrack, ready for a day's work or a drive into the country or on a camping trip.

The day of my worst runaway in my fourteenth year, I undertook to drive a hay wagon load of boys on an overnight camping trip. I had hitched the strawberry roan, Tony, and Buckeroo, the buckskin, to the wagon. Next I drove to the haymow and forked in about three feet of loose hay for the campers to sit on and to feed the horses overnight. I met the boys, about twenty of them from the ages of nine to eleven, at the main corner of town. Here they piled in their duffle, cooking utensils, tents and boxes of food.

Off we went into the country near a lake to camp. When we arrived the boys and one of the men in charge scattered to find a good campsite and to gather wood for cooking and the evening campfire. I began to throw the duffle onto the ground. The horses were restless. The flies were bad. As the duffle hit the ground the horses began to snort. Without my knowledge, Buckeroo had rubbed his head against Tony and worked off his bridle. Just as the last piece of baggage struck the ground, Buckeroo gave a snort and started off at a run down the woods road, pulling Tony and the empty wagon with him. I grabbed the reins to stop them, but I was helpless to check them as only Tony's rein was effective. Off they ran at a gallop. I jerked the left rein and pulled Tony off into the woods. The wagon struck a tree and with the momentum and my tight grip on the reins, I was vaulted over the front rack and onto the ground just in front of the left wheel. My head barely missed the tree. I looked up to see the wheel coming over me. It seemed my last moment on earth. As the wheel was about to crush me, it hit a stump and bounced over me. The wagon broke into two parts, leaving the hayrack and the back wheels against the tree. The team ran down the road with the tongue dragging the front wheels behind them. Dazed, I scrambled to my feet and ran after the horses, yelling at the top of my voice for the boys to get out of the way of the runaway team crashing down the road. My chief concern was the safety of the boys. By that time the horses had disappeared around a bend, but I could hear the bouncing of the two wheels, the clatter of the tug chains and the pounding of the hooves.

At the dead-end of the road I found my horses tangled in the harness and the wheels wedged between two trees. One horse was down and the other rearing to get loose. No one was in sight. The boys had disappeared into the woods and to safety. Unhitching the down horse, I got him to his feet and tied him to a tree with the reins. Both horses were quivering with fright and excitement. The knuckles of both my hands were skinned to the bone from my vault over the front rack. The wagon was completely smashed, the harness torn to bits and the horses unfit for further use that day. I bound up my bleeding hands and sent the other man back to town on foot for another team and wagon to take us back home the next morning. It was my most harrowing experience with runaway horses and left me dizzy whenever I thought of what might have happened to me or the boys.

With the acquisition of western bronchos we kids of town turned cowboy. Our chief ambition was to be able to lasso a horse like the cowboys who brought the wild herd in each spring. I bought a thirty-foot, quarter inch rope and made a lariat. We chased cows, calves and horses without being able to "lay" a loop around their necks. One afternoon I succeeded in driving our horses down to the river for a drink, with my lariat in hand and one end tied around my waist. Standing behind them, I uncoiled the rope and waited for them to turn back to the pasture. Buckeroo, the wild runaway, turned out first and I swung my lasso. It looped around his neck beautifully and settled against his shoulders. Away he dashed past me, jerking me off my feet. I had forgotten to untie the rope from around my waist. The horse galloped on, bouncing me along on the ground. Over and over I went, knocking skin off from end to end. I finally managed to loosen the rope. Buckeroo ran off with the lasso around his neck. It took us several days to herd him into the barn. By that time the rope was just a frayed end. I was afraid cowboy.

Winter Sports

In our northern climate winters began early and lasted late into the spring. The dry, brisk air invigorated our play and we spent many long, happy hours at our favorite winter sports. Skating on the frozen mill ponds, lakes and ice rinks, skiing and tobogganing down the steep hillsides and snowballing were indulged by young and old.

With no Park Department to provide skating rinks, we made our own. A dozen kids got busy on a cold evening shovelling snow from the low spots in neighborhood lots. Using the family garden hose we flooded the space with a fine spray which froze as it struck the ground until the area was glassy with ice. Here games of tag on skates, "shinny-on-your-own-side" and races were held. Fancy figure skaters showed off their skill, while the less competent circled around. A big bonfire was built at one side to thaw out frozen hands and feet. "Crack-the-whip" was played by the older boys and girls and many a spill resulted as the lighter end of the whip was snapped. Most of the skates were the type which clamped onto the soles of our shoes. Only the elite families could afford skating shoes with skates permanently attached. We skated round and round, tumbled on the ice and played games until we were wet to the skin and frozen like snowmen. Then we were off to thaw out at home, warmed by a cup of chocolate and a late snack.

Skiing on the many steep hills about the edge of town was most popular and thrilling of all. Unable to buy manufactured skis, we made our own from split ash, sanded down to a smooth finish on the bottom, steamed in mother's wash boiler and bent up at the front end. We waxed the runners with beef tallow or melted miner's candles. Or, lacking our own skis, we used barrel staves in the middle of which we nailed foot straps of leather from an old harness. We also made a ski seat by nailing a wooden box on a pair of barrel staves and skiied down hill seated. With a cold wind in our faces and bumps and other hazards to avoid, we slid down at racehorse speed, then walked back up to the top of the hill with our skis in our hands. We held amateur skiing tournaments and ski jumping contests, which the more practiced and skilled Scandinavian children usually won. Many crack ski jumpers were developed there and competed in the big jumps in the Upper Peninsula. Our deep snow and the long months of winter gave the natives the opportunity for developing their skill beyond the average. Some of our ski jumpers competed in national events and set some national distance records which stood for many years.

Ski-joring was a combination of skiing and horseracing. Those of us who had riding or buggy horses attached long reins and traces to our steeds which pulled us along at a fast pace over the snow and ice. Balls of snow from the flying hooves pelted our faces and the swift turns often upset us while going at full speed. We organized ski-joring races over the week-ends. To see a dozen horses flying at a swift gallop over the snow, drawing their masters was a thrilling sight indeed.

Tobogganing down Weimer Hill and the mile-long Stambaugh Hill was the height of winter sports. Homemade bobsleds and hand-hewn toboggans loaded from front to back with close-packed kids and adults raced down slippery slides at forty miles an hour. To make it even more exciting and risky, we watered the runways to increase the speed and danger. Hitching onto horse-drawn sleighs held little danger and it was a common sight to see a dozen sleds or toboggans pulled behind a team of horses and sleighs along the village streets.

Snowballing was an everyday event, on the way to and from school and on the snow-covered village streets. We built forts of rolled up snow and staged battles for the capture of the enemy's strongholds. If we sometimes soaked snowballs in water and let them freeze before throwing them at our embattled opponents, it was all a part of the game. Black eyes and bruised faces were the accepted risks of these winter battles.

Sleigh ride parties were ever popular events of the winter season. Couples snuggled in close proximity in the straw-filled sleigh-box under bear robes and blankets. No doubt many a romance was encouraged by the warm propinquity of lad and lass. On occasions we drove to a farm house or a grange hall in the country where a dance or a box-social was held. A roaring fire in the big box stove in the middle of the room soon thawed us out. If the event was a box-social there was hot rivalry among the boys to buy the box of lunch prepared by the most popular girls. These boxes were beautifully wrapped and be-ribboned and often bore some telltale mark to guide the boy friend to bid it in, usually at a high price. By ten or eleven we snuggled down again in the sleigh next to the best girl friend, to hold hands and steal a kiss in the dark. The restless horses went all too fast as they sought the warmth and grain of their home stables.

I well remember my first attempted long ski trip I took with my pal, Cal Haggerty. We both had acquired pairs of new skis. So on a Saturday morning we set out to ski to the homestead of Fred Miller, on Little Hagerman Lake, a distance of about twelve miles over hill and dale. With a light pack and a lunch on our backs the first three miles went well. But by the time we had reached "Fartin'" Brown's clearing five miles from town, I was so exhausted that I could go no farther. Cal was the better and more experienced skier, but I think he too doubted the wisdom of continuing the rest of the way and then back home again that night. It was late that evening when we dragged our tired legs into town, having decided that the next time we skiied to Fred Miller's it would be by horse-drawn sleigh or by means of ski-joring.

During the winters some of us set traps for muskrat and mink along the Iron River and the tributary streams flowing into it. Since we were going to school we set our traps on Saturday mornings and looked at them again on Sunday afternoons. If a fur-bearing animal was caught in the traps between Sunday night and Saturday morning, it stayed there frozen to death until our next trip out. Frequently we found only the bones of our catch left in the trap by predatory owls, hawks or foxes. The income from our trapping went into the purchase of clothes and hunting and fishing equipment.

Born and raised as we were in the country of deep snow, zero weather and virgin woods, lakes and streams, we acquired a love for the outdoors which gave us a healthy and thrilling vocation and hobby. The practical experience we gained in this way was of great value in our adulthood. It enabled us to meet almost any situation which confronted us and required independence of thought and action. Our needs were simple. If we wished a sled, we were able to make it out of materials at hand with elementary tools. We used axes from the time we were able to hold an ax handle. Guns and fishing rods were familiar to us from childhood. All about us in the village and in the woods were competent, skilled men who lived off the land, cut down the forests, cultivated the fields and dug rich iron ore out of the ground. Few ready-made toys led us to make our own. Games were of our own devising on the spur of the moment. Competition began as soon as we were out of our children's clothes. We learned to "stand on our own feet" among the rough kids on the village streets or on the school playground. The sissy soon found that life was rugged and earnest. Quick use of fists, speed in running and skill at games were the marks of a man. We learned early how to "take it and how to dish it out." Hardy food, almost endless chores and simple life was the routine which built strong bodies and resourceful minds. We had to meet competition where we found it. There was plenty of it between the Pine and the Iron.

The Fire Fighters

Every small and large town had its own volunteer fire department, made up of local men who were swift of foot and brave of heart. Our town had no fire department horses and volunteers were always on call. When the fire siren at the waterworks blew the volunteers dropped their work and rushed to the fire hall on foot to haul out the light hose cart and hand-operated pump. Clerks left customers standing at the counter, barbers abandoned half-shaved men in their chairs and the village blacksmith dropped his hammer on the anvil, took off his leather apron, and ran.

Fire hydrants were located at strategic corners on the main street and on a few side streets. The town stretched no more than ten blocks in either direction. When word came to the waterworks over the automatic fire signal boxes about town that a fire had broken out somewhere, the engineer speeded up his pumps and shovelled more coal under the boilers to provide more adequate pressure in the water mains.

Each volunteer had his specific duty to perform and each was at his place when the trucks were drawn out of the station, or joined the others later on the run. Since there was no way of knowing just where the fire had broken out, the truck was rushed from spot to spot until the blaze was located. The fire had often gained considerable headway when the fire fighters arrived. Once a fire was located the hoses were run out, a coupling pair screwed the hose to the hydrant while another turned on the water with his wrench. No uniforms were used except a fireman's helmet, some of which were too small or too large for the wearers, thus giving the department the grotesque appearance of amateurism. Since there was little other entertainment in the village most of the time, great crowds gathered to kibitz and jeer at the energetic efforts of the unpaid volunteers.

Between fires the volunteer firefighting team practiced on the streets evenings. The fastest runners were chosen for the department. The men elected their own "chief" who assigned the personnel to their

specific duties. To promote greater interest in firefighting and in the
work of the department, inter-city firefighting tournaments were organized between towns in the Upper Peninsula. These were always interesting spectacles, for the competition was extremely keen and each town
had its own gallery of rooters. Each town offered prizes of money and
cups. The events consisted of races between teams drawing the hose
carts three town blocks, running out the hose, screwing on the nozzle,
making the coupling at the water hydrant and "laying" a stream of water
in the fastest time. There were relay races, quarter mile runs, 100-
yard dashes and other competition which tested the speed and accuracy
of the volunteer teams.

Among the volunteers I best remember were the Purcell brothers,
Jack and Frank. Both were fast 100-yard dash men who won many of
the foot-races in competition in Fourth of July contests. Jim Henley
was "Chief." There were Dan Van Wagner, Claude Brown, Charlie
Wunder, Bill Little, Jack Counihan and Dan O'Hara. Charlie Wunder
became the employed fire chief when the equipment passed through the
stages of horse and finally motor power.

In the early part of the Century Jim Henley was appointed fire chief
by the town council at a salary of $100.00 a year. Out of this munificent
income he was required to pay for examination blanks for the volunteers,
the fireman's magazine, telephone and other incidentals. At a discussion of the fire fighting set-up, Jim was criticized by some of the councilmen for being a "poor business man", for not conducting the affairs
of the department "efficiently and economically."

In the winter the fire hydrants were banked with horse manure and
covered with a fifty gallon hogshead to keep the water from freezing in
the sub-zero weather which at times went down to forty degrees below.
Even with this precaution the hydrants froze up at times, rendering the
equipment useless. When this occurred the firemen had to resort to
using snow which they threw on the fire with shovels and fire buckets.
Most of the heating of homes and store buildings was by wood-burning
stoves. Overheated stoves resulted in frequent fires and runs by the
volunteers. As the town grew the volunteers found that much of their
time was consumed with fire runs and the demand for more modern
equipment resulted in the purchase of a horse-drawn truck and two big
white horses. These animals were trained to respond to the ringing of
an alarm directly overhead. When the bell rang, they backed out of
their stalls and walked under the overhanging harnesses which hung
over the pole of the truck. The fireman driver snapped the breast collars around the horses' necks, fastened the reins onto the bridles which
the horses always wore, jumped to the driver's seat and was off to the
fire. A few volunteers still served the department and caught onto the
sides of the truck as it came along the street.

At Stambaugh on the hill above Iron River, Dave LeRoy's saloon and
hotel caught fire in January of 1907. The fire pumping station down
the hill drew water from the river, a distance of over half a mile.
When the alarm sounded, water in the river was too low and the pumps
sucked air, so that no water reached the hydrants. Eric Mattson, one

of the volunteers, ran down and placed a log across the river to raise
the water above the intake pipe. Standing on the log, he held it in place
by his weight. When the water rose, it also raised the log. Mattson lost
his balance as the log rolled from under him and he was thrown into the
ice-filled stream. The pressure was not restored and LeRoy's saloon
and hotel was utterly gutted. The only article of furniture salvaged was
a big oak table which "Fatty" Westerberg, a volunteer, carried out. This
table was used in a Stambaugh polling place for many years thereafter
and bore a deep char from the fire.

One evening the boys were gathered in the Stambaugh town hall telling stories and talking politics. A big box filled with sawdust served
them as a spittoon for their liberal libations of chewing tobacco. Un-
noticed, someone had thrown a lighted cigar butt into the sawdust. The
men left for home at ten-thirty. In the middle of the night smoke came
pouring out of the cracks of the building. Oarce Moore, the night marshal, saw the smoke as he was making his rounds of the little town. He
sounded the alarm which was fastened on a pole at the main corner.
Volunteers came piling out of their beds and down the street pulling up
their suspenders and buttoning up their mackinaws. They dragged the
hose cart out of the fire station and ran it down to the town hall, only to
find the building locked. Someone was dispatched on the run to get the
key from the town clerk who lived three blocks away. When the place
was unlocked and the hose cart was unwound, it was discovered that the
hose nozzle had fallen off the cart on the way. Another fleetfooted volunteer was sent to find the nozzle and attach it to the end of the hose.

When the hydrant was turned on there was no water pressure. The
smoke rose thicker and higher. The Riverton mine down the hill furnished the water pressure with their pumps. Someone ran down the hill
to find Bill Wall, the engineer and pump tender. Here he found that Bill
had neglected to keep the pumps going and that the steam pressure in
the boilers was down. Bill had to shovel coal under the boilers. When
he had done that and had gotten the pumps going again, he ran up the hill
to lend a hand at the fire. At the town hall he found Dr. Vilas, a physician and druggist, there in his white suit, in the capacity of Fire Chief.
The little doctor was standing in the hall behind the smoking sawdust
box spittoon, directing the firemen at their work. The hose began to
gurgle with a mixture of air and water. Suddenly the full force of the
stream burst out of the nozzle and hit the sawdust box with such a great
force that it squirted the sawdust and tobacco juice over the doctor's
white suit, giving him the appearance of a spotted leopard. The fire was
put out. So was the sawdust spittoon, to be banished from the town hall
forever.

Folklore and Superstition

Many superstitions and folklore prevailed among both old and young
in the village. Much of the superstitious beliefs had been brought over
from the old countries, handed down and repeated until most people believed them.

We were taught by older kids that if we saw three or more carriages or horse-drawn wagons going down the road in line a funeral was sure to take place within a week. A dog howling in the night predicted a death in the community. We watched carefully in what direction the howling dog's nose pointed, then made cautious inquiries about the health of the people living in that neighborhood.

Pregnant women were especially careful about being frightened for fear that the child would have a birthmark at the spot corresponding to the place where the mother touched her hands when frightened. A sister-in-law of mine who was pregnant was frightened by a rat in the cellar. She quickly placed her hands on her buttocks, so the image of the rat would not be visible on her baby where it would show. I never did ask whether there was a birthmark on her daughter's anatomy in the same place, and now it is too late to inquire.

One of my chums was splitting wood by holding the stick in one hand and chopping with the ax with the other. The wood slipped on the icy ground and the ax severed his left index finger, which fell to the ground and jumped around like a chicken with its head cut off. His pregnant mother witnessed the accident and ran back into the house for fear her baby would be "marked." When the child was born a few months later its left arm was withered. This strengthened the belief that pre-natal fright could mark the offspring.

To find our stray cows we caught a "daddy-long-legs", placed him in our open palm, held one of his long legs and sang:

"Daddy-long-legs
Tell me where my cows is or
I'll pull off your striped trousers."

Then we watched to see in what direction one of his other legs pointed to show where our cows had gone.

Horsehair snakes were created by placing a hair from the tail of a horse in a bottle of water, corking it up and leaving it stand in the sun for a day. Soon the hair began to take on life and wriggle about in the bottle. This belief originated from the fact that a parasite which developed in the bodies of crickets and grasshoppers and on maturity were deposited in stagnant water or horse troughs. These hairlike worms could be found swimming about and captured for exhibition.

For good luck, when we saw a white horse we spit into our palm, said an "abba cadabbra", and struck the spit with the forefinger of the other hand. We were always on the lookout for white horses.

We had a great fear of dead people and the places where they had died. The superstition lurked deep in our sub-conscious minds that something serious or fatal would happen to us if we entered a room where the death had occurred. However, Bob Pelo, the local undertaker, allowed anyone to come into his morgue to view the bodies he was embalming. It seemed to satisfy his sadistic streak to see them horrified at the gruesome sights. A homesteader went berserk and killed his wife and five children with his deer rifle. Their bodies were brought to Pelo's undertaking establishment, where the curious were allowed to view them. A group of my classmates and I went in. We had fidgets for weeks after seeing the frightful sight.

Cemeteries, or burying grounds, as we called them, with their usual tales of haunting ghosts, held a dread even for adults. A miner coming home from work on the midnight shift passed the cemetery and saw the reflection of the first arc lights of the town streets on the tombstones. He ran for two miles for fear that a ghost would overtake him. Everyone gave the cemetery a wide berth when travelling alone at night.

The number "3" was considered especially unlucky. When a match was used for lighting a pipe or a cigar, it was blown out after it was used twice.

When the first cement sidewalks were laid, children carefully avoided stepping on the cracks, for "step on a crack, you'll break your mother's back."

Carrying a "buckeye" or horse chestnut in your pocket warded off rheumatism. The handling of a toad brought warts on our hands. To cure warts a piece of raw meat was rubbed on the warts, then buried in the ground. By the time the meat had decayed the warts were gone. Stump or sump water, found in the top of a rotted stump was just as effective. An onion poultice or turpentine and grease rubbed on the chest was a sure cure for colds. Housewives never cooked a chicken without putting an iron nail in the pot. Fowl cooked that way was never tough.

A graduate of a Chicago dental school hung his shingle up to announce the opening of his office. His practice did not thrive. His body was found hanging from a tree in the woods—a suicide, the coroner said. His body was buried in the local cemetery but his ghost continued to haunt the woods and village for months. His office was a place to be avoided. The landlord completely remodeled and redecorated the room but it was two years before anyone was brave enough to rent it.

Easter was almost as sacred as Christmas in our family. It was observed with awe. The mystery of the Saviour's resurrection was deeper to us than His birth. Our whole family arose on Easter Morn to see a miracle if the sun shone. Mother took us all outdoors to see "the Lamb dance for joy in the sun." It was her sincere belief that the Lamb of God danced for joy on Easter Morn over the Resurrection of the Christ. After our unprotected eyes had gazed into the bright sun long enough we too could see movements which resembled dancing.

On Easter Morning every door and window was left wide open so that the magical Easter sun could penetrate every corner and drive out the "evil spirits." Its real purpose had a more hygienic effect—that of airing out the tightly closed-in odors and the smells of the long winter. Colored Easter eggs were distributed to the neighbors—a symbol of a new life. Giving them signified a wish for brighter things for the year to come.

Whatever we learned about the mysteries of sex did not come from our parents or from the older people of the community. It was a closely guarded secret, not for the ears of innocents. When I inquired as to how I was born, my mother referred me to the midwife, a Mrs. Krauser, who was in attendance at the time. The old lady told me that she had found me in a hollow stump on the hill. Our information about sex came from observing the birth of calves, rabbits and pigs. One day as our gang was accidentally present at the farrowing of a dozen little piglets, my brother Ed observed:

"Gee, that's funny the way they are born."

One of the older and more sex-wise boys informed him:

"Well, that's the way you were born too."

That was the extent of our "sex education" in the day of mysteries and folklore.

When planting time came in our garden or on our little farm, there was always "the right time" to plant certain seeds. Potatoes had to be planted "in the right sign of the moon" to produce a good crop. Much of this folklore was brought from across the ocean and found close observance among the recent immigrants. The signs of the Zodiac and its strange animals and beings governed the lives of many. The month of birth had special significance, for the date had a definite effect upon the disposition and future success of the person born under the signs. "April's child is full of grace; March's child is fair of face", etc.

The yearly calendars published by patent medicine houses were followed more closely than the Gospel. On them the weather was predicted for the entire year ahead. The phases of the moon were pictured in them and advice was given as to "the right time" to do certain things, when journeys could be auspiciously undertaken, what disasters were imminent and what herbs were cures for physical ailments.

Fortune tellers were religiously consulted by the more superstitious. "The lay of the cards", leaves in a tea cup and the lines in the palm of the hand were clues to one's character and fortunes. Weddings, births, floods and other disasters were definitely predicted by these signs. Travelling gypsy fortune tellers were eagerly sought in their dark tents to foretell milady's future after a piece of silver had crossed the gypsy's hand. Fakirs of the future found easy victims for short periods of time, then passed on to more lucrative fields. Each fortune teller told what her patron wished to hear, plus a few dire predictions which lay in the future, in order to make the patron feel that her money was well spent.

Stealing the Courthouse

It is not often that the stake in a poker game is a county courthouse, but what appeared to be a harmless contest between card sharks in our pioneer community ended up by the Iron River hosts holding their guests' money and the Crystal Falls politicians winning the courthouse and the county seat as well.

Back in 1885 the people living in the southern half of Marquette County became politically conscious and irritated over being dictated to by politicians in the north. They petitioned the state legislature to separate them into an independent unit. The result was Iron County with the small, thriving village of Iron River as the temporary county seat. The legislative act provided for a later election in the new county to settle upon the permanent location.

Iron River and Crystal Falls were both infant lumbering and mining towns of about the same size. Intense rivalry had sprung up between them. Each tried to outdo the other in industry, business and sports. The county was split wide open in this competition for supremacy.

The county government records were housed in a small frame building at the corner of Genesee and Third Streets in Iron River, which also served as a meeting place of the county officials.

Crystal Falls was rankled by the legislature's choice of Iron River. It required a whole day of driving by horse and buggy to reach the west side of the county where the meetings were held. Pride alone was cause to do something about the intolerable situation. A plot was hatched to stage a poker game as a blind to the pilfering of the records. The Crystal Falls men resolved that at the next meeting of the county board of supervisors they would remove the books by ruse, if possible, or by force if necessary. Iron River, however, was tipped off that some scheme was hatching and planned to take extra precautions.

The scheduled meeting went off smoothly, though. The Crystal Falls officials moved tables and chairs, with faked excuses but in reality to facilitate the later removal of the books. The meeting was short and peaceful. All suspicion was allayed by the eager, cooperative spirit of the conspirators. The Crystal Falls men invited the whole board to adjourn to the Boynton House and bar for a friendly round of drinks. It was there that the east side men, their pockets lined with gold, contributed for that purpose, proposed a poker game.

The Iron River gamblers fell for the trap and soon the click of the poker chips accompanied the clink of glasses. The liquor flowed as freely down the throats of the west siders as the money found its way into their pockets. Through a haze of cigar smoke all Iron River gathered to watch the redhot game. Stores, usually open until late at night, closed as merchants and customers alike rushed to the saloon-hotel to see the easy money raked in by the Iron River card sharks.

Word spread around that the home boys were cleaning up. The streets were empty save for a bitter wind, deep snow and an occasional cutter and horse hurrying to the home stable.

With the Crystal Falls conspirators was Frank Scadden, newspaper publisher, and Burt Hughitt, an Escanaba lumberman. These two had been elected to sneak off to the temporary courthouse and steal the records. They would be the least suspect. They watched the game with an interest equal to anyone there, while the Iron River officials raked in the chips. But soon they yawned obviously. It was getting late. They excused themselves and left.

The citizens, enthralled by the game, paid little attention, save Andy Boynton, the one-armed proprietor of the hotel. He suspiciously watched the pair return to their upstairs room. Each half hour he sneaked down the hall and peeked through the transom to insure against dirty work. The men were peacefully snoring in bed.

Shortly before 3:00 A.M. Andy, too, grew weary. Reassured by the faked snores of Scadden and Hughitt, he retired to his own room and called it a day.

Assuring themselves that Andy, the Iron River watchdog, had gone to sleep, the culprits lowered themselves through a window onto a shed below. The snow was waist high and the wind howled in the 12 below zero weather. Wrapped in their thick mackinaws and woolen caps and fur mittens, the two sneaked through the deserted streets, cowering against buildings to avoid attention.

The back door of the "courthouse" had been left unlocked, as had the safe, so the men quickly packed the books on a hand sled brought for that purpose and headed for the railroad depot.

Scadden and Hughitt became paralyzed with fear when a stray dog barked as they left the building, but they regained their poise and hurried to make the late freight which was due to leave for Florence, Wisconsin, in a few minutes.

They bribed the conductor, a Crystal Falls man, to allow them to ride in the red caboose. He let them stow the records and sled under a seat. Upon reaching Stager, the pair got off the train, loaded their booty onto the handsled and set off for Crystal Falls five miles away. There the sheriff, also a Crystal Falls citizen, placed the books in a jail cell and set a guard over them.

The next morning the news of the successful coup spread like wildfire in Crystal Falls and a great celebration was staged over the honor of the town's elevation to county seat.

When the theft was discovered by the sleepy-eyed clerk the next day a mass meeting was held in Iron River. Rifles were oiled and put in order. A posse was formed. The citizens decided to recruit an army and clean up the dirty politicians of Crystal Falls and take the books back by force.

What they ran up against, though, was a group of deputies the sheriff had sworn in to protect the county records. A vigilante committee had set up barricades on the street in front of the jail where the books were locked up. They sent spies into Iron River to learn what the enemy plans were.

Against such resistance the victims of the theft were helpless and force was abandoned. A county election was planned to settle the matter in 1888. The west side boys were determined to show those thieves that the majority of voters was on their side. A battle of political wits began.

The day before election Iron River imported 500 lumberjacks from the camps on its side of the county and from neighboring Gogebic county, which was not too sympathetic with such thievery. Most of the lumberjacks had never voted, for they had always said:

"To hell with voting. Politicians are always crooked anyway."

But if there was to be a good fight, where heavy fists and caulked boots were needed, with plenty of whiskey and good grub, sure, let's have a time of it. Lumbercamps were pretty dreary and unexciting anyway.

Crystal Falls hired "floaters" from other sections. The dead in both towns underwent a miraculous resurrection. Coroner's lists of deceased suddenly came to life to vote once more for the old home town. "Ringers" from all over the Upper Peninsula were borrowed and paid well for their votes.

Iron River then went the limit. The town council hired a Chicago detective to guard the ballot boxes at Crystal Falls. The local gentry plied the agent with liquor and money and put him on the train for Chicago on the morning of election day.

On the big day, one of the town councilmen of Crystal Falls took the ballot box home during his lunch hour and fished out the opposition votes. Irregularities which later would rate a grand jury investigation were rampant. Both towns held their collective breaths during the official counting of ballots.

Despite the fact that Iron River had more legal voters on record, Crystal Falls rated a five-vote lead and the county seat was installed there.

To rub salt on Iron River's open wound, a lemon colored stone building, with highly polished floors, marble columns and solid oak paneling was built, to become one of the grandest edifices of the time in the entire Peninsula, with most of the tax money coming out of the pockets of the westsiders. One local wag drew a large design of the Ace of Spades in black crayon on the corner stone to commemorate the poker game at Iron River. Had the tile flooring been inlaid with blue, white and red poker chips the occasion would have had a more appropriate monument.

Iron River citizens now had to travel fifteen miles over rutted and dusty roads to transact legal business at the new county seat. Their defeat rankled for years. Bad blood existed between the rival communities. The county courthouse remained as a reminder of one of the greatest hoaxes and one of the most skillfully planned "robberies" in the Great Lakes territory.

"We wuz robbed!"

Our Organized Athletics

There were few organized sports during my younger boyhood. What games took place were of the spontaneous kind. Older boys and men "got up" informal baseball teams and played other sandlot teams from other town. Travel was by horse and buggy, so there was little exchange between the teams. Cow pastures and empty lots, of which there were many, were the sites of the contests and partisanship was very keen and sometimes rough. Anyone umpiring or refereeing a game took his physical well-being into his own hands.

At Stambaugh "Fatty" John Westerberg organized the first town football team in 1900. He was manager and right tackle. The players furnished their own shoes and nailed on their own cleats. "Fatty" bought twelve football suits for the team from Sears, Roebuck & Company at a total price of $18.00. Parnell McKenna, a former Michigan Agricultural College football captain, was their first coach, to be succeeded by his brother Ed, who was also a football captain at M.A.C. In 1908 Stambaugh's team was champion of the town teams of the Upper Peninsula. This team was unscored upon, had a total of 176 points against their opponents' none, and averaged twenty-two points a game.

Champions Upper Mich. 1905

Stambaugh's Champions
Ed McKenna in U Sweater

The players were Carl Anderson, right end, "Fatty" Westerberg, right tackle, Chester Nettle, right guard, Joe Anderson, center; Jim Drew, left guard; Mac Morrison, left tackle, Hector Ducette, left end; Jim Ducette, right half; Albert Wert, fullback; Hugh Campbell, left half and Rudy Thornberg, quarterback and Ed McKenna, coach. There were no substitutes. Every man had to be an "iron man" and played the full game.

Big Fritz, mentioned in another connection, was a sort of godfather to the team and accompanied them on all their trips. On one occasion he went with the team to Ironwood where they defeated the local boys to the tune of 46 to 0. Across the state line is Hurley, Wisconsin, at that time one of the toughest towns in the U.S.A. Here flourished innumerable saloons, blind pigs, houses of prostitution and gambling dens, unrestrained and entirely lawless. To Hurley Big Fritz took the entire team to celebrate their victory. Fritz lined the boys up at a bar and ordered drinks.

"How much is that?" asked Fritz after the first drinks.

"That will be $57.00," answered the bartender without blinking.

"Fifty-seven dollars?" roared Big Fritz. "Holy, Yumping Yeesus! Fifty-seven dollars!" Then throwing several gold pieces on the bar he yelled:

"Bartender, give de boys anodder round."

When the team reached home from their victory over the Green Bay Packers a week later, they staged a big celebration. Imitating the college boys, they built a big bonfire at the main intersection in Stambaugh and brought boxes and furniture to keep the flames going. A playful riot ensued and Oarce Moore, the town marshal, who had the heart of a lion, tried to arrest some of the team members. The others ganged up on him and took away his prisoners. Then they shut Oarce up in a backhouse and placed a pole against the door. It was a long time before the celebration subsided. Finally someone thought of Oarce and let him out of the "one-holer." He remembered his tormentors and never gave the members of the team a bit of peace thereafter.

Of course, with the rival town of Stambaugh on the hill having a football team, Iron River had to organize one too. Dr. E. M. Libby, who had played football at Northwestern University, and Superintendent of Schools Holbrook, also a varsity star, got some of the town huskies together and taught them some of the rudiments of the game. The play was rugged. Almost anything but open mayhem was allowed or was overlooked as an exuberance of spirit. What the players lacked in finesse and technique, they made up for in brute strength and enthusiasm. There were few rules to govern the game and these were unobserved in the heat of battle. The Iron River team in 1903 was made up of Jess Waite, Jack Purcell, Bob Barnum, Bill Little, Nate Oshinsky, Joe Michaels, Tony Queaver, Norris Hunter, Oscar Anderson, Vern McDonald and Gus Holmes.

Dr. Libby and Superintendent Holbrook acted as coaches. During that first season they played Stambaugh four times and lost three games. The contests took place on Weimer Field near our home. There were no fences around the field, no bleachers and no tickets sold. A committee

took up a collection from the rooters. What was lacking for expenses
for the trips to other towns was made up by the players themselves.
The first football was bought out of a collection taken in the saloons.
The day before the game the players made lines around the field and
across the gridiron with slacked lime. The rules then required the offensive team to make only five yards in four downs. The forward pass
was unknown and the yardage had to be gained by bull strength rather
than skill. The tandem play was used extensively. It consisted of the
backfield lining up in a row back of the center and giving the head man
the ball, to be ramrodded through by the men pushing behind. Ole Olson,
a big, burly Swede miner, played several seasons as the spearhead of
the tandem. One would see his stocking-capped head charge into the
line, then his bald head emerge on the other side of the scrimmage line.
Hurdling over the line was used, with the ball carrier being thrown feet
first over the line by the backfield, to land on his cleated feet on the
ground or on the face of a prone tackler. Another effective play required one of the backfield men to crouch low on the ground behind the
line while a lighter ball carrier used him as a stepping stone to hurdle
head first over the line, landing where he may.

Helmets were unknown and frequent concussions resulted. Most of
the players wore knitted "stocking caps" which offered little protection
and were knocked off in each play. Shoes were ordinary button or laced
hightops which reached above the ankles and were equipped with leather
cleats nailed on by the player at home or at the shoe repair shop. A
few players wore a heavy, wide rubber noseguard which they kept on by
an elastic band around their head and a mouthpiece which they clamped
between their teeth. This afforded ample protection from a kick in the
teeth or face.

Spectators crowded the sidelines and were always on the playing field
when the game became exciting. Some enthusiasts assisted the home
team by tackling the rival ball carrier when he ran too close to the
crowd on the sidelines. Leonard Heppen, the son of a blacksmith, played guard for a few seasons. He was built like a plowhorse and his only
technique on both offensive and defensive plays was to grab his opponent
with his ham-like hands and swing him in a complete arc over his head.

Bob Barnum, a halfback, was my football hero. A terrific, hard-
hitting chunk of dynamite, he seemed to us kids to have no feeling in
his frame. When he hit the line and crashed into a tackler, he nearly
always laid his opponent low, while he himself came out unscathed and
fresh, ready for another plunging drive.

It was from Bob that we first heard about "Big Ten" football. He
had witnessed the great games between Michigan and Minnesota and
told us of the great "Willie" Heston, the piledriving All-Time, All
American halfback who played under "Hurry-Up" Yost. As a thirteen-
year-old I listened in on Bob's description of these great college games
and hoped that sometime I too might be fortunate enough to see some of
those teams in action. I little dreamed that I myself would ever play on
one of "Hurry-Up" Yost's Michigan teams or being selected on a Second
All-American team in 1914 as the result of my "making more tackles

than the entire Michigan team" in that memorable game against Harvard, according to the published athletic records at the University of Michigan.

Soon after semi-professional football began, football was introduced into our high school, despite the opposition of some of the school board members to this "brutal sport." Men teachers were hired to teach some school subjects and to coach football, if they knew how. Few of these men knew much about the fundamentals of the game and as a consequence our success was spotty. What I learned about football awaited the hand of one of the great masters of the game—Fielding H. Yost himself.

Inter-city baseball began early. Martin Bies and his two brothers, "Hank" and "Burrie", were the backbone of our home teams. Martin was the only bare-handed, left-handed catcher ever known. He caught the hot ones behind the plate without benefit of a glove, yet he threw out many a player attempting to steal second base. Herb Hagelin, a member of the town football team and a runner in the Volunteer Fire Department inter-city contests, had the distinction of playing in a Fourth of July baseball game against Crystal Falls and being the first man at bat, hitting the first ball pitched, a three bagger, in the first game held in the first Fairgrounds built in Iron River.

In one of the bitter inter-town baseball games at Weimer Field, one of the fans became very abusive to the umpire, a newcomer in town. He called the official all the foul names in his lumberjack vocabulary, which was a complete one. The umpire finished the game and then invited the burly 'jack to settle their differences of opinion with their fists. They headed for the Buckeye lumber mill yard, followed by a big crowd of fans. There on a sawdust ring they went at it. The lumberjack swung his big fists and the umpire ducked neatly and landed a terrific blow on his opponent's jaw. Back came the 'jack but his punches landed only on the dodging umpire's back. Thereafter it was hit and dodge, with the 'jack taking an awful beating without landing a single telling blow.

The crowd would have liked to have stopped the carnage but none had the courage to interfere. Finally, after the blows on the 'jack's face became sickening to witness, little Arthur Quirt, a highly respected and fearless citizen, stepped between the fighters and told them in no uncertain language to quit and shake hands, which they did. It was learned after the fight that the umpire had been a professional boxer "down below."

School Daze

Our education consisted principally of the "Three R's" in the lower grades and an additional light sprinkling of physics, chemistry, Latin and German in high school. Classes were small and the instruction fair, dependent upon the education, interest and the inspiration of the teacher. With the construction of a new high school, more attention was given to some of the "frills" of education, such as manual training and athletics. Art, music and debating did not have a chance with the

"practical" members of the board of education and the average taxpayer.
Boys and girls had to be prepared to work after they had dropped out of
school or had graduated. College education was a far cry and few had
ever attained that goal. As a result the great majority of pupils awaited
the day when they became sixteen and could "take a job", and the number
graduating from high school was low. Many dropped out of school before that age and little was done to enforce the attendance, although the
law required it.

We had no extra-curricular activities except those which we pupils
developed on our own. When our senior class of eleven pupils proposed
that we present a class play during commencement week, Attorney I. W.
Byers, president of the board, vetoed it as being too much of a departure
from the accepted norm. Our best and most understanding and sympathetic friend on the board was Arthur Quirt, whose daughter, Leila, was
in my class. One evening as we seniors were giving the juniors a rough
initiation in the school building, Arthur appeared through a window to
see what was going on. He listened for a while to learn what was taking
place, then went out by the window and called back:

"Go to it, kids. Have fun."

One teacher made a practice of reading books of adventure which had
much to do with our enjoying school and continuing our education longer
than some of us would have otherwise. Few of the teachers had more
than two or three years of college or normal school training and some
of these had to burn the midnight oil to keep ahead of us in their study
assignments. The majority of the women teachers came from other
parts of the state, to teach a few years before moving to a better school
or until they married. There was little opportunity in the town for
social life or for meeting eligible and desirable males. Since ours was
a small school the women teachers had little private life of their own.
We knew all about their activities and love affairs and we made their
lives unbearable by teasing them about their sweethearts. I am sure
that we discouraged several matches by our open ridicule.

Charles Keenan, who taught history and coached football, was my
greatest inspiration. A good teacher and a loyal friend, he was interested in every pupil. It was he who introduced me to some of the best
literature and encouraged me to go on to college. However, he was too
liberal for the board of education and for some of the mine officials,
who wanted to keep the status quo. He taught only one year and his contract was not renewed. My last contact with him occurred years later
when I received a telegram of sympathy from him in a distant city on
the death of my father. He had not forgotten me. I shall never forget
him.

For me school had become dull in my sophomore year. Coming
from a large family whose means were very limited, I was anxious to
earn my own money, buy my own clothes and have some of the advan-
tages some of the other lads had. Algebra became a bore. I would
rather have split a cord of wood than do some of the problems handed
to me to solve. So one day after I had been unjustly disciplined by one
of the teachers, I quit school and secured a job in Alfred Larson's

bakery. I worked there for over a year, baking and delivering baked goods in town and surrounding mining locations. As I looked ahead to a long life of hard and uninteresting work, I thought of Charles Keenan and his belief in me. I decided to return to school and go on from there to college. The last two years in high school were serious years for me. I continued to work at the bakery from six o'clock until eight each morning, then hurried home to breakfast and on to school. After school I delivered baked goods by horse and wagon. During the fall I played football on the high school team and occasionally on the town team. It was during these last two years that I became interested in social problems, the labor movement and in Shakespeare and Tolstoy, to whom I had been introduced by Charles Keenan.

Upon graduation I took a full-time job at the bakery and saved my money for college. My evenings were spent in reading. I consumed all of the Bard's works and other books. In my spare daylight hours I rode horseback and fished. I learned a good smattering of the Swedish language from my fellow workers in the bakery. When the second fall rolled around I had $600.00 laid up for my college education at the University of Michigan. At the University I continued to work for my board and room and other expenses. I did everything from cutting lawns to waiting on table, scrubbing kitchen floors and washing dishes—everything but "baby-sitting" which had not yet been invented. I worked in a bakery on Friday nights, starting at five o'clock in the afternoon and stopping at seven or eight the next morning, without the benefit of extra sleep. At times I fell asleep while standing on my feet mixing cake batter or kneading dough. After five years of this I became convinced that anyone who wanted a college education could achieve it if he wanted it hard enough and was willing to pay the price. Some of my high school friends said they too would like to attend college but their parents could not afford to send them. They did not want a college education hard enough.

If only a small percentage of the students who graduated from our high school went on to college, it was not surprising. The buildings and equipment supplied by the town were not very inspiring. The quality of teaching varied each year. The majority of the teachers attracted to their positions in our school system used them merely as stopgaps or stepping stones to something better elsewhere—either a higher salaried job or as a means of "meeting the right man." However, there were a few choice individuals who were interested in the personal problems of their pupils and were devoted to their profession, inspiring some of us to go on to make good on our own.

The mixed nationalities and the types of industries in the area made teaching a rather discouraging pursuit. While there was little actual poverty and most of that among the fatherless families and in the homes with drunken fathers, the dress and odors within the classrooms, the lack of ambition and encouragement at home, the conflict between old-country parents and the new generation, left much to be desired.

We had a succession of superintendents, principals and teachers, each staying a year or two or three, then moving on to other cities.

When a pupil quit school to go to work he would remark that he didn't mind the school but he hated "the principal of the thing."

My experience was a mixture of pleasure, ambition and dislike. My first unpleasant contact with school discipline was in the lower grades. I had an abundance of energy which led me one day to crawl along under the fixed desks and seats, pulling off the shoes of the girls, who reported me to the classroom teacher. She sneaked behind me when I was back in my seat and wrapped her long fingers around my face with a stinging slap. She reported me to the "office", which meant a strapping and no questions asked. The principal used a rubber hose on my bare legs. I yelled at the top of my voice that "I won't do it again", thinking that the louder I yelled the less severe and shorter the punishment would be. I found that it worked. Upon my return to the classroom I found myself a hero to the other kids. From that time on discipline was easier to take and less dreaded.

One of our superintendents, a Mr. Hughes, was a physical culture faddist. A big, square-shouldered individual, he put us through exercises which he insisted were body and character building, as if we kids with a multitude of chores and hard work to do at home needed body building. Most of us could whip our weight in wildcats. After school was dismissed in the afternoon he hiked out into the country where he gathered rocks and boulders with his big hands and piled them in heaps, without any practical objective except that of building up his muscles. One day a neighbor woman coming home from picking berries beyond Weimer Hill saw the school man picking up rocks, holding them over his head and piling them up in a heap. Frightened by this unusual sight she ran all the way to town and reported to the village marshal that a crazy man was loose.

A superintendent imported from New England came to our community with his wife and three children. He was a refined, cultured gentleman with a black Van Dyke beard, smart clothes and a dignified bearing which impressed all the pupils but set him off from the rougher townsmen. The new high school had just been completed and he had modern furniture shipped in from Grand Rapids to give color and an air of refinement to the edifice. Davenports and easy chairs lined the offices and the hallways. The new man was an excellent Latin scholar who could translate Caesar so rapidly that it amazed us all. One morning we came to school to find that he was no longer there. Word had rapidly spread around that he had "gotten one of the new teachers in trouble." The soft davenports were said to have been "an accessory to the fact." To our unsophisticated minds it was a puzzling thing. There was no trial or hearing. The teacher's landlady had rushed with a sense of importance and a taste for gossip to the president of the board of education to make her report of the scandalous affair. No one ever knew whether the man was an innocent victim of malicious gossip or was in fact guilty. He was summarily "fired" by the board and turned out of his position. Having no financial resources of his own, he rented a tent and pitched it on a field near the waterworks, where he and his family lived for several months in the most primitive fashion. He resolved to "live the gossip down." Now faced with the necessity of earning a living at the only work available to him, he labored as a ditch-digger helping to put in a new water main. His soft hands became blistered and his long back bent by this unaccustomed work. The only sympathy he received in that town was from his fellow ditch-diggers, who admired his courage and doubted the wives' tale concerning his delinquency. While his wife was cooking an evening meal over an open fire one of his daughters was severely burned and had to be hospitalized for several months. Relatives back in New England learned of his plight and forwarded money for the family's return to a more friendly environment.

"I'll Never Forget The Time When— "

A boy of fifty years ago in that early pioneer settlement lived a life of thrilling and wonderful adventure. With his ears full of listening and his eyes full of seeing, he retained many restful and stirring memories in rich contrast to the later mass-production times.

His entertainment was self-made. He sought and provided his own leisure-time activities. The clear streams and the azure lakes with their tree-lined banks beckoned him and his fishing pole. With a can of angle worms, a hook, a nail for a sinker and a lunch in his pocket, he and his comrades could spend a whole summer's day without care or worry. His games were of his own invention. The shack on the back lot was his castle.

Work, yes, plenty of it. It was a day of hard work for all members of a family. The family vegetable garden or farm was a source of most of the family food. Each child had his share of work and each had a feeling of importance in the family circle. Each learned the value of work, the use of the hands and the head in productive labor. Girls worked beside their mothers at the household arts—cooking, baking, sewing, knitting and housecleaning, while the boys learned the use of an ax, a shovel, a rake and a saw. What city-bred boy of today can swing a double-bitted ax without running the risk of chopping off a toe or weed a garden without digging up vegetable plants instead of weeds? How many can harness a team of horses, hitch them to a wagon and drive them without mishap?

One of our major projects after school and evenings and during our spare time in the summer months was building and operating a "shack" on a back lot. It was a one-room structure about ten by ten feet, made of lumber salvaged and most times "just borrowed" from the backyards in the neighborhood. With hammer and saw and nails drawn out of used lumber, we spent laborious hours gathering and building our castle. Just our own neighborhood gang of ten boys did the work. It was our pride and joy and we had to spend part of our time driving away curious boys from other parts of the town who wanted to join our project with bribes of materials, candy and other treats. Ours was a "closed" brotherhood. The shack was fearfully and wonderfully made, never square, patched here and there to keep out the weather, and had a roof made of flattened number ten tin cans gathered from the town dump. But it was our own and we were proud of it.

We made our own tables and benches. We "found" an old cookstove and two lengths of pipe for heating in cold weather and for cooking our meals. A smoky kerosene lantern served for illumination. Here we brought an assembly of food—pickled pigs feet, pickles, potatoes for roasting, meat and vegetables for stews and such cookies and cakes as we could confiscate from our mothers' kitchens.

Our shack was the center of our play life for several years until the neighbors began to object. Finally one cold morning we gathered to find our beloved shack in ashes. We never did learn how it occurred, but we suspected that the cause of its destruction was tied up with the fact that a certain, too curious and vicious neighborhood dog had met his death in the vicinity on a dark night the week before. There may have been some basis for this suspicion. We never did like that mongrel!

Our project caused much jealousy among the other gangs of boys in the village and we had many battles of fists and rocks in defense of our "home." Since I was the biggest of our group it was my lot to have to fight the white-headed Oberg boy who led an opposing gang. Surrounded by our cohorts, we squared off. I shook in fear and so did he. I measured the distance to his nose with my fist several times to make sure that my first blow landed. Then I let go with a right-handed punch which reached its mark. Down he went and me on top of him. Soon both gangs were in a melee. Rocks and sticks flew. We retreated to our shack, barricaded ourselves and ducked as rocks bounded against the sides of the structure. We would have been in for an all-night siege had not Ed Lott, who operated a livery and horse sales stable next door, witnessed the battle and drove the besiegers away. We showed our appreciation for the rescue by cleaning Ed's stables for a week.

I must say in all honesty that our gang activities never led to law-breaking, but were merely expressions of the gang instinct seeking an outlet. There was no juvenile delinquency in the whole town, although some of the citizens must have often feared it.

Every early village had its favorite meeting places for youth. We had several hangouts in addition to our shack. One was the blacksmith shop operated by Gottfried and August Hane three blocks from the center of town. Here we watched the brawny men shoe big farm and woods horses. Our only excuse for being underfoot was our willingness to shovel out the horse droppings and to switch the flies off the horses' backs and legs while the smithy held up their feet during the shoeing operation. Our switch was the tail of a defunct horse nailed on the end of a broom handle. We watched, fascinated, while the blacksmith heated the shoes to a white glow in the hand-pumped forge. When the shoe was heated to a proper degree he placed in on the anvil and shaped it with his heavy hammer to fit the horse's foot. Sparks flew against his leather apron and on the plank floor. Then he carefully pared and rasped the hoof and while the shoe was still hot placed it on the bottom of the hoof to burn a level place. Then cooling the shoe in a tub of water near the forge, he tacked it on the horse's foot with horseshoe nails. At times the acrid smell of burning hooves was almost overpowering, but we liked it.

Two livery stables operated by Phil Boynton and Bill Moss drew many of us too. We made ourselves useful and necessary by cleaning the stalls and grooming the horses, which were used for travel into the many places where the railroad did not reach. Both Phil and Bill took great pride in their horses and equipment. Should anyone bring the horses back too heated or too exhausted, they were never allowed to hire a rig again. I was present at Moss' stable when a pair of drunks brought back a team so exhausted from overdriving that the horses fell to the floor as they entered the stable. The drunks had driven them under a lash all the way from Crystal Falls, fifteen miles. Dan Van Wagner was the stable boy in charge that day and he administered the inebriates a sound beating before they got away.

Foster's poolroom was another meeting place for the younger sporting element above high school age. It was run by Mr. Foster, a little dude with a waxed and curled red mustache. His portly wife who, frog-like, overflowed the biggest chair in the place, presided at the candy counter. I was too young to frequent the establishment. My parents objected. Furthermore, I had too little money to waste on pool, so I never did learn the game. Every night the dudes gathered there for their games and "bull sessions." The income of the business was never big and by the time I was old enough and independent enough to participate, it was closed. A poolroom was considered as one of the lowest places to spend one's time—"dives of iniquity", in the estimation of most parents. Here, they said, the youth learned to gamble and to smoke cigarettes, which were made from "Bull Durham" which came in small cotton sacks and advertised by a picture of a big bull with the hind part of his carcass hidden behind a rail fence. Bull Durham was rolled in rice paper and was smoked by the more daring boys.

As we grew older and some of the high school graduates returned from college with tales of fraternity life, we decided to organize a high school fraternity of our own. Up to that time our social groupings were on the basis of neighborhood friendships.

Our first fraternity consisted of a half dozen of us. We adopted Greek letters, which of themselves meant nothing to us. We set to work on a ritual and an initiation routine. Our chief interest was to give the neophyte as rough a time as we could dish out and still have him live through it. With the help of one of the boys, whose father was a councilman, we got the use of the town hall which had a big room with a stage at one end. We did not have to know how college fraternities initiated their victims. We made our own "hell."

We tied up the candidates and rolled them down the long stairs. If they lived, we melted a pot of lead in their view, then blindfolded them and substituted a pot of quick silver into which they were forced to plunge their hands. A few fainted. We taught them the fraternity whistle—three shorts, one long and four shorts. We ordered them to follow the whistle blindfolded through every obstacle in their path. This usually subdued the most durable and the most obstinate candidates seeking to enter our sacred order. We got behind fences and watched them crash into them. We whistled across creeks and saw them flounder. We took them through briars, crosslots and hedges, until utterly exhausted, they begged for mercy.

The last rite took place on the stage in the town hall. Here we bound them to a chair and shot off firecrackers and rockets around them. This latter stunt was kept up until one day the stage scenery was set afire. We finally managed to put it out but thereafter we were obliged by the alarmed town fathers to shift the scene of our unholy initiation to other, more fireproof quarters.

Most of us kids had a private library of juvenile literature of the time. It consisted of nickel and dime paper-covered adventure novels sold at the local drug store. There was "Nick Carter, Famous Detective", "Diamond Dick, Gunman Deluxe", "The Merriwell Boys" and the like. Our literary tastes did not reach to the "Police Gazette", which was found in the barber shops. We bought the novels with our spare money and read them in our shack or in our bedrooms, surreptitiously, keeping them hidden from the sight of our parents. The most gruesome one I ever read was entitled "The Grave Diggers", which kept me awake long into the night with its tale of ghouls and the disinterment of bodies in the graveyards. This thrilling literature was used as a medium of exchange among us. There were always dozens of the novels floating around. We exchanged them for jack knives, candy, gum and baseballs.

Occasionally our parents made a raid on our libraries, to our deep sorrow and loss. This literature evidently gave us an "escape" and furnished us an outlet for our hero worship. It gave our parents deep concern over our futures, but I knew of no boy among us whose life was blighted from reading it. There seems to be a time in the life of every boy when he craves exciting reading which takes him out of his humdrum world and wafts him among the daring characters of fancy. Despite my early devotion to the paper-covered novels of my boyhood, my taste for this "degrading" literature did not persist.

Indian Incidents

The Indians who roamed the Upper Peninsula were of several tribes, chiefly the Pottawattamie, Chippewa and Ottawa tribes. While by 1870 they were quite subdued by the aggressive whites, they gave trouble on occasions when the white men's firewater was involved.

In one of the towns Joseph and Pauline Nolden operated the first brewery in that northland. In connection with the brewery they ran a saloon and a bowling alley. It was Nolden's custom to furnish the Pottawattamie Indians who lived near Ford River Mills with free beer as long as he could afford to do so. The town lacked sewers and he had difficulty in his cellars due to high flood waters during the spring thaws. The floods at times raised to a height of five and six feet in the low section where the brewery and saloon were located, entailing considerable damage and loss of business.

Chief Sunshine of the Chippewas Traded Indian Ponies

One day two Indians came into the bar and asked for free beer. Nolden explained that this would be the last time they would be able to secure free beer as he had had a lot of expense and could no longer afford to give it away.

A quarrel ensued. One of the Indians stood at the bar and pulled out a long knife and tried to stab Nolden. The saloon keeper stepped back and reached under the bar for a large wooden mallet which he used to tap the beer kegs. He swung it on the Indian's head and floored him. In the meantime the second Indian also pulled a knife and tried to stab Nolden across the bar. Nolden grabbed him by the wrist and they wrestled together to the end of the bar. Down they went onto the floor. Nolden held the Indian's knife hand and prevented him from using it. They rolled about on the floor in a desperate tussle.

In the meantime the first Indian recovered from the mallet blow and came at Nolden with knife in hand. He struck the proprietor twice in the back. At that both Indians struggled loose and ran out of the saloon.

Nolden's main back artery was severed. Mrs. Nolden heard the racket from her apartment upstairs and came down to find her husband lying on the floor in a pool of blood. There was only one physician, Dr. Tracy, in town. He was summoned and came to the saloon on the run. He stemmed the flow of blood and said that the victim must have lost at least a quart of blood.

A specialist was called from Milwaukee and he succeeded in putting in a silver tube to connect the artery. Nolden was then about thirty-five years of age and lived to be eighty, with the silver tube in his back giving him no further trouble.

Nolden did not prosecute the Indians for this deed, but after he had discontinued his business and whenever he met any of the tribe of Indians from Ford River Mills they paid him deep respect.

Mrs. Nolden had a number of encounters with the local Indians. Chronic thieves, they tried several times to break into the house. She kept a loaded revolver on hand which she was obliged to use to frighten them away. On occasions she shot above their heads but never did fire directly at them.

The family had a safe in their bedroom. Nolden always kept a loaded rifle beside his bed, for he never knew when the Indians might attempt to break in and rob them. One night as Mrs. Nolden was sleeping on the inside of the bed and Nolden on the outside, the door began to creak. Mrs. Nolden raised her head and saw an Indian crawling along the floor on his hands and knees. She gave a yell and Nolden grabbed his rifle. The Indian got up and started to run out of the room but got his feet tangled in a baby carriage and could not free himself immediately. As he regained his feet he picked up a chair and threw it across the room at Nolden but missed. He started running out the door and down the dark road. Nolden drew a bead on him but fortunately missed his target in the darkness. The Pottawattamies avoided any contact with the Noldens thereafter.

Our Indians inhabited the woods and back country and lived on venison, rabbits and bear and by fishing, trapping, berry picking and trading.

The squaws did all the work about their camp from cutting firewood, processing wild meat, skinning deer and tanning the hides, making moccasins which they decorated with beads and porcupine quills, cooking and caring for the children. The bucks did the hunting and fishing. The women cultivated small garden patches and raised ginseng roots for the medical trade.

The tribes came into town a few times a year to trade their furs, ginseng, venison, tanned buckskin and bead work for flour, salt, beans and other staples which they did not raise. Whole tribes came in at one time, with the chief and the bucks riding their little Indian ponies, while the squaws carried their papooses on their backs in blanket packs and led other ponies hitched to small travois or landboats loaded with trade articles. They had little money and their trade was chiefly on a barter basis with stores, saloons and housewives of the town.

Bright clothing, knives, axes and firewater held their primary interest in the deals made with the natives. They frequently came to our home to barter or sell their wares. Most of us children were outfitted with brightly beaded buckskin mittens and moccasins made by the squaws. There was little restriction on the shooting of deer by the Indians and we often had a venison hung up in the woodshed as the result of a trade for something in our house which took a squaw's fancy.

At one time I owned a beautiful spotted Indian pony. I had him tethered before the stable where one of the chiefs saw him and wanted him. We entered into a long and elaborate negotiation and I finally wound up by trading my pony for one which the Indians had hitched to a landboat and a buckskin jacket to boot. My horse had never been trained to draw anything, but he was a fine saddle animal. The chief hitched him to his conveyance and they sailed off at top speed through town. Soon they came back past our barn and the spotted pony wanted to go home. A dozen bucks and squaws collected and pushed and pulled him but he refused to budge. Finally the chief came into our house and said:

"Dat pony crazy!"

They finally got him started and set off to their encampment in the woods. The last I heard of my nice, fat spotted pony was that he had died of starvation, not being able to survive on the diet of brush and cedar browse which the Indians fed all their ponies in winter.

One of the bucks had become so intoxicated on the white man's firewater that the others could not drag him out of town, where he stayed for two weeks in a drunken stupor, the butt of mean tricks and practical jokes of the whites, until a few of the tribe came in to get him. They hoisted him on the back of a pony and tied him there until they reached their bivouac in the woods.

When a group of my friends and I were on a fishing trip at Chicaugon Lake near an old Indian encampment we came upon a tribe which had come over from Lac Vieux Desert reservation in Wisconsin. They were on their way back home to secure their government pension money. Chief Sunshine was head of the tribe at the time. He was a wizened old Indian and his face was wrinkled like an apple that had been left out to dry in the sun. His raven black hair was braided and tied with red and

yellow ribbons and the strands hung down below his shoulders. A battered and faded brown derby sat on the side of his head. His white man's
coat had been patched with many colored pieces of cloth. His pants were
a faded green and the seat had a bright red patch across the entire bottom. He smoked a stubby, frayed stogy which he kept clenched in the
corner of his mouth. A new pair of buckskin moccasins, encrusted with
colored beads and dyed porcupine quills, was on his small, pigeon-toed
feet.

Chief Sunshine took a fancy to one of my handsome blonde buddies
and told him that if he would marry his daughter he would never have to
work the rest of his life but would have a government pension as a member of the tribe. My blonde friend was not interested in this romantic
proposal but he was curious to have a look at the dark "princess." The
chief entered an elm-bark shelter and led her out for inspection. She
came out with bowed head to see her "intended." She was attractively
attired in a long buckskin dress which reached her ankles, beaded head-
band, with a white wild goose feather in her jet braids which hung to her
waist. Comely for an Indian maid, she was rounded at the proper places,
young and rather pretty. Her deep brown eyes took in the blonde white
youth and seemed impressed with the prospect.

Chief Sunshine pressed my friend for a decision, offering to throw
in five Indian ponies and a shotgun. The young man, embarrassed and
blushing, asked for time to make a decision. As soon as the opportunity
afforded, we struck out for home, needling our friend over his lost romance and opportunity to become a full-fledged Chippewa.

We noticed in the Indian camp meager supplies of corn, a pot of
beans and a small amount of jerked venison hanging from a pole. With
an abundance of game, fish and a forest of wood, the Indians provided
for the day only. They would kill a deer in winter and sit around in
their smoky shacks or elmbark wigwams until the meat was gone, then
go out to hunt for more. When they were asked why they did not kill
enough meat or catch enough fish for the winter, they would reply with
a grunt and their chins out-thrust to the sky:

"Ugh! Mebbe winter never come!"

When we asked why they did not cut enough wood for the winter instead of sending the squaws out each morning with an ax in the deep
snow to cut wood for the day, they would reply:

"Ugh! Mebbe winter never come."

In the land of the free, where foresight was the price of comfort, the
Indians had little of either. Foresight and worry for the future were
qualities that were brought to the Upper Peninsula from Europe and
passed on to the sons and daughters of Europeans. To this day the two
kinds of freedom live there side by side, unoppressed, though one is
victor and the other vanquished.

Chapter VI

THE MEN WHO WERE

The Town Marshal
Dan Seavey—Lumberman and Pirate
"Pigface" Conley and His Contemporaries
Jim Murphy—Woodsman Supreme
"H'African" Bill
Men About Town
Fabulous Characters
Pat Kelly's General Store
The Oldest Profession
I Remember When—
The Sharpened Tongue
Billy, The Blacksmith, and Hay, The Baker
The Birch Bark Will

Alex Quirt's Hardware Store

Chapter VI

THE MEN WHO WERE

The Town Marshal

It is easy enough to lump men off by nationalities, to measure them by class or social measurements, but sooner or later one comes up against the fact that men are individuals, and that when each man was made the mould was broken.

None of the men in these pages was great, or even important, but some of them were bright sparks of interest in the too frequently drab struggle for existence in that land between the open mine pits and the pine stumps.

Our town marshall was such a man. . . . .

Oarce Moore didn't appear to be a strong man. His general make-up deceived you, for he was small and self-effacing. He was the Stambaugh town marshal and kept law and order in that early rugged community by his fearless bull-headedness. Oarce was never known to retreat from a dangerous situation or from the fiercest antagonist. Whenever he encountered a tough customer he fought him if necessary with the free-for-all tactics of his town and the day in which he lived. It didn't take him long to discourage his opponent. While he could slug it out with the best of them, he could absorb more punishment than a half dozen fighters. No matter how many sledge hammer blows his system had to withstand, he packed a wallop in either hand that sent many a roughneck into the land of dreams in the end.

Plank sidewalks, muddy streets and no water or sewer systems to the homes was the Stambaugh in Oarce Moore's day. Saloons ran full-blast on every corner of main street. Many a miner and lumberjack had his pockets picked clean of his wages and woke up in the mud under the board walks the next morning with a terrific headache without knowing the cause.

Only the graver and open infractions of the law were punished and Oarce never concerned himself about infractions of which he was not a witness. Wife beatings and drunkenness were overlooked. Only the most persistent complaints by people of the upper crust could stir Oarce to do anything about closing the saloons after hours or keeping them closed on Sundays.

In combating extreme lawlessness Oarce never worried about methods. His idea was to settle fights, make arrests, chastise wife beaters on the spot or beat up a swindler. He took the law into his own hands. Few of his cases reached the justice of the peace.

"Minor infractions", as he called them in his French-Canadian dialect. "Dose is not for Oarce."

Years went on and Stambaugh grew. Order and justice crept in and Oarce was made a mere night patrolman. A more progressive man was made the chief of police. The sidewalks were now cement and the red iron rock streets were paved. Oarce was just an old tradition. Only the oldtimers knew the courage that lay deep inside his breast. The young bucks of the town looked upon Oarce and his traditional fearlessness as a Paul Bunyan tale.

Nothing exciting ever happened any more. Oarce was kept on, not for his ability as a law enforcement officer, but because the town fathers could think of no easy or polite way of brushing him into the discard. Too many of the older citizens remembered him from his hey-day. Night after night he patrolled his beat in a slow, sad way. His heart wasn't in it any more. His hair was getting grey. The world was getting soft. Nothing ever happened, so he made no arrests. Even the youngsters on the streets after curfew mocked his helplessness.

June, the month of weddings, came. The weather was beautiful. Ramponi was giving a reception for his brother. The wedding had taken place two days before. Ramponi's beer tavern was the scene of great hilarity. Dago red wine flowed like water. The public was barred and only the Ramponi family and the friends of the bride and the groom were invited.

The guests were happy on this June evening. They danced in the large livingroom which was part of the family quarters at the back of the saloon. Gaiety was in full swing when a group of young roughneck miners crashed the party. How the front door of the tavern became unlocked is still a mystery. A fight started as the male members of the wedding party attempted to bounce out the invaders just as Oarce was coming up the main street.

Oarce never hesitated. There was a fight going on and his place was in the middle of it. Into the tavern he went, night club swinging as he barged in. The young bucks were slammed right and left. In the melee Ramponi's brother, with true Latin temperament, lost his head. When the fight started he had run for a gun and came back with a .32 pistol in his hand, just as Oarce had cleared a way into the center of the tavern proper. The groom had no intention of using the gun. Now he faced a police officer. His mind went blank and madness reigned in his head.

"Drop that gun, you Dago " roared Oarce and started for the groom.

The latter's mind was filled with anger, fear and liquor and he could not distinguish between friend and foe. Instead of dropping the gun, he fired point blank at Oarce. The bullet made him wince but the old peace officer never stopped.

"Drop that gun, I tell you," he roared above the tumult and kept coming toward young Ramponi.

The latter fired twice more before Oarce's night club laid him cold on the barroom floor.

Two bullets took effect but Oarce was still on his feet with blood streaming down his pants legs and onto the floor. Singlehanded he put the groom in the town lockup, then staggered up the street to a doctor's office.

Newcomers to the town who were near the scene were astonished at the old man's display of courage. The oldtimers nodded their heads in an "I told you so" attitude. They remembered Oarce of the good old days.

Oarce was not hit in a vital spot and the gun was of a low calibre, so he was back on his beat within a month. He refused to testify against Ramponi's brother.

"Dose tam Dagos not responsible when dey get full of Dago red," explained Oarce.

The gunman was jailed for three weeks and fined fifty dollars to replace Oarce's bullet riddled uniform. He left town shortly thereafter, for he could not face the antagonism of the oldtimers.

The town council passed a resolution to the effect that Oarce Moore could remain a night patrolman as long as he lived. In addition, they voted to buy him a gold badge to wear on his bullet-scarred chest.

Dan Seavey—Lumberman And Pirate

Perhaps one of the most colorful characters of those early days was Dan Seavey, described as a Klondiker who came back broke, a lumberman, Great Lakes pirate, liquor smuggler, operator of a gambling ship and, according to an Escanaba woman, "the handsomest man I ever saw."

The big, square-chested, six-foot-six Dan was born in Portland, Maine, in 1865. At the age of twelve he ran away from home and made it to Peshtigo, Wisconsin, arriving there five years after the great forest fire had leveled that mill town and killed more than fifty people. He spent some time in the lumber camps in the Upper Peninsula where he worked as a chore boy, swamper and canthook man. He began sailing on the Great Lakes when he was twenty, with time out for a gold rush fling in Alaska, which he ended up some salt water sailing around the world.

Tales of this incredible man were told wherever old-time mariners gathered, each tale growing in magnitude through the years. Out of these stories came undeniable reports that he was "the last pirate on the Great Lakes", that he engaged in such varied activities as transporting fruit, smuggling contraband liquor, operating a gambling ship, raiding harbors at night and sponsoring lake cruises offering exotic and unusual outlawed entertainment.

Seavey stole a two-masted schooner with a full cargo at Chicago and sailed her to Frankfort, Michigan, into which port he was chased by the U. S. Government vessel, "Tuscarora." As he came into the harbor he drove his vessel full sail up on the slab pile in front of a sawmill, jumped over her bow as she struck and disappeared. The boat was confiscated and A. C. Frederickson, the son of an old sea captain, salvaged her compass.

Dan appeared again in Milwaukee where he was engaged in the fish market business. At the same time he acquired two saloons and a farm on the outskirts of the brewery city. These properties he sold for

$ 14,000.00, which he invested for a one-tenth interest in the Rosebud
Mining Company in Alaska. This was the beginning of his gold rush
adventures. But, he said:

"The only real money I made in Alaska was the $500.00 I got for
hoisting a large safe that had fallen through the floor of a saloon. There
was a lot of gold in the safe and the owners had been trying for a couple
of weeks to raise her up to the main floor. One of the owners asked me
how much I would take to do the job. I told him that if he would give me
an eight man crew and $500.00 I would do it. He accepted. I got some
rope and poles and in half an hour the safe was out of the cellar."

When he returned from Alaska in 1890 he acquired the schooner. The
Wanderer. Under the guise of freight hauling he would sail into a port
without lights and clear out again before daylight, taking on board anything that was loose. When his trail became too hot, he disappeared
again to pop up in an early movie depicting the wrecking and salvaging
of an ore carrier on the Great Lakes with Dan doubling for the heroine
as a deep sea diver.

Later he was reported to have made a business of killing deer on
Summer Island in Lake Michigan, and taking the schooner load of
venison to sell in Chicago. Deputy Sheriff Charlie Olmstead, himself a
husky, fearless fellow, was asked to go to Summer Island to arrest
Seavey. But Olmstead, who had lived all his life on the mainland with
the island in full view, asked innocently:

"Where's Summer Island? "

As an adjunct to his illegal operations, Seavey brought "women" on
his boat to "Squeaky" Swartz's "house" at Frankfort and took those who
had been with Swartz too long to be attractive any more to another
bawdy house in the Soo area.

A man of courage, ready to fight any comer, but with few to take him
on, Seavey would sail in any weather. His was the last schooner to dock
at Escanaba in late winter, the bow ice-covered and the spars white
with snow. His call for drinks brought every man to the bar. Those who
hesitated to join the pirate felt his big hand on their collar and his boot
on their pants. Only once was he bested in a fight, and that when a professional fighter imported from Chicago to do the job tore him in
shreds.

Rumor had it that many a man was rolled off his vessel into the icy
waters of Lake Michigan when he displeased the owner. He was suspected of burning down a sawmill at Gouley's Harbor, the flames of
which also destroyed The Wanderer. He never came to trial, escaping
as he always did and turning up in some other district to carry on his
lawlessness.

The only other antagonist to overcome the "Pirate" Seavey was
death itself, whom he met in a convalescent home back in Peshtigo, a
colorful character in the exciting chapter of those stirring days before
the turn of the Century.

"Pigface" Conley And His Contemporaries

Rough as were some of our early characters, many had "hearts of gold". In their sober moments they were generous to a fault, willing to give their last dime to a friend or to a family in need.

"Pigface" John Conley was another well-known personality who had been a saloon keeper and a bawdy house operator in a small way at Elmwood, up the tracks a piece. He had given up drinking and lived a sober and respectable life in his latter years.

"Pigface's" eyelids sagged down between his cheekbones and nose and showed a bright red on the inside as the result of his early years of dissipation. His eyes watered continually and the tears ran down through his nose, despite frequent dabbing with a red handkerchief, keeping his long upper lip wet in all weather. His mustache, which looked as if he had carelessly trimmed it with a dull brush-hook, hung down like grey icicles and was stained a bright amber by the short Irish clay pipe between his snagged teeth. His nose had been flattened in a barroom brawl in his youth and spread sideways over his ample, fleshy face.

He was a staunch Democrat in that predominantly Republican community and an uncompromising critic of the Catholic Church, although a former Catholic himself. Every evening found Conley sitting before the pot-bellied stove in Pat Kelly's general store, discussing politics with Pat and Mike Kelly and the few other Democrats of the town. He was an enthusiastic admirer of Eugene V. Debs, the perennial Socialist candidate for the Presidency of the United States. Arguments waxed hot and heavy wherever the clan gathered. Insults flew back and forth, but the same "hot stove league" assembled evening after evening. In my late teens I became interested in politics too and joined these cronies around the stove.

It was "Pigface" who introduced me to the radical literature of the time—"The Appeal to Reason", "The Menace" and others. He became my warm friend and we had many intimate discussions on politics and religion at the store and in his little shack in town. He had a keen wit, a vitriolic tongue but a real sense of fairness. It was he who loaned me several hundred dollars to attend the university. When I returned to repay him, he remarked that he would not have cared if I had never paid the loan, as long as I had gotten my education.

"Tonic" Webb, another Irish pioneer, lived on a little farm a few miles from the village. He trained oxen to work and did some lumbering on a "haywire" basis. He was noted as the fiercest rough-and-tumble fighter in those parts where fighters were plenty. Sober, he was a quiet citizen. Periodically he came to town and got roaring drunk, but drunk or sober he was carefully avoided. Woe to the careless native or unsuspecting stranger who crossed him or challenged his fighting ability. Those were the days when everything went in a fight—fists, teeth, gouging and caulked boots. In a previous fight an opponent had bitten off "Tonic's" left nostril, giving a falcon-like expression to his grizzled face.

One particularly tough lumberjack nearly bested him in a rough and tumble fight. The next time they met, they were locked in the back room of a saloon and told to fight to a finish and the best man come out. Once the door was locked "all hell broke loose". Walls bulged, furniture crashed, fist blows resounded through the partition. Then suddenly a body struck the floor and all was quiet. A rap on the door and "Tonic" appeared, cut to ribbons, bloody, clothes torn to shreds, but a crooked smile showed through his swollen mouth. His antagonist spent three weeks in the   hospital.

One late afternoon "Tonic" drove into town and tied his horse to the hitching rail in front of Pat Kelly's store. Going into the store he gave Pat an order for supplies. He asked Pat to open a can of sardines and weigh out some crackers from the barrel for his lunch. As "Tonic" was munching his food a half-drunk Finn came into the store and asked Pat whose rig that was tied up outside. Pat said it belonged to "Tonic". The Finn staggered up to "Tonic" and said:

"Ay skal like for to take dose horse and buggy and tak my gurl for a ride to Stambaugh. All right? "

"No," replied "Tonic" between bites. "You can't take my horse but if you'll wait until I buy my groceries and eat these sardines and crackers, I'll take you and your girl up myself. I've never seen a Finlander, drunk or sober, who could drive a horse right."

The Finn became abusive and threatened "Tonic" with a thrashing.

"Well, if you want a fight." said "Tonic", "I'll tend to you as soon as I get through eating."

Wiping his mouth with the back of his hand, he led the Finn out to the feed barn back of the store. Pat Kelly wanted to see that fight and started to follow them as soon as he could get off his grimy apron. He got to the barn just as "Tonic" was coming out of the door. The Finn was lying in the dirt, out cold. "Tonic" smacked his hands together to shake off the dust and calmly said to Pat:

"Bedad, that Finn can't fight worth walking this far."

"Tonic" was elected township road commissioner and proceeded to build a big, wide road to his little farm. Asked why he built such an expensive road to such a little farm, he said:

"Who in hell would build it if I didn't? "

When "Tonic" died two decades later, the local newspaper, after giving an account of his exploits, commented:

"The whole community celebrated his death."

Many French-Canadians drifted into the Upper Peninsula to assist in the harvesting of the pine, hemlock, basswood and elm in the early 'Nineties. Skilled with ax and crosscut saw, they cut a big swath through the timberlands of that northern empire. Many of these swarthy Canadians could neither read nor write, but they loved the woods and all that was in them.

"Black Alex" was a French-Canadian who had come down from the Quebec province to seek a new life and opportunity amid the big pine of the Iron River district. What his surname was I never knew. Everyone knew him only as "Black Alex." He knew nothing of the three R's but

he did know how to "make his mark, X". His French-Canadian accent
set him off as a colorful character apart. He had many imitators and
was the principal actor of countless tales told about him.

Alex raised a family which often did not know where their next loaf
of bread was coming from. His wife, Lizzie, and his children bore their
lot stoically. Alex did odd jobs about town and some work in the lumber
camps but steady work of any kind was inimical to his desire for freedom and distaste of restraint. He refused to work in the mines.

"Beejees, dat mine work she is for da dago," he held. "Not for a
French-Canadian from da nort' countree, like me."

Rabbits were the chief source of meat for the family. Alex set snares
in the rabbit runs. This was the easiest method of securing them. It
took little effort and the snares needed tending only once or twice a
week. When snaring was good, the family lived well. Rabbit stew,
rabbit boullion, rabbit fried and rabbit roasted gave variety to their
palates.

One morning Alex got up early and made the rounds of his snares.
When he returned empty-handed, the children were gathered around
the breakfast table hungry for food. Alex burst into the shack and made
this report:

"Lizzie, we 'ave to pos'pone da breakfas'. Da rabbit she jump da
snare."

Alex lived off the land and the woods. Blueberries, raspberries,
cranberries and hazel nuts were abundant and there for the picking.
With the help of his wife and children they fared not too badly in the
summer and the fall. Come winter, it was another matter. One day Alex
bestirred himself to assist the women in picking two pails of blueberries. As he was carrying the buckets down the road, one of his neighbors asked him:

"What are you going to do with those blueberries, Alex? "

" What I'm goin' to do wit' dam? " rejoined Alex. "Don' chu know dat
de blueberry make better apple sauce dan da prune? "

Alex drove a team of horses and a sleigh down the street one very
cold winter's day. His black whiskers and long jet hair were frosted
with frozen breath. He flailed his arms to keep warm. On the side of
Smith's drygoods store hung a large thermometer. He stopped the team
and ran over the creaking snow to look at the thermometer. As he
jumped back onto the sleigh, someone yelled:

"How cold is it, Alex? "

"By gar," reported Alex, "she's a foot and a 'alf below!"

Alex always participated in our Fourth of July celebrations. He had
a keen sense of humor and loved to attract attention. His first money-
making ventures on the Fourth was to make and sell ice cream at a
stand. But after one serving to a customer he never sold him another.
After each dipping with a big spoon, Alex would lick off the spoon and
dip for the next customer. One look at his black beard and his stubby,
unbrushed teeth convinced the buyer that he was not hungry for ice
cream at Alex' stand. Thereafter Alex was engaged to dodge eggs
thrown at him while he stuck his head through a split in a piece of

canvas which was nailed to two upright poles. He stood this until one Fourth Heinie Bies, a terrific baseball pitcher, mixed the eggs with baseballs. Heinie had perfect control and never missed Alex's black head.

Poaching game, fish and furbearing animals was a common practice in those days. Natives claimed that since domestic raised meat was expensive and hard to get, nature's game was theirs for the taking. Alex lived close to nature. He felt that what nature had she should give without interference from game wardens. He was looked upon as the most successful poacher in those parts until his eyes went bad. Game wardens set traps to catch him but he was never convicted even though he was arrested and tried several times. He always asked for a jury trial and his attorneys were careful to select jurors who themselves felt as Alex did about getting a venison occasionally out of hunting season. Even justices of the peace who held the first hearings knew about the slim fare Alex's children and wife had to face and were sympathetic and lenient.

Alex and Harry Hane were headlighting deer from a canoe on Ottawa Lake, which was a violation on two counts—headlighting and shooting deer from a boat. While waiting for darkness to settle, Alex decided to have a smoke. He laid his rifle across the gunwale of the canoe to fill and light his pipe. Harry shifted himself in the canoe and the gun slipped off into the deep water.

"Wait, Harry," yelled Alex. "Mark da boat, mark da boat, so we can fin' da place tomorrow!"

Max Jaeger, a successful poacher in his own right, was appointed game warden. It seemed to be the policy of the state game commission to "set a thief to catch a thief", for poachers knew all the tricks used in evading the law. Max set out to hang a game law violation on Alex. He hid himself beside an old logging road where Alex often hunted, and waited. Just at dusk he spied Alex coming down the road carrying a deer over his shoulder and a rifle in his hand. Max stepped out into the road as Alex approached and faced him.

"Well, Alex," smiled Max. "I got you at last, haven't I? "

"What you mean, you got me? What I do? " replied Alex.

"That deer on your shoulder."

Alex looked down at the deer's leg hanging in front of him and said in innocent, hurt surprise:

"Who in 'ell put dat dare? "

Jim Murphy—Woodsman Supreme

Not all the woodsmen were addicted to alcohol and women while on their vacations from the lumber camps. Some of the men who migrated to the big pine country were skilled timber lookers, timber estimators, surveyors and log scalers. Some of these select woodsmen were employed by the big lumber companies to seek out large stands of pine and the best means of cutting and hauling it to the rivers. With a compass, a small cruiser's ax, a blanket, a rifle, a small sack of flour, a tin of tea and a slab of bacon, these men would spend weeks at this estimating. So skilled were they that they could walk through a stand of pine and calculate in their heads how many thousand feet of logs per forty acres the trees would produce. Upon their judgement alone the companies bought great areas of timberland.

Jim Murphy was one of the most respected and skilled timber estimators of the north. Born in Canada in 1868, he came to the Iron River district at the age of eighteen to work in the woods. A handsome, alert and refined Canadian, he soon found his place with the lumber companies looking for merchantable pine. He grew up with the rugged country and among rough men, acting as timber cruiser and estimator, camp foreman, surveyor and boss on the spring drives. He saw the country change from black, limitless pine forests to denuded and burned-over slashing, then to farm land and finally to a summer resort area.

Jim finally retired because, he said, "my legs couldn't stand the traveling through the woods any more." He settled in a little house beside the Chicago & Northwestern Railroad tracks at Elmwood, a symbol of the tribe of men who devoted their lives to the woods and tall timber.

Jim had just sold his last surveyor's instruments and retired to a more leisurely life amid the scenes of young manhood. When I knocked on his door, a spritely man with grey hair beginning to appear in his black locks and mustache invited me into his simple one-room dwelling. He prepared a lunch of pasties and blueberry pie and a pot of black coffee. In one corner was his bunk bed and above it hung his rifle and shotgun and fishing tackle which, he explained, he had not used for several years. An overly-fat old hunting dog lay on the bed and wagged his tail in welcome.

"Yes," said Jim, as he lit his old stained pipe, "I've been here since 1886. I've seen many changes, some for the better and some not so good. Do you see that watertank across the track over yonder? I remember when that was first built. The railroad had just been finished from Iron River to Watersmeet to haul the pine from the camps along the right of way. The first tank was just completed and filled for the first time. The crew knocked off for lunch that hot summer day and sat in its shade. They had just finished their lunch and were smoking their pipes when the piling supporting the tank gave way and fell over and killed eight of that crew.

"I well remember the first county jail built in Iron County. The first prisoner was Jack O'Rourke, a drunken lumberjack. During the night the jail burned down and Jack lost his life in the fire.

"How cold did it get in those early days? Well, I worked for the Kirby, Carpenter-Cook Lumber Company in 1898 when the thermometer went down to fifty degrees below zero. On top of that came five feet of snow. The camp operations were closed down and it took twelve teams of horses and a big crew of men twelve days to plow the roads out so we could haul the stuff again. No, we don't get weather like that any more. Guess it was the big trees which held the cold and brought down the snow.

"Maybe you were too young to remember the Harrington House. Well, I attended a lumberjack dance there one night. It was run by Kate Harrington, who later married Jim Piper and changed the name to Piper House. It was a well-known boarding and rooming house and a bar in those days. When the men started drinking and fighting that night, I got up on a table and saw as many as four and five fights going on at the same time. One lumberjack got particularly nasty. Kate came in and knocked him down, jumped on him and slugged him with her bare fists. She didn't need a bouncer.

"Right over there near the north branch of the Iron River," he pointed through the window with his pipe, "'Pigface' Conley ran a blind-pig and a bawdy house. You can't see it. It was burned down in the big fire years ago. Some of my Indian friends were making maple syrup one spring. One of the bucks got a pint of 'rotgut' from 'Pigface' and started for the sugar camp. Before he got there he decided to drink it all himself before the other Indians got a smell of it. He drank the whole bottle, gave a warwhoop, jumped high in the air and came down dead in his tracks.

"At another time the Indians were having a drinking party near Elmwood. Bucks and squaws all got drunk. One of the squaws hit Chief Edward's squaw over the head with a club and blinded her. After that Chief Edwards led her over the trails with a rope around her waist. When they came to a windfall, he would jerk the rope—one jerk for a low windfall, two jerks for a high one.

"When an Indian died the tribe buried him in the ground and built a house of boards or poles over the grave. They placed tobacco, a pipe, matches, fish and crackers or bread in the house for his use in the Happy Hunting Grounds. You know, there is a big Indian burial ground over at Chicaugon Lake, where the Chippewas had their original camp before the whites drove them out. The Iron County road commission keeps the houses in repair now.

"I never had any trouble with the Indians. I saved my old clothes and shoes and gave them to Chief Edwards. When I gave him anything he would say:

'Now I tell God.'

"After he talked to God in Indian, he would say:

'Now God know. He put your name in the big book.'

"The Indians brought me maple syrup, venison, wild rice and maple sugar in return for my presents. I never could use the syrup because they strained it through their woolen blankets in which they slept and never washed.

"When the Indians had firewater in them they were bad actors. Chief Edwards' son, Jim, married a Pottawattami squaw. On the way to Lac Vieux Desert to the Pottawattami reservation over in Wisconsin, young Edwards and some of his Ottawas got into a fight with some of the Pottawattamis. Edwards cut the throat of one of the bucks with a knife and left him beside the trail to die. The party visited the reservation for two days, then went back over the trail for home. As they came to the spot where the fight took place they found the wounded Indian sitting along side the path with his back to a tree, singing his death song.

Edwards made his squaw hold the Pottawattami while he himself severed the Indian's neck completely. Edwards was caught and sentenced to
Waupun State Prison in Wisconsin for twelve years, but he died a few
years after he was placed there. No Indian could live long in prison.
They were outdoor people.

"About six miles up that old road," pointed out Jim, "Mike McGraw
had a shack and it was there that Mike shot Mike Kane for trifling with
his wife, Jen. Both men had had too much of "Pigface" Conley's bootleg
liquor. Kane made a pass at Jen and McGraw shot him in the leg with
his rifle. The couple tied up Kane's leg and came running into my place
and asked me to telegraph Dr. Sturgeon at Iron River to come up on the
next train to see what he could do for the wounded man. I went out to
see if I could help and found Kane in serious condition but the bleeding
had stopped. We placed him a boat and rowed him across James Lake,
then transferred him by wagon to the railroad just in time to flag the
down train to Iron River. Kane's leg was saved but he limped the rest
of his life.

"At another time, a lumbercamp roustabout died of bad whiskey at
Mike McGraw's place. It was probably some more of "Pigface's" rotgut
again. McGraw and Jen came to my place and asked me to go back with
them in order to hold an Irish wake until the coroner could arrive by
train the next day. There was only one bed in the house. The corpse lay
on a bed in the shack nearby. After some fried salt pork and strong
coffee and whiskey, Jen told me to go to bed, as she had to clean house
before the coroner came. Finally Mike got into bed next to the wall and
I in the outside position. I told Mike we had better trade places in case
Jen decided to go to bed too. I told him, 'I don't want to have two corpses
around tomorrow morning.' Mike was a jealous man.

"In the morning when I woke up I found that Mike had gone out to feed
the horses and there was Jen in bed with me. Well—.

"When the coroner got there he pronounced it death from alcoholism
and loaded the corpse into his basket and onto the two-horse sleigh. We
went at breakneck speed, with the basket sliding from side to side on the
slippery sleigh box. We got there just in time to catch the down bound
train for Iron River.

"Yes, those were great days," reminisced Jim as he knocked the
ashes from his ancient pipe and loaded it up again with Peerless.

"We had rough men and rough times, but, believe me, I wouldn't
trade them for the free and easy life people live now. That's why I still
live here in this little shack. I love the woods. Last night I saw nine
deer grazing near the railroad track. The only noise I hear is the trains
going by four times a day. I like it better here than in that noisy town
of Iron River. This country is getting too crowded. A new neighbor
moved in two miles from here. But I don't have much longer to live. I
guess I can take civilization for a while yet."

"H'African Bill"

"H'African Bill" was a Cousin Jack miner at the Dober mine. He kicked his H's far and wide and ate his pastie in his dinner bucket three times a week. No one ever told a taller story or had roamed a farther field than he.

Work in the underground wasn't Bill's long suit, for he had been in the British army too long, but he could sing a lusty baritone in the small Cousin Jack church choir at Christmas time. He wasn't satisfied with the vim and vigor the boys put into their choir practice.

"Why, h'over in Hingland a man would sleep with 'is feet 'anging out of the window on cold nights for three weeks, so 'e could sing bass on Christmas Day," was Bill's choice remark.

Bill had fought in the Boer War. He bragged continually about the way he had stuck to his night sentry post when sick with jungle fever while the rest of the sentries couldn't stand it.

"Those bloody Boors could creep up to you under a blade of veldt grass and cut your bloody throat without makin' a bloody sound," he said.

He recounted how 'e saved 'is company when 'e uncovered a Boer night attack by crawling on 'is belly into the enemy outpost. Kitchener had written 'im a personal letter of thanks, so 'e claimed, but through some h'oversight 'e never got the Victoria Cross for 'is bravery.

Bill preferred to work on the surface at the Dober mine, which in itself caused the miners to suspect his alleged bravery. Any real Cousin Jack looked upon surface workers as "hunkies". The boys never tired of kidding him about the time he stuck to his army post, but he didn't back down on his claim. He always said:

"Byes, that's the God's 'onest truth and h'im 'ere to tell you."

Someone had made a mistake in his calculations and the ore had been stripped too close to the rock on the fourteenth level. Dober rock was high in sulphur content. Its exposure to the oxygen in the air caused spontaneous combustion and started the sulphur to burn. It started slowly at first but soon a subdued flame burst over the surface of the exposed rock. Before many days the thin, blue, misty smoke started to curl up out of the open pit which connected the fourteenth level with the surface. Within a week all the rock surface was on fire.

The heavy sulphur fumes drove the miners out. No one could work underground. The engineers were panicky. The superintendent decided to shut the mine down until bulkheads could be built and sand filled into the burning stope.

For two weeks the crew fought the fumes. Pumpmen went home sick, their eyes closed tight with the acrid smoke. By Saturday night the shift pumpman and his partner reported themselves unable to endure it any longer. What was to be done? The entire mine would soon be flooded with water if the pumps were not kept going. The damage and delay in mining operations would reach into a ruinous figure.

Phil Jones, the surface foreman, went to his crew.

"Boys," he said in earnest tones, "we need some volunteers to go

John Airey's Butcher Shop When the Spring Floods Came

down to keep the pumps going tonight. Will some of you boys go down?
We'll spell off every hour and at no time will there be less than three
men in the underground pump house. How about it? Who'll do down?"

Old John Saderna, an Italian, and Tony Shubat, a Slav, stepped out.

"Good, that's two," said Jones, casting his eyes on "H'African Bill."

"Here's your chance to prove that story about the Victoria Cross,
Bill."

Bill gave the surface boss a look like that of a hurt calf and stepped
forward. He was no mechanic and, besides, he had told the boys many
times of his dislike at playing the part of a "bloody ground 'og".

Three others then volunteered and the crew was rigged out with
waterproof clothes and wet turkish towels to cover their faces against
the sulphur smoke. The shift boss went underground with the first crew
and instructed them how to man the pumps and when to pump. The first
crew stayed one hour, then came up pale, vomiting, with tears streaming from their smarting eyes, cursing the smoke.

There was no need to go down for another hour, for the mine water
would not fill the sumphole or catch basin before that time. So "H'African Bill", John Saderna and Tony Shubat sat around the dry house,
sweating, smoking their pipes, awaiting their turn.

It was ten o'clock that morning when they were lowered on the skip
to the seventeenth level pump house. The smoke was pouring out into
the shaft in greater volume. Tony, an old, experienced miner, knew that
this was no ordinary job. The risk was great, for in the semi-darkness
a man could be overcome and not be found until too late. Bill and John
followed him. The drifts and the pump house room were dark with the
sickening smoke and gas. Tony started the pumps.

"Go back to the shaft and I'll stay here for ten minutes," Tony directed his partners. "When ten minutes are up, come back and I'll go
to the shaft. The air is better there."

The men followed the instructions for two cycles. Then the pumps
stopped. Tony worked hard to start them again. John and Bill did what
they could to help. After another ten minutes John looked at the lights
over the pumps.

"Tony," he said in a frightened whisper, "there's a rainbow around
the lights. I'm going up!"

"Go ahead," was Tony's only comment as he worked on the pumps.
When he looked up again, John was gone.

Bill helped Tony for five minutes more, when suddenly Tony fell on
his face on the dirt floor. Bill dragged Tony to the shaft just as the skip
came back to the level. Tony was dumped into the skip and was carried
into the dry house by the frightened surface crew.

What happened down below is pure speculation. Swanson and Olds
went down and ran into the pump room. The pumps were going, but Bill
was out like a light with a pump wrench in his right hand.

Tony had been revived by the time Swanson and Olds got Bill to the
surface, but the Boer War veteran never came to. He had died at his
underground post.

Phil Jones went to Bill's rooming house the next morning to look

through his belongings and papers for some clue to his relatives. In the
top tray of his shabby trunk, in an old badly-worn and patched envelope
he found a letter. It was a personal achnowledgement from Lord
Kitchener to William Malet for heroic and distinguished service beyond
his call of duty at his sentry post. The place and the name of the company was there but Jones couldn't see them. His eyes had suddenly
became misty and he felt very, very small.

Men About Town

Every pioneer town attracts its quota of interesting and colorful
characters. We had many. The impression they made upon the young
minds of the day lasted throughout their lives.

The town butcher, John Airey, was an institution all by himself. He
had migrated from Switzerland in his youth and learned his trade in
this country. His butcher shop and small, cluttered grocery had become
well-known before I was old enough to remember his first coming. Short,
stocky, with a heavy black mustache, often flecked with beer suds, he
ruled his family of a wife, two daughters and one son with old-country,
masculine discipline.

John's business thrived lustily, for he always gave extra weight in
meat and staples. It was the day of "baker's dozen". A dozen of eggs
always meant thirteen. A pound of meat was a pound and a quarter,
without John's hand included. He had a large charge business. Each
customer was furnished by him with a pocket-sized charge book in which
John entered the articles and the price with a stubby pencil dipped in
saliva. His large scrawls were had to decipher. The same charges were
entered in his large, greasy charge account book in the same manner.
How his poor wife, who was his bookkeeper, was ever able to transfer
these illegible accounts was a mystery to all his customers.

Airey slaughtered his own beef, veal and hogs in a barn back of his
shop off main street. He was assisted by a Hollander called "John the
Bear", so nicknamed because the latter boasted that he had killed a
bear with an ax. Others held that he had found the bear in a deadfall
trap and struck the dead animal over the head with his ax. We kids
were chums of the butcher's son and were always on hand to watch and
help with the butchering, which took place after dark. We held kerosene
lanterns for the men to work by. Airey was a bit cross-eyed when he
had a few drinks under his belt. "John the Bear" held the critter's head
while Airey struck it on the head with a sledge hammer. Once in the excitement of holding a steer, "John the Bear" looked up into Airey's
crossed eyes. He dropped the critter's head and said:

"If you're going to hit where you're looking now, you better get somebody else to hold this cow."

When the beef lay on the ground, stunned, Airey cut its throat. As
the blood streamed onto the ground, the two Johns drank a glass or two
of the hot blood, saying that it gave them strength. None of us kids ever
wanted to be that strong.

Airey had a terrific temper. Anyone present when he lost control had to hide behind boxes and counters. His favorite expressions were: "Holy, Jumping Jesus, I'll kill you with a cleaver", and "Go home to your father and get his blessing while his eyes are still open!"

Once he threw a cleaver at "Burrie" Bies, his delivery boy. "Burrie" promptly threw it back at John. Too bad—both missed!

Airey's fancy meat supply came from Swift and Company and Armour and Company of Chicago. Every Friday these packers shipped crates of liver, hearts, kidney and tongue to Airey for free distribution to his regular customers. We always had liver and onions on Saturday. With a big family of thirteen children and a raft of boarders these free gifts were very welcome and helped out on the budget.

Another popular custom which prevailed at the time was that of giving turkeys and chickens to good customers as Christmas gifts. Whenever a bill was paid, John gave a valuable gift of food without charge. When Nels Fisher opened a butcher shop in connection with his grocery store, the new butcher, Ernie Fisher, never gave more meat than was actually bought. Often the weight included his fingers on the scale. However, because Airey gave such liberal weight and kept such a slovenly set of books, the new shop survived and John finally failed, giving way to the new economy in business.

At one time Armour and Swift tried to put the squeeze on the local butcher shops and attempted to force them to buy meat exclusively from them. Packers' prices were getting higher and higher and the local shops resorted to patronizing local farmers for their meat supply. As the pressure became more and more severe, Airey and Paul Minckler, who operated a large cattle and hog farm, organized a "meat" strike. John had the bulk of the meat trade of the town and Minckler his herds. Between them they started to buck the meat trust. They organized a parade with horses and wagons which drove through town with noise makers and a big sign which said:

"Go to John Airey for your Steak
And the Meat Trust you will Break!"

The strike went on for several months. John bought his meat from Minckler and the farmers until the supply of local cattle and hogs gave out. Then John had to beg the Chicago packers to sell to him again.

One spring when the snow and ice melted and flooded the streets, John's store basement, which was filled with groceries, became flooded to the top. The village council had haggled for years over building a sewer system but nothing was ever done about the annual floods. John came out of his shop to survey the flood waters as they went by his place in an ever-swelling stream. A plank placed to the door of his shop was the only dry place for him to stand. As he looked across the street he spied Jim Long, one of the village councilmen, standing on a high plank sidewalks.

"Say, Jim," called John, "what are you fellows going to do about the water in my basement?"

"I guess you'll have to suck it up through your chimney, John," replied Long, laughing.

Literally foaming at the mouth, John shouted to Long:
"Holy Jumping Jesus, I'll cut your bloody heart out!"

Airey's delivery horse was old Billy, an emaciated, fleabitten grey. Billy's performance varied from sleeping standing up while hitched to the delivery rig until his legs buckled under him to balking when he had too heavy a load. One day "Burrie" Bies, the delivery boy, was hauling a load of loose hay in from the country when Billy decided that the load was too heavy and he was too tired to go farther. Despite coaxing, whipping and leading, Billy wouldn't budge. "Burrie" decided to try an experiment he had heard of. He took an armful of dry hay and placed it on the snow under Billy's belly. Then he lit a match to it. When the fire blazed up under him, Billy merely squatted down to get warm. As the fire scorched him, he pulled the load up just far enough to set the hay on fire. The flames became too hot for Billy's behind. He started for home on a dead run, with "Burrie" chasing after him on foot. By the time the flaming load reached the stable the hair on Billy's tail was burned off. The hay and the sleigh burned down to the runners. But that was the last time Billy ever balked.

We had three negroes in the community, all of them having been slaves in their youth. They had escaped to the north country through the Underground Railroad and settled there. The most colorful and most deeply colored was "Old Black Joe" Herrin. He first worked for Paul Minckler on the farm and later as night watchman at Minckler's iron foundry. His last dwelling place was a little shack on the back lot in the middle of town near Airey's butcher shop. The land was low and during the spring thaws the lot was flooded and the shack inundated, causing Joe to seek temporary shelter elsewhere.

How Joe survived, no one knew. He was too old then to work. But he was a happy and friendly darky, who sat before his little home strumming on his old banjo, singing and entertaining anyone who came his way. He had been married to a white woman before he arrived at the village but she did not accompany him to his new home. He had a handsome son of light color and excellent athletic ability. We younger kids often watched him with deep admiration playing football and baseball on the town teams.

Joe was a sober and inoffensive character. When he entered a saloon he became the center of attention, for he brought along his banjo and sang for the crowd. He had only two songs which he sang off key. They were:

"Oh, I feel, I feel, I feel,
I feel like a big sunflower.
Oh, I feel, I feel, I feel
I feel like a morning star."

and

"Shoo fly, shoo fly,
Don't you eat my grub,
For I belong to the baseball club.

"Sho fly, shoo fly,
    Don't you bother me,
    For I belong to Company B."

One of Joe's best tricks which gained him applause and drinks was
to stand on his head while drinking a schooper of beer.

Darius Falkner was a big, burly, friendly Negro who had a draying
business and was quite prosperous. He claimed to have been a former
slave and that he was used by his plantation owner for the propagation
of slave children before the Emancipation Proclamation. He said that
he never did know how many offspring he had for he never saw them.
His big team of horses was the envy of all horse owners. He was a
veterinary without diploma and was called upon whenever an animal
needed attention. He also had charge of Phil Boynton's breeding stock
at the livery stable.

"Branch" Harris was the other negro. He was a respected citizen in
the village and a dependable worker. He and his white wife raised a
large family of light colored children who made good on their own. Race
prejudice was almost unknown there in those days and colored children
mixed on equal terms with the whites.

Johnny Shay was an Irish immigrant. He had all his fingers, except
his thumbs, missing on both hands. He had become completely asphyxi-
ated with liquor one night and froze his hands as he lay in the snow in
sub-zero weather. The fingers had to be amputated. After that experience he led a rather sober life on a little farm. My father and I hauled
bailed hay from his farm one winter with Johnny's help and his loss of
fingers was no handicap. He lived alone and did his own cooking and
housekeeping despite his missing digits. With his stumps we saw him
knead his own bread, milk his cows and paddle his own butter. He lived
a lonely life by our standards but he was independent and could still
"thumb his nose" at the outside world.

There was one individual who was always pointed out to us by our
parents as an example of what would happen to us if we drank liquor. He
was "Billy the Drunk". Billy spent his time mooching drinks in the
many saloons of the town, although he was able-bodied and well. It was
held by the natives that he had contracted "indolent" fever in his childhood and had become senile in his youth. He was the first person seen
on the streets in the morning, looking for an open back door of a saloon
where he could beg an "eye-opener". He was the last one in the saloons
at night to get a free "nightcap". For these necessary favors he swept
out the saloons and cleaned the big brass spittoons. When not making
the rounds of the saloons he slept peacefully in the town lockup, where
he earned his lodging by emptying the "thundermugs" in the cells.
When someone asked him how he slept, he said:

"Well, at night I sleep like a baby. In the mornings I sleep pretty
well too. But in the afternoons I just turn and toss."

There was one thing in which "Billy the Drunk" excelled in and that
was swearing. When he cursed a man he started back in his dim history, named all his ancestors by their dog titles and ended up by casting aspersions on their doubtful family status. It was said that he

"swore by note." On cold winter days Billy often appeared at the bakery where I worked for a while, to warm himself before the oven. As he became warm he would reach under his shirt to scratch himself and, as he said, "to give the other lice a change for a square meal."

"Fartin' " Brown was one of our early homesteaders who "took up a claim" on a section of land about six miles from town. Most of the pine had been logged off the claim and the land had reverted back to the government, as was the case after the cream of the timber had been skimmed off. Here Brown grubbed out the pine and hardwood stumps, made a small clearing in which he planted a few hills of potatoes, transplanted some cabbage and scattered a package of rutabaga and turnip seeds in the scratched-over area. His rude little log cabin sheltered him during the late spring, summer and fall until he harvested his crops. Then the lumber camps called him for the winter.

A kindly, indolent bachelor, Brown got along well with his neighbors and the rough element in the camps who gave him his nickname. It came about because of his "rear-end tooting." Too many beans, he claimed. One day in the lumber camp his companions teased him about his indelicate accomplishment. He bet them a plug of Spearhead chewing tobacco what he could "toot" every time he pulled a saw through a log. He reached the count of forty-two when the saw reached bottom. From that time on he was "Fartin' " Brown to everyone, even to the women who knew him. His clearing in the woods thereafter was known as "Fartin' " Brown's clearing, a halfway mark between town and the first lumber camp on the Brule River.

Porcupines were plentiful and a very destructive pest in the woods. They gnawed anything that tasted of salt. Ax handles, peavy stocks, harness, shoes and cabin doors were considered delicacies by these big, lumbering, quilled but otherwise harmless sloths. "Fartin' " Brown was on his way to his cabin in the woods with a pack of groceries on his back and a load of firewater on his insides. Night overtook him in the deep woods. The air was balmy and he was tired and groggy. So he lay on the ground to sleep with the pack under his head for a pillow. The next morning when he started for home his shoes felt as soft as moccasins. Looking down at the soles he discovered that a porcupine had eaten off the bottom leather while he was sleeping.

Billy Sullivan and his father, M. T., operated the Sullivan House, a third-rate rooming house, and a saloon at the east end of main street. Billy's hobby was collecting wild animals and keeping them in cages back of the saloon. At times he had four black bear, caught while they were cubs, wild foxes, woodchucks and snakes. He fed them out of his hand. The more intoxicated he was the more fearless he became. He was often mauled by the bear and bitten by the snakes, but like most drunks, he was never seriously injured. Any gifts of snakes, woodchucks, foxes or other wild animals brought to him were good for a round of drinks. As the menagerie increased, so did the stench, until the neighboring storekeepers appealed to the town council to close the place for fear their customers would think the stores were harboring spoiled meat.

M. T. "Empty" Sullivan was appropriately named. Red-nosed and bleary-eyed, he was the saloon's best customer. He spent most of his waking hours fighting off delirium tremens and imaginary snakes twining around his neck.

On one occasion Billy wanted his father to give him some money which the old man refused to do. Billy, who always carried a gun, shot at his father and nicked his throat. Si Sensiba, the sheriff, attempted to arrest him. Billy, with a revolver in hand, threatened to shoot anyone who tried to enter the house. Sensiba crawled through a back window and caught Billy from the rear as he was guarding the door. A hearing was held but Billy was released as soon as he was sober enough to realize what he had done.

Early in his checkered career Billy was both town marshal and police judge, as well as tavern keeper. When he arrested anyone and brought him to "court", Billy asked him how much money he had in his pants pocket. Then he would fine the culprit the full amount and pocket the same. On his backbar hung a sign:

"Don't Leave The Bar While The Floor Is In Motion."

A bunch of the boys were sleeping it off on the tables of his saloon one day. Trade was slow. Most of the lumberjacks had spent their winter's stake. Drink moochers were aplenty. Billy fired his revolver over the sleepers into the plaster and ordered them to wake up and buy more drinks or get out.

Billy was a fast sprinter in his youth and ran in the volunteer fire department tournaments. He owned a black racehorse which he entered in a race on the Fourth of July. Just before the race Billy poured a pint of whiskey down the horse's throat and said:

"Now you b------, you'll win the race this time."

Quarter way down the track the horse staggered and ran into the crowd. That was as near as he ever came to winning a race.

Jerry Mahoney, all dressed up, walked into Billy's saloon and asked for a drink of whiskey, then another and then another. Turning on his heel, Jerry said:

"Thanks, Billy, That's on you," and started to walk out.

"Don't you move," yelled Billy, "until you pay for those three whiskies."

"Oh, no, Billy, this is your treat," laughed Jerry, continuing toward the door.

"If you take another step," threatened Billy, "I'll shoot the damn heels off you."

Jerry reached for the handle on the door. Billy leaned over the bar and shot the heel off Jerry's left shoe.

One of the boys had a fighting cock which he matched with those of his neighbors around. He was a mean bird and would take pieces of flesh out of the fingers of his handler as easily as he would disable another rooster. He acquired a deserved reputation as a killer.

Billy, not to be outdone by any of the sporting gentry, bought a dunghill rooster which he thought was a sure winner. The two birds were matched on the floor of the saloon. In a few minutes Billy's bird lay on floor with his neck pierced by the game bird's spur. Billy was so disgusted with his dunghill that he rung his neck on the spot.

Fabulous Characters

Ed Lott, Jr. was the town's most successful horse trader. What he couldn't do to make a forty-dollar horse look like a hundred and fifty dollars no one else could. He never told a prospective buyer or trader the horse's faults, but should he be asked point blank if the horse had heaves or was an outlaw, Ed told the truth. The only persons who were sharper horse traders than Ed were the wandering bands of Gypsies who trailed their strings of windbroken, spavined and outlaw horses from town to town. It was always a matter of speculation among the natives as to who would get the worst of a trade. Ed seldom lost.

When local option came to Michigan, Wisconsin was still wet. Ed opened a saloon just across the border opposite the Michigan town of Pentoga. Here he made a sizeable fortune catering to the weak and thirsty on both sides of the state line. On one occasion I saw Ed banking a fistful of big bills which would have choked a buffalo. I remarked to him that I would feel ashamed to make my living at the expense of other people's weaknesses. Ed replied with a trace of guilt in his voice:

"Well, if I didn't do it, someone else would. I might as well make it while it lasts."

An itinerant sign painter, known as the "Artist", came into town and stayed for a few weeks. He was a refined looking individual with a skilled hand at painting signs for the merchants and pictures on barroom mirrors. When he had completed all the available work in town he went on a "bender" and landed in the jailhouse. In his stupor he set fire to his mattress. The jailhouse nearly burned down. He was rescued in the nick of time by Jim O'Brien, the town marshal, and was "sent up" to the county jail at Crystal Falls for ninety days to cool off. At the end of the term, he appeared in town a paler, thinner and a more contrite man, vowing to "never touch the stuff again." A few days later, under the influence of sympathetic friends he was in the same "picked" condition. This time the justice of the peace "shipped him out of town" rather than have him become "an expense on the county." This was my first look at an "artist."

The Englehart brothers, Conrad and Matt, were an interesting pair who drifted into town in the late 'Nineties. Both were artistic and industrious. Both affected small, waxed mustachios, wore flashy clothes and were interested in cultural activities.

Matt was a taxidermist and plied his trade locally with some degree of success. One of his helpers was Milton Hopkins, the son of a drygoods merchant. Milton was also artistic and talented as well as an outdoor man. His interest in taxidermy began when he shot and killed a cub bear. He sighted the she-bear and her two cubs while he was hunting rabbits with his .22 caliber rifle. The she-bear and Milton saw each other at the same instant. She cuffed one of her cubs up one tree and the other up a nearby sapling. While she was busy with her second cub, Milton shot the first one out of the tree. Running in quickly, he placed the body in his packsack and made off with it. He could hear the mother crashing through the brush searching for her lost baby. As Milton ran he thought of all the stories he had heard of she-bear tearing men to bits for disturbing their young.

He put on another burst of speed despite his heavy load. When he reached an open clearing and saw the town ahead he dropped exhausted on the ground. As he rested he thought he heard the she-bear searching through the woods for her missing cub. Off he dashed again to reach home and safety, overcome by fright and fatigue. He stuffed the cub skin under the supervision of Matt and did such a good job of it that he stayed to be Matt's assistant. Thereafter he continued to get his own wildlife specimens and had a veritable museum of his own. But that was the only bear he attempted to shoot.

Conrad Englehart built and operated an outdoor ice skating rink during the fall and winter. This rink was surrounded by a six-foot board fence and was the gathering place of those boys and girls who could raise the necessary fifteen-cent admission. It was operated for several years. Then rumors began to circulate among the town elders about "the goings on" in the rink shelter house. One night the volunteer fire department was called out to extinguish a fire that had already consumed most of the shelter and part of the high board fence. That spelled the end of our only "commercialized" recreation for the time being.

"Pie Plant" Archie McDonald lived on a back street in a little unpainted shack. He was a little, weazened ex-lumberjack who had given up the struggle and haunted the saloons for what treats he could beg from the incoming woods boys or from the bartenders in a weak moment.

"Pie Plant" was suspected of never washing his face or hands. Dirt of long vintage filled the creases of his neck and face. His hands were invariably greasy and black. He lived on the free lunches always found at the end of the long saloon bars—cheese, rye bread, pretzels, and smoked herring. These lunches were for the purpose of keeping the patrons in the saloons as long as their money lasted. Although "Pie Plant" was repeatedly driven away from these free snacks, he always came back for more, often in the company of a sympathetic friend who could buy drinks for both and take the curse off taking the lunch.

The only contribution Archie ever made to industry was from his little patch of pie plant or rhubarb, which grew in his front yard. This he watered and manured carefully from the fertilizer he obtained from Bill Moss' livery stable a block away. It grew in profusion each spring. As soon as some of the stalks were large enough, "Pie Plant" cut an armful and peddled them on his arm to the local grocery store for a few cents a bunch. When the pie plant season was over, Archie was "on the town" again.

With a few thin dimes in his pockets, "Pie Plant" went into a local hashhouse and said to the waiter:

"I'm so hungry I could eat a horse."

"Well," responded the waiter, "you certainly came into the right place."

Joe Bedore was a French-Canadian who ran the "Lumberjack's Friend" saloon. His place was patronized largely by his fellow Canadians. He seldom "treated the house" and was particularly resentful of the professional drink "moochers" who came in.

"Pie Plant" came in one quiet morning, desperate for an "eye-opener." Seeing no one in the saloon he approached Joe for a drink. Joe merely pointed to the door and told him to get out:

"If you don't go out, I get somebody that will go out."

"Which door, Joe?" asked "Pie Plant" innocently. "There are four doors in your saloon."

"B' da Holy Mary, you crazy, 'Pie Plant'."stormed Joe, "Der' is only two door in dis place."

"No, be jees, Joe, there are four doors in your saloon," said "Pie Plant."

"You show me der' four door in my place, I give you a drink."

"Well, Joe. There is the front door. There is the back door. Then there is you, Joe Bedore," laughed "Pie Plant."

"Dass right," smiled Joe, "but dat only t'ree door."

"Then there's the cuspidor," chuckled "Pie Plant."

"B'cris, 'Pie Plant', das a good joke. Here is your whiskee!"

Later when a crowd had gathered, Joe decided to try the joke on his customers. He yelled:

"I bet any man in the 'ouse a drink der is four door in my saloon."

One of the "bar flies" moved up and took the bet.

"Well, der's da front door," pointed Joe. "Der's da back door. Den der's me, Joe Bedore. Dass t'ree."

Then looking around the room he yelled:

"Who in 'ell move dat spittoon?"

Barney Krom was one of the first drygoods merchants to buy a large store building. He had begun his trade as a peddler with two telescope suitcases which he carried from town to town, selling from door to door. When he had accumulated enough cash he bought a two-story building across the street from the Boynton Hotel. It was a half block long. The upper floor was rented as a dwelling flat. There was a two-story Chic Sale in the rear serving both floors. A long balcony or bridge reached from the second story door to the high backhouse. When Barney decided to build a bigger and better store, he hired my father to raise and move the old building to another location. While the structure was being raised, Barney didn't want to lose any of his trade, so he had a plank walk constructed from the street to the front door and had a big sign erected on the front of the store, reading "Business Going On As Usual" to keep the customers coming. As the building was on its way down the street some of the boys took down the sign at night and nailed it solidly on the Chic Sale restroom, which was still standing bold and straight on the back lot.

Nels Fisher's General Store

A fish market was opened by an enterprising Scandinavian who hung out a sign:

"Fresh Fish For Sale Here."

It was an odorous affair, for refrigeration was in its infancy and the ice boxes of the day did not keep the fish supply fresh for long Some of the neighbors became concerned and cooked up a plan to discourage the business. One of them went to the proprietor and said:

"Your sign is too long. Besides people know you are 'here'. So why don't you paint out the last word? "

The owner did this promptly to please a possible customer.

The next told him:

"Everyone knows that your fish must be fresh or you wouldn't be able to sell it. So I suggest that you paint out the word "fresh", to which he complied, to be a good neighbor.

The third conspirator came along and suggested:

"You don't need a sign, 'Fish For Sale'. We know you want to sell them. Furthermore, everyone can smell your damn fish two blocks away."

Pat Kelly's General Store

The favorite gathering place of the older men of town who were interested in liberal politics was Pat Kelly's general store at the main business corner. On the other three corners stood the Boynton Hotel, Barney Krom's drygoods emporium and Martin Lalley's elite saloon. Kelly's was a low, one-story frame building, built flush to the plank sidewalk with a false front rising two stories high to give it an appearance of height and importance.

The old building had had one coat of blue paint which now had become a grimy grey from the buffeting of the wind, snow and red road dust. Along the bottom of the front ran an eight inch ledge of pine plank where in summer roosted from ten to a dozen men, smoking their pipes and expectorating tobacco juice between the cracks of the sidewalk, talking politics or damning the "gov'ment".

The front windows were piled high with dust-covered goods consisting of horse collars, mackinaws, straw hats, a barrel churn and a variety of work clothing. Inside was a combination store which on one side held a long counter displaying men's and boy's wearing apparel of the more practical kind while on the other side was another long counter displaying cases of groceries, salt meat, tobacco, pipes, cheeses, a big red coffee grinder and candies and gum. Along in front of the grocery counter tin bins on the floor held bulk rice, oatmeal, cornmeal, brown and granulated sugar and an assortment of other food which was scooped out for weighing on the balance scale on the counter.

In the middle of the front end of the store were tables piled high with underwear, men's and boy's shirts, caps and jackets. At the far end were hung harness, pails, lanterns, small farm equipment and miscellaneous tools. The back wall was decorated with ancient calendars advertising patent medicines, staples and farm machinery. In the center of the establishment stood a big pot-bellied stove which heated the big room. On the floor around the stove stood several old straight back chairs. Flat wooden boxes filled with sawdust served as spittoons. Brown splotches around the boxes showed evidences of the many misses that occurred in exciting moments of arguments.

The whole store reeked of a mixture of odors, a combination of harness oil, kerosene, coffee, molasses and spices. The floor was of one time planed pine boards, now scarred deeply by caulked boots. The place had the appearance of never having been scrubbed. Pat's method of sweeping the floor was to scatter sawdust over it each morning and sweeping it with a big, red handled broom. The sweepings were pushed through the front door and out over the plank sidewalk and into the street.

Pat was a very genial, easy-going Irishman, who spoke in a soft twitter interspersed with gentle grunts. His once-black felt hat was greasy around the band and grey with the dust of the store. His faded green shirt was grimy around his tieless, open collar and his elbow length black sleeve-protectors were frayed at the cuffs. His grey wool trousers were baggy at the knees and gave the impression that Pat was ready to jump at any time. They had never had a cleaning or pressing. They could stand alone. His long, black finger nails at the end of his stumpy digits must have held a great assortment of food and candy and kerosene which he had handled over the years.

Kelly evidently had been a victim of small pox during his boyhood in Ireland. His face from the hairline to his neck was pitted with deep scars. His little, scraggly black mustache under his sharp pointed nose was continually wet.

Pat's sense of humor appeared in the signs which hung about the inside of the store—"Chewing Tobacco and Kerosene", "Molasses and Woolen Underwear", "Pickled Pigs Feet and Middlings", "Graham Crackers and Shoepacs." Over the tobacco case hung a sign: "Chew Copenhagen Snuff and Live Longer." Pat had struck out the word "Longer."

On the grocery side of the store old-fashioned candy cases with their rounded fronts held an assortment of gum drops, horehound bars, old licorice sticks, white and pink peppermint lozenges, sweet-wood for chewing, Yucatan gum in yellow wrappers, lemon drops, rock candy crystals in a jar, cheap chocolate mounds and barber pole stick candy. Here the young fry spent long minutes pricing the display before buying a penny's worth, while the patient Pat stood behind the counter, paper sack in hand.

The town and country trade bought a gallon of kerosene out of the barrel in the warehouse or a jug of molasses from the keg next to the kerosene. It was there that I learned what was meant by being "slower than molasses in January." In another case was a variety of packaged smoking and long bars of chewing tobacco and a few cheap stogies. A chewing tobacco cutter stood on the counter next to the coffee grinder.

Pat frequently cut off a plug of the sticky tobacco, then without wiping his stained hands scooped up a sackful of bulk candy. The most popular smoking and chewing tobacco was the brand called "Peerless." It was stout enough to peel the lining of an amateur's mouth and strong enough to send the new smoker into a dizzy drunk. It was the tobacco of he-men. To the town dudes, Pat sold many packages of "Bull Durham" and rice cigarette paper encased in pink wrappers as "makin's" for cigarettes which were just coming into use.

The large red coffee grinder on the end of the grocery counter was turned by a handle on a big wheel to pulverize "Arbuckles Bros." coffee from one pound paper containers. Pat sold "coffee essence" sticks made of chicory which he ground up with the coffee to give the brew more body and flavor. It "stretched" coffee served in boarding houses.

Along the floor in front of the counter were large covered tin bins containing loose sugar, rice, flour, cornmeal and other dry food, to be scooped out by Pat with a common scoop and weighed on the balance scales on the counter. Pat was liberal with his weights and measures and enjoyed a flourishing trade with the old town families, homesteaders and farmers.

On the other side of the store were piles of men's and boys' clothing and furnishings in disarray. Here customers searched for the garments they wanted until they found them, and took them to Pat to wrap up and charge. There were rubber boots, heavy work pants, plaid mackinaws, mittens, work gloves, long and short woolen socks in assorted colors, summer and winter caps, heavy red and white woolen underwear, sheep-skin lined jackets and bright plaid wool shirts.

Red woolen underwear was worn by miners and lumberjacks, some-times the year 'round. Some held that woolen underwear was cooler in summer than light cottons, because the wool absorbed perspiration when one was working. It was a common sight to see whole families gathered on their front porches facing the street on warm evenings, with the men wearing trousers and their red underwear tops. Every store had the reds for sale. For economy sake it came in two pieces—the drawers and shirt part. Whenever one of the pieces wore out it could be replaced without buying a whole suit. Pat Kelly sold quantities of the red under-wear.

Every evening the amateur politicians of the village gathered around Pat's hot stove in winter or sat on the ledge in front of the store in warm weather to smoke and chew and bandy about the "condition of the country"—how the Republicans were spending the nation into bankruptcy and how if the Democrats "got in" things "would be different". My fri-end, "Pigface" Conley was always the leader in the attack. He was well-read in Socialist literature, "The Appeal to Reason" magazine and other Eugene V. Debs publications. Pat and his brother, Mike Kelly, were middle-of-the-road politicians and attempted to keep the arguments on an even keel. Both old and young men joined the circle and we had a liberal education in progressive politics. Here many a town election slate was discussed and candidates chosen. Mike served as village president several terms although he was an avowed Democrat in that predominantly Republican town. Under the hanging kerosene lamp which cast a yellow light upon the group, arguments continued long into the night until "Pigface" stretched himself and broke up the meeting.

The cracker barrel with its ever-present cat ensconced was nearby and was patronized by us all. Farmers and homesteaders came in, bought a wedge of cheese, a can of sardines, a slice of sausage and a pound of crackers from the barrel. They sat on the counter, eating their lunch and listening to the debates before returning home for the night. Few of the men were drinkers but the discussions waxed hot and heavy. Insults flew back and forth and some of the participants went out in a huff when the heat was turned on too much, only to return to the fray the next evening.

"Soapbox" orators came to town periodically and spoke on street corners or in halls hired for the occasion by the so-called "radicals" of the town. These speeches were largely of a Socialistic nature and lent fuel to the debates in Pat's store. Sitting silently at first, I soaked up enough social and economic information and bias to start me off on my liberal attitudes which I continued to hold in later life. Local merchants, fearing the wrath of the mining officials, frequently got into arguments with the soapboxers, only to come off with a sound verbal shellacking for their pains.

Tom Lewis, the Oregon labor firebrand, was scheduled to speak on the main corner one evening. The members of the county Socialist party distributed handbills in the stores and tacked some on the telephone poles, announcing Tom's coming. The local priest was satisfied with the status quo, being a close buddy of the mine management. The afternoon before Lewis' appearance the clergyman made the rounds of the town and tore down all the handbills he could find. Late that night after the speech some of the "boys" pasted one of the bills on the front door of his church. While Lewis was orating on the soapbox, a large crowd gathered, most of them miners interested in better wages, safer mines and shorter hours. Two mine superintendents appeared and walked through the crowd to see who was in attendance. Soon the miners were seen leaving and disappearing from the scene—a sort of "economic pressure" to discourage radical thinking and action.

A farmer politician was a frequent participant in the arguments in Pat's store. Accustomed to early rising and early retiring, he found it difficult to keep awake when nine o'clock rolled around. His wide yawns and cavernous gaping helped to put some of the others to sleep.

One evening he remarked between yawns:

"Well, I killed a hog today. Guess how much he weighs."

"Two hundred pounds," guessed Pat.

"Guess again," the farmer replied, covering his gaping mouth.

"I'll say two hundred and fifty pounds," put in "Pigface".

"Guess again."

"I guess three hundred pounds," tried Mike Monahan, the budding attorney.

"Guess again," repeated the farmer.

"See here," said Pat, irritated, "we're not going to sit here all night

guessing the weight of your damn hog. How much did he weigh? "
"I really don't know," yawned the farmer, stretching himself. "I ain't
weighed him yet."

The Oldest Profession

My semi-pioneer town had its quota of lawless and border characters.
Most of them had drifted in from other parts, some attracted by the free
and easy life of that lumbering and mining region, some seeking new
opportunities that these new industries afforded, and some, no doubt,
came because "they had gotten in trouble with the authorities" in their
previous locations.

The southern Michigan pine had been cut off and the woods boys who
had worked and drunk and "loved" in the Saginaw and the Cadillac areas
moved into the virgin pine country of Iron County. As they moved north
they attracted women from the towns they left behind—women who were
not so "virgin." With them came gamblers, pimps and ex-saloon keepers
looking for new opportunities too where the lumberjack's hard-earned
money was spent like water for whiskey and "women."

The most notorious gambler and bawdyhouse operator was Dave
LeRoy. He had the appearance of the typical gambler—tall, spare,
aristocratic looking, a cold blue eye, a flowing black mustache and a
hard, coldblooded character.

LeRoy drove a tall bay horse called Napoleon hitched to a fancy
buggy with a swanky fringe on top. He ran a "house" in Iron River and
in Wisconsin just across the state line from Pentoga, Michigan. He also
operated a saloon and hotel in Stambaugh where he and his wife lived in
elegance.

Mrs. LeRoy was a pillar in the local church and knew nothing about
her husband's nefarious business at Pentoga. Whenever she visited
LeRoy at his house of prostitution in Pentoga all the "girls" would have
mysteriously disappeared. Once she asked her husband what all those
bedrooms were used for. Dave told her that they were used to put
drunken lumberjacks in to sober them up. When she asked what the piano
was used for, he replied:

"Oh, when the lumberjacks become happy they like to drum on it."

We often saw LeRoy and his "ladies" with their heavily rouged lips,
their artificially reddened cheeks and their ample bosoms riding about
town for an airing and to flaunt their wickedness before the respectable
citizens. My first recollection of the gambler was when I saw him pitch-
ing silver dollars at a line in the dust on the main street of Iron River
against a half-drunken farmer, Josh Coffin, who was principally noted
for the fact that he had never had a shave in his life.

When LeRoy was in Iron River and Stambaugh he was "like a lamb"
but in his Pentoga house he never allowed anyone to cross him. There
he became a "roaring, fighting, gouging lion."

He had a shortened left leg. On one occasion Herman Holmes, the
county sheriff, and his deputy, Irving Jackson, drove a team of mustangs

and a buckboard to Pentoga to arrest LeRoy for some offense. What the offense could have been in those lawless days is hard to conjecture. They apprehended him, placed him between them on the buckboard and headed for the county jail. On the way the half-broken horses became frightened at a bear crossing the road and ran away. In attempting to jump off, LeRoy caught his leg in a wheel and broke it. It was several days before the leg could be set and it was shorter than the other. Thereafter he wore a wide basswood sole under his shoe, which gave him an even more sinister appearance as he shuffled along the streets.

Frank Long had charge of the Pentoga "house" in LeRoy's absence. Dick Rogers, another hard character from "down below", frequented the place often and though he was married made use of its purpose. He gave Long a lot of trouble because of his drinking and fighting. Long told Rogers:

"We run a respectable house and if you can't behave yourself when you are here, I'll have Dave handle you."

One night Rogers was in bed with someone else's woman when LeRoy burst into the bedroom and yelled at Rogers:

"You dirty bastard, I can lick you on less ground than it takes you to stand on."

As LeRoy came toward the bed the woman reached under her pillow and gave Rogers a revolver hidden there in the expectation of trouble. Rogers shot from his lying position and pumped three slugs into LeRoy's body. LeRoy staggered out of the room to get his gun and fell dead near the dog house where he kept a pair of vicious dogs to protect his place from raids of the law.

The next morning the body was loaded into a baggage car and taken to Stambaugh. There it was loaded onto a sleigh and covered with a blanket, to be taken to the undertaker's. On the way the driver stopped before a saloon to go in to get a hot whiskey sling. A crowd gathered around the sleigh to have a look at the notorious gambler and bawdy house operator. Willard Goodhall, a timid little barber with pince-nez glasses tied to his ear with a black ribbon, threw back the blanket, viewed the frozen corpse and remarked so the crowd of onlookers could plainly hear:

"That's the best I've ever seen you look, you dirty S.O.B. !"

Dick Rogers was arrested and had a hearing before Circuit Judge Goodland. The judge released the gunman on his own recognizance and stated that he would be back later at the Iron County courthouse and clear up the case. Dick was never tried for the shooting. Local citizens were heard to remark that Dick should have received a bounty for his act. There was little mourning on the part of the local people and the only persons who attended the burial were Frank Long and five of LeRoy's "ladies" in black dresses and thick black mourning veils.

There were other "houses" on back streets with their red doors and red window curtains to advertise the profession. As the pine thinned out and the lumberjacks moved to the great stands of timber in Minnesota, Washington and Oregon, the demand for camp followers lessened. The town filled up with families and laws became stricter. Bawdy houses were resticted and then outlawed.

A few of the older "ladies" who had passed their prime of physical attractiveness continued to operate on their own, appealing to the less fastidious and the rougher element which remained behind. One such was old "Kate Pie", who had more or less "grown up with the town" and lived in an old log cabin on the edge of town. She was known for her profession by every man and woman in the community and was frequently the butt of ribald and coarse jokes and ridicule from the youngsters when she appeared on the streets. She had her "sweethearts" who lived with her for a period of a few days to a few weeks, to be succeeded by others when their money ran out. Although she was "one of the cheapest", Mike Kane, the old limping lumberjack, who had lived with her for two weeks, was heard to remark:

"I can say this for Kate. She was always true to me."

"Boxcar Mary" was a big, powerful female of doubtful reputation. She had her succession of private consorts whom she bounced out when their money gave out or when she became tired of them. She later married little Billy Willlams, half her size. The "marriage" lasted for several months. Billy was the "log jammer" at the Buckeye mill where he was employed to roll the great decks of saw logs into the river. One day Billy missed his footing while using his canthook at the bottom of the deck and a big maple log rolled over him and flattened him out. His "widow" went into deep mourning. She wore a heavy black veil which hung down to her waist and was a sad picture of despair when she appeared on the streets in her long black dress. Three days after the funeral she married another lumberjack of the same size.

Every "lady" had her nickname hung on her by her patrons. There was "Buckskin Lottie", the "wife" of Dick Rogers, who shot Dave LeRoy; "Dirty Dott" from Peshtigo, Wisconsin; "Goldtooth Sharkey" who had seen her best days on the riverfront in Saginaw; "Kate Pie", our own local product; "Liverlip Lil", from Escanaba; "Lumberjack May" from Minneapolis and "Broncho-the-One-Eye" from Chicago, who lost her right eye in a brawl with "Liverlip Lil" over the patronage of a young lumberjack with a big poke.

I Remember When--

Andy J. Boynton was a Civil War veteran who had lost his left arm from a sniper's bullet near Huntsville, Alabama. For three years after the War he prospected for gold in Montana. It was alleged that he had won $ 500.00 gambling in the army and with this money he bought a farm in Wisconsin. A farmer neighbor on seeing him for the first time scoffed:

"What can a one-armed S.O.B. do clearing a farm? "

Andy said:

"I'll show you," and promptly threw the farmer back over his own fence.

Andy did not enjoy grubbing land too much. He heard about a new territory opening up where iron ore had been discovered and big timber operations were under way. He would see if there was greater opportunity in this new country for an ambitious young man. He took the train to the little hamlet of Stager. There shouldering his pack of worldly goods he walked over the Indian trail to Iron River, then just a cluster of small log cabins in the valley, arriving there in 1881.

New people were streaming in to cut the timber and dig the rich ore. The town would grow and Andy with it. He bought a lot on the main cross roads in the town and built the first hotel in the district. No sawmills had yet been erected, so Andy had lumber hauled in from Florence, Wisconsin, thirty-five miles distant. It took six horses and a strong wagon three days to haul 1500 feet of lumber over the forest road.

It was a combination hotel and saloon, with handy access from the lobby to the barroom. A wide pine plank served as the first bar. Both hotel and saloon did a thriving business. A few years later the hotel burned to the ground. Andy had carried no insurance. In fact, with no fire protection in the village, insurance was prohibitive. He went deeply into debt to build a new structure of forty-five rooms which stood as an example of Upper Peninsula architecture—an oblong, two-story building with two covered porches. It was from the second story balcony that patriotic speeches were made on the Fourth of July.

Andy was an enthusiastic fisherman. His favorite fishing spot was at Uno dam on the Iron River near the Chicago & Northwestern Railroad tracks. Carrying his long cane pole in his only hand and his creel with worms and lunch over his shoulder, he would hail the morning freight, board the caboose and go. When the freight came back on its return trip, the engineer knew where he could find Andy and tooted his whistle before getting there. He always found Andy standing beside the track ready with his catch. Andy's fish stories were classics and no one dared to dispute his tales of big catches. At one time I saw him fill his empty creel with marsh grass and place his only fish on top of the grass. When anyone asked him how many fish he had caught he let him peek through the hole in the creel and said:

"A whole basketful, damn it. See, they're all the same size."

No one openly disputed his claim but it was generally an accepted fact that where fish were concerned the partition between Andy's memory and imagination had completely broken down.

Speckled trout fishing was usually best in the late spring when rivers were at flood and the fish could not get up over the dams to spawn. The trout would crowd below the dams in such numbers that the bottom of the stream was black with them. One spring Andy took some of his traveling salesmen guests for a day's fishing at Burnt Dam on the Brule River. As they were loading the buckboard with their gear, he threw in a five-tined manure fork and tied it under the seat.

"What is that fork for, Andy?" asked one of the men.

"Oh, that's to pitch some hay to the horses when we get to the river," replied Andy with a twinkle in his eyes.

On reaching Burnt Dam he sent the others down stream while he stayed at the dam on the pretext of feeding the horses and preparing the noon lunch. When the fishermen were out of sight Andy used his manure fork to spear a basketful of trout from the pool below the dam. He cleaned and fried the fish, then called the men to lunch. All the fishermen came back with empty creels. Amazed at the big panful of crisp brown fried trout, they asked him what he used for bait.

"Hell," said Andy, "what the devil do you think I used? Just worms, the same as you did."

Andy was proud of his prowess with a rifle. He took two women guests to his farm beyond the James mine to hunt deer and on the way bragged what a crack shot he was. As they walked around the clearing they sighted a big buck standing broadside to them. He threw up his gun and called to the women:

"Watch him fall."

It was a clean miss. The buck flagged his white tail and leaped off into the woods.

Andy was a staunch Republican and whenever anyone went wrong, he remarked:

"Well, he must be a Democrat!"

Andy was very fond of his nephew, Jess Waite, the son of Mansville B. Waite, a sheriff for many terms. Jess stayed with the Boyntons each summer at the hotel. Andy would never give Jess money but always schemed some way by which he could earn it. Andy had a pony which belonged to his late son. In order to give Jess the impression that he was earning money, Andy would let the pony out of the barn and into the pasture. Then he would call Jess and say:

"That damned pony got out again. Go get him back into the barn."

This happened every day and Andy gave Jess a quarter to round up the pony each time.

After Andy retired from the hotel business and turned it over to his son, Phil, he lived in a home near the Catholic parsonage near the railroad tracks. Here he spent his leisure time raising flowers and vegetables in his little garden. The loss of his left arm was no handicap in handling garden tools. But when the freight whistle blew for its trip north, Andy dropped his hoe and grabbed his cane pole and creel, ran down to the tracks to flag the train. The train crew knew him well and always stopped to pick him up. He never had to pay a fare for his ride to Uno Dam. When he heard the train whistle for the return journey, he walked to the tracks and went aboard again.

A. J. died on November 15, 1923, a typical pioneer, sportsman and hotel man of his day.

Solberg was the engineer at the first waterworks of the town. The pumping station was erected in a big swamp at the foot of Stambaugh hill, through which ran a cold, clear stream of water. The thick brush of the swamp was a sure place to snare or shoot rabbits.

The Solbergs and a French-Canadian homesteader living near the mill town of Atkinson each bought a milch cow at Florence, Wisconsin, and walked them home through the woods to Iron River, a distance of thirty-five miles. These were the first cows in the district. The homesteader built a small log barn for his critter and turned her out loose in the woods to find her own forage. Solberg kept his cow in a shed back of his house in town. He made arrangements with Mrs. Behnan to milk the cow for half the milk. A few weeks later the homesteader found his cow's hide stretched over a log in the woods. Some deer hunter evidently preferred beef to a steady diet of venison. A few days later the Solberg cow was missing. A search was made of the fields and woods in the vicinity, without success. A lumberjack living near Atkinson reported seeing a cow near the homesteader's place. It was the first cow he had seen in that country. The Solbergs investigated and located the cow. The homesteader claimed she was his original cow. Mrs. Behnan was taken out and identified the cow as the one she had been milking for the Solbergs, who led the animal back home. The two families were never on speaking terms thereafter.

Frank Camins was one of our local blacksmiths and later a beer peddler. His beer vault was an underground root cellar dug into a bank beside the Chicago & Northwestern Railroad spur at the east end of Main street. Over the cellar he had erected an icehouse to keep the cellar cool for his beverage kegs. Here he rolled the big kegs of Schlitz and Blatz from Milwaukee out of the iced boxcars down a chute into the vault. Frank's giant, steel-grey Percheron pulled the heavy loads of beer kegs and chunks of ice to the saloons every morning and afternoon.

One hot and muggy summer's Saturday morning while Frank was maneuvering his clumsy horse around a box car to take on a load, three high school boys, Bob Solberg, Cliff Haggerty and Roy Morrison, came around, bent on some vacation mischief. The heavy door of the vault stood open. The big padlock hung on the door hasp. Cold air was coming out through the opening. It looked inviting on that hot morning. The boys decided to duck into the vault and get a few bottles of cool beer. The cellar was pitch-dark. The only light Frank used was a wax candle which was stuck in a crack. Here, thought the boys, would be a cool, pleasant place to hide, drink beer and await Frank's return trip of the afternoon to duck out again.

Quietly as mice the boys hid behind the beer kegs. Frank loaded up his wagon, closed the heavy door, locked it and drove off. The boys began to search their pockets for matches to light the candle but found none. Dressed in light summer clothes, they began to feel the damp, chill air creeping over them. To keep warm they jumped up and down. They hugged each other and rubbed themselves. The cold was beginning to stiffen their muscles. It was hard to move around. On all sides was the clammy wall. The wet floor chilled their feet.

The long afternoon passed but no signs of Frank and his Percheron. Suddenly they remembered that Frank did not peddle beer on Saturday afternoons. They became panicky but no release appeared and none was expected. Saturday night passed. They lay down on the damp, cold marsh hay which was used for insulation in the vault. But no sleep came, except nightmarish fits.

Sunday morning dawned bright and sunny but inside the vault all was black and cold. The boys recalled all the wicked things they had ever done and prayed aloud for forgiveness. Suppose Frank had decided never

to return? Perhaps he had work to do at his blacksmith shop which
would delay him longer.

Sunday passed. Then Sunday night. At 7:00 o'clock on Monday morning there was a rattle at the heavy door. They heard a key turned in the
big lock. A bolt was slammed back and the light of day flooded into the
arctic cavern. Frank's short, stocky frame came toward them. Blinded
by the bright light the boys decided to made a dash for the opening as
soon as the door swung open. But they were so stiff from the cold and
dampness that they stumbled and fell at Frank's feet. The beer peddler
picked up a board and belabored the three. The beating did not hurt their
numbed bodies but rather warmed them up and frightened the boys the
more.

Stiffly they set their legs in motion and started for home. When they
told their separate stories to their parents they received another sound
thrashing. Someone asked them later how they liked the bottled beer.
Bob Solberg replied:

"We were scared so badly when that door slammed shut that we didn't
think of beer."

Gus Ruus, who later operated a grocery store of his own, worked as
a delivery boy at Nels Fisher's store. Nels sent him to Beechwood to
collect a long past due grocery bill from a Finnish homesteader. When
he knocked on the door of the humble log house the housewife appeared
and asked Gus his mission. She said that her husband was out working
in the woods but would soon appear and pay the account. A little girl lay
sick on a cot in the room. After sitting for an hour or more, Gus asked
the mother what was wrong with the child. Her mother said casually
that she had diphteria. Gus grabbed his cap and ran out of the house
without closing the door. As he ran he pulled a package of Peerless out
of his pocket, stuffed a handful into his mouth and swallowed the juice to
kill the germs. The cure was worse than the disease, he found, for soon
he was retching his insides out along the road. The bill was never collected. Nels Fisher never learned why.

The Sharpened Tongue

Jerry Mahoney, a lumberjack, frequently got into trouble because of
his sharp and biting tongue. Sober, he was a very mild person, minding
his own affairs and doing a good day's work on the job. But, lubricated
with liquor, his tongue ran on and on, abusing everyone in sight. Even as
he staggered along the sidewalk with no one near him his tongue rattled
on against imagined opposition.

Jim Summers, the protector of the homesteaders in the Canal Company steal, had a bad reputation in the town which he had been invited
by a posse to leave. Jerry evidently knew something about Jim's trouble
and reputation and in his cups would publicly tell the world about it.
Jim warned Jerry to keep his information and abuse to himself. Late
one afternoon Jerry was sitting in the back room of a saloon belaboring
Summers with his vile tongue. Jim stood it as long as he could, then said

to Jerry:

"If you don't stop abusing me, Jerry, I'll shoot that damn tongue out of your mouth."

Jerry kept on. Jim went to the Piper House where he kept his rifle and came back to get Jerry, who was still keeping up his tirade in the back room. Jim pointed his gun through a crack in the partition and pulled the trigger. The bullet pierced Jerry's right cheek and came out of his left cheek, taking with it several of Jerry's teeth and a good slice of his tongue. That silenced Jerry until the wound healed. Jim left town. It was difficult for Jerry to overcome a lifelong habit and before long liquor again loosened the brakes on his tongue. However, it was only necessary to yell at Jerry: "I'll shoot your damn tongue out" to silence him.

Jerry got into a fight with Bill Noske, the lumberjack with a crooked nose and crippled little finger on his right hand. Bill would not listen to Jerry's tongue lashing any longer and knocked him down repeatedly. Finally, tired of the one-sided battle, Bill asked Jerry, lying on the ground with his nose bleeding:

"Do you want some more?"

"No," mumbled Jerry, looking up at Bill's cocked fists above him. "I ain't no hog!"

Mike Mahaney was foreman at the Menominee River Lumber Company camp on the Brule River where I spent my two weeks' Christmas vacation as a "cookee". In the off season Mike was the barkeeper at Kate Piper's saloon. He was a jolly six-foot-four giant, good natured but tough when the occasion required. Jerry Mahoney was a short five-foot-eight. In the presence of a crowd of lumberjacks in the saloon Jerry remarked in a loud voice that he and Mike were brothers.

"Mike, aren't we brothers?"

"Sure, Jerry," replied Mike. "Sure we're brothers. In fact we're twins. I was born first and you were the afterbirth."

Fred Hanold was a saloon keeper and a shoe repair man in Stambaugh. He had two fine dachshunds—father and son—and Fred was very fond of them. A whiskey salesman remarked to him:

"Those are a fine pair of dogs you have there, Fred."

"Yah," answered Fred. "You know der'se somding funny about dose togs. De oldes' von iss de junges' von."

"Ach," interruped his wife from behind the bar. "Fritz iss crazy. Der bigges' von iss der smalles' von."

My father and Fred were close friends and neighbors while we lived in Stambaugh. In fact, Fred was one of the three godfathers at my christening and gave me the name of Frederick. When my parents became interested in buying the boarding house in Iron River and moving the family there, my father approached Fred for a loan of $350.00 as down payment on the property. Fred had become rather prosperous with his tavern and shoe repair business. However, Fred refused to make the loan.

"But, Fred," my father reminded him, "who loaned you money to set you up in the saloon business?"

"You did, Louie."

"And who was it who helped you when your daughter was in the hospital and you had to have money for an operation? "

"Dot vass you, all right, Louie."

"Who was it who pulled your son Charlie out of the river when he was drowning? "

"Yah, I guess dot vass you, all right."

"Then, Fred, why don't you loan me the $350.00? "

"Dot's all true, Louie. But vot haff you done for me lately? "

"Tom Guts", a local product who lived in our neighborhood, spent considerable time in federal and state prisons for burglary and holdups. He was an expert at opening safes. He was in Schaefer Brothers stationery store when the owner was locking up his safe and closing the place for the night. Tom watched the procedure and said to one of the brothers:

"What are you locking up that bunch of junk for? Anybody could open it with a hairpin. Let me show you."

With a few flips of the combination knob he had the safe open.

Tom broke into a Greek restaurant and stole a bagful of silverware and took it to Shook's saloon and offered it for sale for $5.00. He at times posed as enforcement officer during state prohibition days and collected blackmail money from the Italian bootleggers. He acquired a considerable knowledge of medical terms and posed as a doctor. He visited doctors in various parts of the country and got on friendely terms with them. He proceeded to "case" the "joints", then broke in and robbed the safe and office, taking both surgical instruments and narcotics which he both used and sold at high prices.

Mike Mahaney finally decided to get married to one of the waitresses at the Piper House. He asked Kate and Jim Piper to "stand up" for them. Mike hired a double rig from Bill Moss' livery stable and the four drove over to the Catholic parsonage to have Father Lenhart perform the ceremony. When that part of the ritual came where the groom was to place the wedding ring on the bride's finger, Father Lenhart asked Mike for the gold band.

"Ring, Father? Ring? Do I have to have a ring? " asked Mike.

"Of course you are supposed to have a wedding ring," replied the priest. "I'll loan you the 'Bishop's ring' until you can get one of your own."

After the ceremony Father Lenhart admonished Mike to go down town to a jewelry store immediately for the ring. Mike and Jim Piper got into the buggy and left the bride and Kate to walk back to the Piper House alone. Mike and Jim never reached the jewelry store. The Boynton saloon was the first place they stopped in. Then they made the rounds of all the drinking establishments in celebration of the marriage. Three hours later Mike and Jim staggered into the Piper House without the ring but with a terrific load.

Tommy Windsor drove a horse and buggy for Captain Wall at the mine. He had never attended a baseball game in his life. One Sunday he appeared on the street dressed in his best suit and a clean collar and tie.

Captain Wall asked him where he was going.

"To Weimer Field,"" responded Tommy. "I'm going to see the Boston Bloomer Girls play our town team in a baseball match."

Tommy was standing in the crowd cheering lustily for the girls when Father Lenhart slapped him on the back and asked:

"You God damn old woman, what are you doing here?"

"The same as you are, Father," answered Tommy. "I'm like you. This is my only chance to see real girls in action."

Fred Woempner, the butcher, staggered down the street on his way home, supporting himself by placing his hands against fences and buildings along the sidewalk. When he came to the end of the street where there were no more buildings to support him, he held out his hands and cried:

"More houses! More houses!"

Barney Burns inherited $45,000.00 from his father's estate and spent it all on booze over a period of two years. One cold winter's day he went into a saloon and the barkeeper noticed a white spot on Barney's nose.

"Barney," he called. "Your nose is frosted. It's all white at the end."

"Bee Jeesus,"" said Barney trying to look down at his frozen proboscis, "here I've run $45,000.00 worth of alcohol through this damn nose of mine and still she freezes!"

"Uncle" Alt, said to have been of Royal Dutch birth, was perpetually under the influence of liquor. He worked as a chore boy at Kate Piper's hotel. Here he peeled potatoes, scrubbed floors and fed Kate's big flock of Barred rocks. Kate treated him like a close relative. If a drunken stupor overtook him when he was down town he would grope his way to Bob Pelo's undertaking establishment and crawl into a "rough box" where he slept it off. Kate always knew where to find her chore boy.

In 1889 Bert Blessingham and his wife owned a home near Gus Ruus' grocery store. They decided to separate for a while and Bert took a job at a lumber camp in Wisconsin. He was gone over a year when a copy of the Iron River weekly paper was sent him. In it he read that his wife had a new baby. Bert took the next train to Iron River. He stopped at Billy Sullivan's saloon and borrowed a revolver. On entering his home he found the man with whom his wife had been consorting and poured five shots into him. The victim was not quite dead, so Bert pounded his head on the floor until there was no sign of life in the man.

Paul Minckler, the mill and camp operator, was a hard driver of his employees. He hired Herman Holmes, a stocky young lumberjack, to work at his camp at $1.25 a day with the understanding that he would stay at the job until the work was finished. Herman, who was destined to become one of the biggest road building contractors in the United States, could not stand having Paul "ride" him all the time. He called at Paul's town office and asked for his pay. Paul wrote out the check and handed it to Herman, who looked at it and found that he was being paid at the rate of $1.00 a day. He demanded his $1.25 a day rate.

"You'll take $1.00 a day," countered Paul, "or I'll give you a damn good beating."

Herman was a rugged, blocky individual. He reached over the desk and grabbed Paul by the collar. He dragged him out into the street and gave him the worst trimming he had ever had in his life. He nearly killed him. It took Darius, the big negro teamster, and two other men to pull them apart and rescue Paul.

Minckler owned one of the largest cattle and hog farms in the Upper Peninsula. The land was cleared of its hardwoods to make charcoal for the furnace smelting the first ore at the bottom of Minckler Hill. He had a horsepower churn to make butter. It was run by a tread mill which was turned by tying a big white stallion to the ramp and his weight turned the wheel and churn. Paul's farm manager was a religious man who carried his Bible to church and taught a Sunday School class of boys. The two men finally had an argument over wages. In the heat of the word battle Paul grabbed a pump handle and struck his manager over the head. The Sunday School teacher said a short prayer and proceeded to give Paul his second worst licking in his life.

Henry Yakle was the eldest son of a large German family which owned a small farm across the river. While his father was a hard taskmaster, Henry was notorious for his laziness. One early July day the father told Henry that the next day Henry would have to cut a certain field of hay with a scythe. That evening Henry purposely cut the palm of his right hand with a piece of rusty tin so he would have an excuse for not working. The next morning his hand was puffed up twice its natural size. Blood poisoning set in and he nearly lost his arm. Telling us about it later, Henry confessed that he had intended merely to scratch his hand but that the tin was sharper than he thought.

Billy Winters lived in Bates township and came in to town for his periodic sprees. He was a stout fighter and was the only man whom I ever saw pull a knife on an opponent. One day he went from saloon to saloon until he had such a load that he staggered along with widespread feet. As he tried to enter "Long" Hanson's saloon his hands fumbled uncertainly for the door latch just as another drunk fell headlong through the opening and onto the plank walk outside. Billy looked at him in disdain and said alcoholically:

"Good, good, lay there you drunken bum, if you don't know better than to drink!"

Every community had its neighborhood bully and my town was no exception. He lived across the alley back of our house and he gave me many beatings. He was several years older than I and considerably bigger. Whenever his younger brothers got into a quarrel with my younger brothers, he fought their battles for them. We hated him thoroughly and feared his beatings. Whenever his brothers ganged up on us his whole family entered the fray. They were too many and too big for us, so we had to endure occasional beatings at the hands of the bully.

My younger brother Art and the bully's younger brother got into a kid's argument and came out about even in their fisticuffs, when the bully appeared and knocked Art unconscious. As an older brother it was my duty to take up the argument from there. At that time I was playing football in high school and was a pretty husky kid of 150 pounds. I met the bully on the street the next morning on my way to school and asked him not to repeat the performance but to let the kids fight their own battles. He said that he would do the same thing to me and made a lunge at me. My right and left fists met his face as he came in. He got me down under him because of his greater weight but I managed to get a strangle hold around his neck. I held on and we were at an impasse. We finally let go and got up. The next day I had to make a deposit at the bank where he was a teller. He was the only one in the bank and had to accept my money. He sat sideways to the window but I noted that his left eye was closed and his upper lip had a deep cut.

The next evening he and his whole family with the exception of his father came to my home demanding that I come out and fight them "like a man." Caution seemed the better part of valor, so our meeting was postponed. He alibied that I was in football condition but that he would go into training and take me on. For two weeks thereafter we saw him take long walks over the hills after banking hours, but the battle never took place. He was the brother of "Tom Guts" mentioned in this saga.

Danny Kane and Billy Bone were inseparable woods and drive pals. Danny was short, stocky and handsome. Billy was tall, skinny and boney. Billy was an artist of abuse and could insult with ease. He had the fighting ability to back it up. One fall they came to town from Danny's shack on the Brule River and entered Boynton's saloon. Their life in the woods was getting monotonous. They craved excitement. A good crowd was gathered at the bar and the tables. Billy invited everybody to the bar for a drink. Within half a minute Danny and Billy were surrounded by the thirsty. When they had had several rounds apiece, Danny whispered to Billy:

"Let's start something. You do the insulting and I'll do the fighting."

Looking down at Danny's five foot five frame, Billy said contemptuously:

"Why you sawed-off, chisel-faced runt, I kin insult enough in five minutes to keep you fightin' for two weeks."

Billy, the Blacksmith, and Hay, the Baker

Billy Windsor was a blacksmith. He shod oxen and horses, repaired wagons and buggies and helped run town politics as well. He was a wiry little fellow but he was not afraid of anyone, no matter how big and tough they came. He was never known to fight but his clever tongue and his picturesque language slayed many antagonists.

He was a member of the school board when a discussion arose to replace the old wooden firetrap which had served as a school for many years. Billy was there and spoke his piece:

"Huh, build a school! Build a jail and lock 'em up! The kids are getting too damn smart now!"

His daughter, Pearl, was the first Iron River high school product to graduate from the University of Michigan. Later she taught in our high

Home Talent in the Town Hall

school and became its principal. When a new superintendent of schools
was sought Pearl was chosen and served successfully for many years,
one of the few women superintendents in the United States. She promoted
the building of several schools long after her father had served on the
board.

Another daughter of Billy's, Myrtle, is a professor in one of Michigan's normal colleges. His eldest son, Clifford, graduated from the
U. S. Naval Academy at Annapolis and rose to the heights in the Navy.

Father Lenhart, the Catholic priest, was the authority for the story
of Billy's experience with skunks. Billy was having trouble with a family
of shunks which had taken up residence under his house. The house was
built on high cedar posts and offered a refuge for stray animals chased
by dogs. Billy asked someone how he might get rid of the skunks. He
was advised to bait a muskrat trap with a chicken head, tie it to a long
pole and push it under the house.

"Isn't that damn risky?" asked Billy.

"No," he was assured. "When you find a skunk in the trap, just pull
out the pole and carry the critter down to the river and drown him. It's
simple."

So Billy took the advice with some reservations. The next morning
he looked under the house. Sure enough, there was a big black and white
polecat waving his long plumed tail and trying to get out of the trap.
Gingerly Billy pulled him out, according to his instructions, and carried
him at the end of the extended pole down the alley toward the Buckeye
mill pond to drown him. On the way he passed the back of the Catholic
Church and encountered Father Lenhart.

"What are you going to do with that smelly skunk, Billy? Eat him?"
asked the Reverend Father with a gleam in his eye.

"Indeed, Father, I'm not going to eat him," shot back Billy. "I'm
going to take him down to the river and make holy water!"

Bill Poquette was the sexton at the Stambaugh cemetery. He could
neither read nor write. As a consequence he got his records terribly
mixed and frequently buried people in the wrong lots. A town councilman
asked him:

"How many people do you have buried in the cemetery?"

Bill replied: "Every damn one!"

Bill had trouble with stray cows and horses which broke down the
fences around the cemetery to eat the luscious grass there. Sven Nielson came around that way looking for his cow one morning and encountered Bill. Bill knew Sven's cow too well. Shaking his spade at Sven,
Bill yelled:

"You keep your damn cow to home. You ain't no man at all. Many's
the time I got out of my grave to chase her away!"

Hay Davison, a Scotch immigrant, operated a small bakery for forty
or more years next to our boarding house. A crack trout fisherman,
every afternoon when his work was done he would be seen going down
the street with a long cane pole to the river below the Buckeye mill to
fish the quarter mile stretch to the C. &N. W. R. R. depot. He never
came back empty-handed, to the puzzlement of the local fisherman, who

claimed that Hay could catch fish on dry land.

Hay went into John Airey's grocery and meat market and asked John: "John, how much are eggs today?"

"Well, Hay, today the good ones are twenty cents a dozen and the cracked ones are fourteen cents," replied John, opening up a paper bag.

"Crack me up three dozen of the good ones," ordered Hay.

Iron River's contribution to the entertainment world was Frank Davis, the son of Hay. As a boy and young man Frank worked in his father's shop mornings and delivered baked goods in the afternoon. But his heart wasn't in his work. Hay's chief complaint was that Frankie never took his work seriously and spent most of his time putting on comedy acts in the shop and along his route. Frank practiced his acts whenever and wherever he was not kneading dough or selling bread. The boys would gather on the plank sidewalks or in the alley back of the bake shop to see Frank do his "take-offs" of Jewish and Irish and Scotch characters. He would don an over-sized brown derby which drooped over his ears and assume the characteristic attitude of a Yiddish peddler, with his hands outthrust and his chin stuck out. Even Io Oshinsky, the son of the Jewish proprietor of the big bargain store, admitted it was a good imitation.

Frank broke into vaudeville one day when a one-night stand, hicktown vaudeville team needed a fill-in. He was an immediate hit with the company. Brushing the flour dust off his clothing and bidding goodbye to his over-worked dad and weeping mother, he joined the cast on the road.

As Frank Davis, he returned to town in 1907 as a partner of Nate Cole in the vaudeville team of Cole and Davis. They performed in town halls and livery barn theatres in the small villages and had trouble meeting expenses. Thereafter Frank went into burlesque and rapidly rose through vaudeville to musical comedy and the legitimate stage. The early movies of Hollywood soon called him and there he wrote scenarios and directed, acted in and produced film shorts. Some of the pictures in which he had a hand were Lord Jeff, The Devil Was A Sissy, Petticoat Fever and Saturday Wives. He gained experience along the way by his association with Ziegfeld, Garrick, Schubert, Claws and Erlanger and other big producers. He did a stint on the RKO Orpheum circuit when vaudeville was still in favor.

Frank's keen wit and adaptable personality enabled him to vault the sharp transition between each succeeding popular entertainment medium until he landed on his feet in radio and did well enough to become a radio production advisor.

Frank, the son of Hay, the town baker, is another boy from the town "which was so far away from anywhere that it would never amount to anything." Another home town boy surmounted the drab surroundings of a small pioneer town and make his mark in the broad world.

The Birch Bark Will

Large families were the rule rather than the exception in that era and place. While a few individuals were busy amassing fortunes from the big pine and the red ore, the majority, despite the struggle for food,

clothing and shelter, produced large numbers of offspring. As one wag
stated, the rich got richer and the poor got children. Families of ten
and twelve children were common. Our family of fourteen was exceeded
only by the Baker family who lived in the Spring Valley region and had
fifteen. Nor were children considered a handicap in that day, for as they
grew they were enlisted in the work on the farms, in the small towns
and on the homesteads. Every child had his part of the labor required
in the family circle, each according to his size and energy.

The Pete Charbeneau family was typical of the French-Canadians
who moved into the Upper Peninsula to help get out the pine. Nine
children had '"blessed" the couple and another was on the way. Every
child was blackhaired and swarthy and spoke with a French patois dialect—half English and half French-Canadian. They attended the little
rural school a few terms, then dropped out to find work or to stay at
home. Every Sunday morning would find the brood at mass. The original log shack had been added to with frame lean-tos, as two or three
additional children were born until it was a patchwork of shed attached
in several directions to the log house. Other sheds were strung about
the half acre to serve as cow and chicken shelters. An accumulation
of old sleighs, decrepit wagons, discarded cooking utensils and other
trash cluttered the premises. Pete had "accumulitis" and gathered odds
and ends of castoffs but never threw anything away.

Charbeneau, short, black and rugged, worked in the lumber camps
in winter and cut and sold stove wood in the summer and fall. Life was
always precarious for the big family. If the father could be headed off
after the lumber camps closed and before he reached the nearest saloon
with his winter's pay check, the wife and children lived well for a time.

It was in the middle of a hard winter when Dr. Robert Sturgeon, the
lone physician of the town, was called by a neighbor of Charbeneau's
to attend a childbirth in the little shack. When his big bay mare drew
him in the cutter to the place, a midwife was already on hand. The good
doctor found Mrs. Charbeneau in serious child labor. She was making
little progress and was in great pain and fear. She lay on a low, handmade bed in a little bedroom. The blankets were torn and filthy. Dim
light entered the room through a small window, one pane of which had
been broken and was now stuffed with an old discarded coat. There was
a smell of "painkiller" in the room. Frightened, black-eyed children
peered from out the gloomy lean-to sheds. The little, worn-out woman
writhed as the spasms struck her. Dr. Sturgeon ordered the midwife
to set a kettle of water on the kitchen stove to boil and prepared for the
delivery, which could not be far off.

Turning her thin face to the doctor, the mother cried:

"Oh, Doc, I know I won't live through this. I've had nine kids but I
never had such a hard time. I don't know what will happen to this baby
if I die. Pete is always away in the woods and we don't have enough to
live on."

"Don't you worry, Lizzie," replied the doctor. "I have delivered
babies for many years and I know that you will live through this one.
Why, the Garseaus have fourteen children and they are expecting another one next month."

"Doc, Doc," she said, wrenching with pain. "If I don't live will you take care of my baby? Will you see that he has enough to eat and clothes to wear and a chance to go to school? Will you?"

"Sure, sure. I promise," said the little physician, kindly.

"But Doc, I want to be sure my baby is taken care of when I die. Will you write it out if I give you the baby?"

To comfort her, the doctor sought a piece of paper on which to write the agreement. He looked around the mean little hovel and finally found a piece of white birchbark in the woodbox. Taking it to the kitchen table he wrote:

"I, Dr. Robert Sturgeon, physician to Mrs. Pete Charbeneau at the birth of her tenth child, agree in the event of Mrs. Charbeneau's death in child birth or from the after-effects therefrom, promise to care for the child, feed and clothe it and send it to school until it reaches the age of sixteen.

Signed:
Dr. Robert Sturgeon"

He then called Mrs. Dominic Naretti, the midwife, to place her "X" at the bottom of the birchbark agreement as witness.

When he read the agreement to Mrs. Charbeneau, the woman smiled and relaxed on her bed, saying in a tired voice:

"Now, Doc, I can die in peace. You are so good to me and my baby."

A half hour later the first cry of the baby was heard in the little home—a big, husky boy.

The doctor unblanketed his restless mare and set off in the dark night for home and a well-earned sleep. As he drove down the snow filled street he saw the kerosene light in Pat Kelly's store still blazing. He stopped in and saw a dozen of the town's politicians still arguing over the recent election. Opening his fur coat and hanging his wet mittens near the hot stove, Dr. Sturgeon showed Pat the birchbark agreement.

"I have it here to register with the county clerk tomorrow."

When he had read the strange instrument, Pat hitched up his baggy pants and said:

"I'll be damned. I never in all me born days saw such a thing. I'd like to sign it too."

Then Pat read the agreement to the whole group.

"Boys," sniffed Pat, "don't you want to help th' Doc?"

"Sure, be gorrie, we'll sign it," said "Pigface" Conley, wiping his dripping grey mustache.

Within a few minutes a dozen new "godfathers" affixed their signatures to the birchbark scroll.

Mrs. Charbeneau lived to have three more babies. Years after Dr. Sturgeon rummaged through his papers and found the "will" which he had neglected to register at the county seat. The baby boy who was born on that stormy night in January lived and followed his parents' example of producing another big French-Canadian family. The baby outlived the kind old family doctor.

THE ABSENTEES

The Songbird Of The North

Carrie Jacobs Bond

THE ABSENTEES

The Song Bird Of The North

By the turn of the century the "endless" supply of pine was nearing exhaustion. The timber which was to have lasted forever had been exploited by a succession of lumber companies and private operators. Mill towns began to disintegrate for lack of saw logs. Ghost villages were left to decay. Grass grew on the skidways and logging roads where rough men and giant teams had made the woods ring with their shouting and clanking chains.

Fire leveled the cut-over forests. Streams once clear and filled with speckled trout ran for a few months, then dried up. Lumberjacks moved west, to Minnesota and Oregon, to cut the virgin stuff in a new country. Their shouts and street fighting were things of the past. A few broken-down woods boys remained behind as a reminder of the "days that were."

The fortunes which had been wrested from the woods moved to Chicago and other big cities to be reinvested in other, more lucrative ventures. The exodus of men and money left the village poorer but unafraid. Those stranded, with no better place to go, turned to the mines and to the denuded woods and farmland to eke out an existence and find a new way of life. The cities called many, there to find life routine and mechanized, a dreary existence after years spent in the deep pine woods and on clear lakes and streams.

One Absentee took nothing from Iron River but her poverty and extracted from her experience there such simple, haunting melodies as "When You Come To The End Of A Perfect Day", "Just A'Wearyin' For You" and "A Long Time Ago."

Carrie Jacobs Bond was the most distinguished citizen Iron River produced. She came to our town as a bride, saw its poverty and struggles for a livelihood and left it with nothing in her hands or purse but an urge to put into song and music the saga of those brave souls who opened up the new country, saw it decline, then come back again to new life and usefulness.

Mrs. Bond, a cousin of John Howard Payne, who wrote "Home, Sweet Home", was born Carrie Jacobs in the little town of Janesville, Wisconsin, in the second year of the Civil War. A trained musician and a skilled china painter, she became the fiancee of Dr. Frank Lewis Bond. who began his medical practice in Iron River in 1881. Living with her was her young son by a previous marriage. The doctor was somewhat of a politician and to supplement his meager income accepted an appointment as town postmaster under the Grover Cleveland administration from 1885 to 1889. His sister Lillian served as his assistant postmistress.

In 1888 Dr. Bond returned to Janesville to claim his bride and brought her to our pioneer town. Few residents were interested in classical music or china painting. In fact, the native women shunned the refined newcomer at first, thinking that she was above them because of her interest in the finer arts. However, her sincere friendliness, her ability as a homemaker and cook and her interest in the little Presbyterian Church gradually won them over. She gave piano lessons to some of the children of the mining officials and merchants. She played the organ in the church for seven years. She was active in the ladies' aid and helped with the church suppers, where she learned to "cut a cake so it would go farther."

Gus Ruus as a boy delivered groceries at the Bond home and his pockets were usually filled with Mrs. Bond's cookies. A little girl who delivered milk to her often went away with her pail filled with cookies or a huge piece of cake.

On the doctor's rounds to see his patients, Mrs. Bond frequently drove the horse and buggy. At times when she learned of destitute patients she brought a basket of food and clothing as a gift.

Dr. Bond continued to serve as postmaster and the town physician until 1894, while Mrs. Bond carried on with her piano teaching, china painting, recitals and early compositions to supplement the family income. As was always true in those early days, the doctor's bills were the last to be paid. In lieu of cash patients brought him gifts of eggs, chickens, beef and farm produce, so the family of three managed to get along.

It was in the summer of 1894 when a group of young people was gathered on the high wooden sidewalk in front of the postoffice awaiting the distribution of the mail which had come in on the upbound train. Dr. Bond came down the street and stopped to chat with a bevy of girls gathered there. In a friendly scuffle one of the girls playfully pushed the doctor. He fell headlong off the sidewalk into the hard iron rock street three feet below, bursting his bladder. He arose and walked across the street to his office where he lay down on a cot. Mrs. Bond had had a recital at the town hall and had just returned to their flat above. The doctor used a long stick to pound on the ceiling to summon his wife. Mrs. Bond telegraphed Dr. Minnehan, a noted surgeon of Green Bay, Wisconsin, who came in on the next train. Dr. Minnehan made a careful examination and told Mrs. Bond it was only a matter of a few hours.

For the balance of that year Mrs. Bond and her son stayed on in Iron River, where she tried operating a boarding house for school teachers. The doctor's assets were small and want soon faced the mother and boy. In the fall of 1895 they moved to Chicago where they lived in a small flat on the south side. The rent was fifteen dollars a month. The room was gas lighted and usually cold. They often lived on one meal a day. On one occasion a friend visited her in her flat and Mrs. Bond served her last tea and crackers. Wealthy friends interested in music came to share her scanty bounty—pulling their fur coats about them when the grate fire went out. Remembering her own struggles in Iron River, she welcomed beggars and homeless strangers who came to her door and gave them out of her little, even allowing some of them to sleep in one of her empty, fireless rooms. One of her later songs reflected her

warm heart—"It Ain't So Much The Doin' As the Way the Thing Is Did."
Mrs. Bond sold her few possessions bit by bit, to buy food and pay
rent. At the age of thirty, she travelled hopefully to the music publish-
ers with some of her first compositions, only to be told that her songs
had no demand but that children's songs were needed. By noon the next
day she composed the music and words to "Is My Dolly Dead?". The
publisher accepted it and the song was sung five days later in the comic
opera "1492."

It was about that time that she rummaged through an accumulation of
her husband's papers and found a $1,000.00 insurance policy, the pay-
ment of which helped her eke out an existence and enabled her to work
on her compositions for a while.

Her success came, not gloriously, but grudgingly. To put her songs
across she sang them in vaudeville theaters of Chicago—at first to be
hissed, then skeptically accepted. Finally with the help of an old friend,
Walter Gale, she organized her own Bond Publishing Company with her
son as her partner. In 1910, after fifteen years of poverty and struggle,
her first big check for $8,500.00 came from royalties from "A Perfect
Day", which eventually resulted in the sale of over five million copies.
She wrote over forty songs and composed the music, which later became
household pieces, sung wherever music lovers gathered. Among them
were "To A Wild Rose", "I Love you Truly", "Just A'Wearyin' For You",
"The Flying Flag", and "I Am The Captain Of The Broomstick Cavalry",
the latter written in Iron River for her son who, she said, was the inspiration for many of her songs and much of her music.

When success and acclaim came at last, she moved to San Diego,
California. Her greatest sorrow after her departure from Iron River
came in 1929 when her son was killed in the San Bernardino mountains.
At his death she moved to Los Angeles, where she continued her com-
posing and added many new songs to her list of successes—a total of
over two hundred.

Mrs. Bond's greatest thrill came when she listened to 40,000 American soldiers sing "A Perfect Day" during World War I. She heard that
song wherever she travelled—Jerusalem, Monte Carlo, at a Turkish
wedding in Constantinople, the English Derby at Epsom Downs and in
New York when that town went wild on Armistice Day.

Mrs. Bond scored her greatest success in London where she sang
in a musicale with Enrico Caruso. The audience proclaimed her "I Am
the Captain of the Broomstick Cavalry" with almost as much enthusiasm
as it accorded the greatest tenor of all time.

She repeated that song at the White House upon the invitation of
President Theodore Roosevelt and was invited to sing again by President Warren G. Harding. "A Perfect Day" was sung at the latter's
funeral as his favorite song. She often said that that song was inspired
by a California sunset.

The climax of Mrs. Bond's life came when her songs were featured
at the Tenth Chicagoland Music Festival before 100,000 people at Soldiers Field, Chicago, in 1939. At the Festival luncheon she heard Edith
Mason, opera star, sing "When You Come to the End of A Perfect Day."

On either side of her sat George Ade, the famous American humorist, and John T. McCutcheon, the Chicago Tribune cartoonist, who forty years years before had aided Mrs. Bond when her struggle for a livelihood was bitterest.

At Soldiers Field Mrs. Bond entered on the arm of John Carter, the Metropolitan star, who sang some of her songs. At the climax of the evening a great set piece in fire reproduced a towering portrait of the composer and then a porch scene and the setting sun to the accompaniment of "A Perfect Day."

Before her death in Los Angeles on December 29, 1946, Mrs. Bond had repeatedly revisited Iron River and the scenes of her happy married life. It was for the occasion of her last visit there that she wrote "A Long Time Ago", which recalled her earlier life as a bride. She was asked to sing her "Perfect Day" while being entertained at the home of Mrs. Ben Quirt. She replied that she did not sing any more but she would play it on the piano. She said it should not be played as a sad song but "quickly and brilliantly."

Her one request in the midst of her public appearance in her former community was:

"Let me talk to the schools, if I may. I can do some songs and I want to do all I can for the children."

So she sang to the children whose parents and grandparents had known her as a bride forty-five years before.

At the age of 84, Mrs. Bond had risen on the wings of faith and hope and charity, above the bitter grief and desperate poverty of her early days. On her last visit she looked like her music sounds. She was the perfect portrait of her melodies. Her Iron River friends who survive her proudly claim her as their own. She was to those of us who had been through the struggle of boom and bust a symbol of courage, hope and fortitude. She had brought into the little pioneer village no wealth in her hand or in her purse, but a talent for friendship and making life a little brighter. She left with a sorrow in her heart but also with a message in her soul which gave the world- peace, pleasure and purpose.

The Upper Peninsula too has come through its days of peril and poverty, and it may well be that days of greater prosperity and opportunity lie ahead. Those courageous souls, who left their home shores to sail across a broad ocean to seek their fortunes in an unknown region between the iron and the pine, have passed on to their children a heritage of hope in the future.

Those contemporaries of mine who were dispersed to distant states by the panic of 1893 and the depressions which followed and by the wars between nations, still look upon the Upper Peninsula as a state and home apart—the U. P. of their childhood and the scene of their struggle to wrest a life and a living from the trees and the ore.

Whatever the future may hold for that Northern Empire which is the U. P., its past needs no apology. Its pine still houses millions of its nation's citizens and its iron bridges streams and sends skyscrapers soaring for prouder cities than Iron River to be proud of. Whatever lies ahead for this scarred and rugged land, it is certain that its blue northern skies and its clear, cold waters will earn the love of generations far removed from ours.

Just as the generation which succeeded ours has made an adjustment to modern ways of life, so have the denuded forests begun to spring up again. The red ore resources still scarcely tapped continue to serve as the backbone of our factories, our ships and our industries; and that other kind of backbone, the kind that mined in the stopes and labored in the woods, is as strong in its way as our way in our day.